NEW GEOGRAPHIES
10 Fallow

Printed in China

Logo Design: Johannes Breyer, Elias Hanzer

ISBN: 978-1-948765-09-1
LCCN: 2018946431

gsd.harvard.edu/newgeographies

Harvard University
Graduate School of Design

New Geographies is a journal of design, agency, and territory founded, edited, and produced by doctoral candidates at the Harvard University Graduate School of Design. *New Geographies* presents the geographic as a design paradigm that links physical, representational, and political attributes of space and articulates a synthetic scalar practice. Through critical essays and projects, the journal seeks to position design's agency amid concerns about infrastructure, technology, ecology, and globalization.

New Geographies 10: Fallow has been made possible with support from the Graham Foundation for Advanced Studies in the Fine Arts and the Harvard GSD Office of the Dean.

All attempts have been made to trace and acknowledge the sources of images. Regarding any omissions or errors, please contact:

New Geographies Lab
Harvard University Graduate School of Design
48 Quincy Street
Cambridge, MA 02138

Distribution
Actar D
440 Park Avenue South, 17th Floor
New York, NY 10016
Actar.com

We would like to acknowledge a debt of gratitude to all previous editors of *New Geographies.* A special thanks to Mariano Gómez-Luque, who proved to be a resilient sounding board as we navigated the process. We would also like to thank the Harvard GSD Dean's Office, the Harvard GSD Publications Department, copy editor Kari Rittenbach, proofreader Elizabeth Kugler, and all the people who offered their help and insight through the making of this issue, especially Neil Brenner, our dissertation advisor and comrade.

Fallow

MICHAEL CHIEFFALO & JULIA SMACHYLO

I

A dialectic of devaluation and renewal today produces profound and varied transformations in both built and unbuilt environments. Global economic restructuring has led to the decline and abandonment of urban environments in shrinking cities but has also engendered new forms of social relations and new modes of self-organization.[1] In other locations, vacant, underused, or foreclosed properties emerge as loci of tension in processes of transformation, as activism and insurrection rise in opposition to speculative capitalism.[2] The programmed obsolescence of buildings produces erasures in built environments that rack communities with cultural loss, while also offering the possibility for more progressive forms of social and ecological relations.[3] Areas of industrial decline may become sites of effervescent biological productivity, as plant-based remediation detoxifies soil polluted through industrial exploitation.[4] Vibrant manifestations of the devaluation-renewal dialectic are also evident if we extend our gaze beyond the city, to a broader geographic scale. We find, for instance, that land abandoned by large-scale logging and agriculture has become a key focal point in an expanded project of biodiversity protection that emphasizes industrial hinterlands rather than pristine natural areas.[5] Similarly, despite mainstream representations of coastal retreat as a politically unfeasible response to sea-level rise, many seaside residents are self-organizing to promote retreat as a basis for greater community resilience.[6] Many other examples could be enumerated here, but the preceding are sufficient to highlight the contemporary interplay between proliferating contexts of decline and corresponding efforts to recapture neglected and marginal spaces to restore social, ecological, or economic capacity.

This issue of *New Geographies* (NG10) seeks to open a conversation exploring this set of issues, and in particular, the tension central to this dialectic: the hinge between devaluation and revaluation.

This hinge is both process and condition. As a process, forces of transformation unfurl at different scales and across diverse geographies, producing variegated social and ecological effects. As a condition, the moment of pause—of fallowness—is replete with potential to forge new social and ecological relations. How can we, as designers and members of allied disciplines, intervene to bend vectors of transformation toward more just modes of social or ecological organization? Beyond traditional project proposals that perpetuate the status quo, can design thinking engage the heavy work of analysis required to reveal the operations that structure these moments and spaces, to instead offer proposals that redraw political and cultural horizons? As agents deeply enmeshed within the forces producing these transformations, designers and planners are implicated in shaping the future of these challenging contexts.

Against this backdrop, NG10 borrows the term "fallow" as a metaphor to examine this critical juncture in cycles of devaluing and revaluing built and unbuilt environments. In agriculture, fallowing is understood as a process of restoring latent ecological capacity through periodic idleness. NG10 proposes to extend this concept to a much broader spectrum of conditions, including many that are not immediately associated with crop rotation, but which are inscribed in diverse forms of devalorization and revalorization associated with geographies of industrial capitalism. Lack of productivity in urban contexts, for instance, is often described in such negative terms as abandonment, marginality, or wasteland, circumstances often produced through industrial exploitation.[7] What insights might be gleaned from viewing the dynamics that shape sociospatial and socioecological relations in this and other contexts by instead using fallow as a lens? Rather than assume a strict binary of fecund or barren, the texts assembled in this volume critically reflect on the sites, strategies, scales, and imaginaries of the devalued, the dormant, and the wasted, and explore revalorization in all its forms: cultural, ecological, economic, and social.

We are not the first to propose the concept of fallow be applied to non-agrarian contexts. Franz Oswald and Peter Baccini, for example, use it in a short passage in their book *Netzstadt: Designing the Urban* (2003). Here they gloss the problem of "vacant and decaying" buildings as "fallow resources to preserve and enhance the quality of city life" without unpacking how fallow resources emerge or what their broader position might be in the built environment.[8] Studio Basel mobilizes it more specifically in *Switzerland: An Urban Portrait* (2006) to explore the situation of formerly industrial alpine zones under conditions of accelerated contemporary urbanization.[9] And the edited volume *Terrain Vague: Interstices at the Edge of the Pale* (2013) is closely aligned with such ideas, albeit without explicitly using the term. Invoking the work of Catalan architect Ignasi de Solà-Morales, editors Patrick Barron and Manuela Mariani present a group of essays that recast spaces in cities often considered marginal in a more positive light, claiming them as complex and dynamic sites of engagement for planning and design.[10] In an epoch increasingly defined by a skein of human activity that stretches across the planet, where built and unbuilt environments are subjected to the machinations of speculative capital, and where the appropriation and instrumentalization of space is everywhere imminent, now it is critical to further analytical work on this fundamental moment in the transformation of the environment.[11]

In his work on industrial agriculture, geographer Tony Weis helps to broaden the relevance of fallowness beyond questions of soil fertility by demonstrating how crop rotation techniques allow for alternative uses. For example, by alternating the planting of various grasses and roughage with crops meant for consumption by humans, fallowed fields were opened as a site for livestock grazing.[12] In turn, livestock became a valuable asset in nutrient cycling and soil fertility as their dung, previously dispersed in open fields, became a concentrated form of fertilizer.[13] In a closely related analysis, Weis shows that the temporal deceleration of fallowing increases the possibility for crop diversity and, importantly, can energize the reemergence of small farming communities that form more ecologically viable models of agrarian production than those associated with industrial farming systems.[14] That is, in addition to its ecological healing capacity, the process of fallowing may also influence social organization in potentially progressive ways. Beyond its circumscribed origins within agricultural production, today we propose building on these insights to further expand the concept of fallow to contexts of economic production and the built environment.

From its etymological root, fallow has accumulated various meanings and can be used as both verb and adjective to describe different aspects and dynamics of agricultural land use.[15] In our expanded field, fallowing (*v.*) is a concomitant phase in the process of both producing and demolishing built and unbuilt environments. Fallowness (*adj.*) as a condition within the production process—a state of pause—becomes a field of potential, a moment or site in which human and nonhuman actors have the opportunity to rework those relations that structure their environments. Here new strategies emerge, countering many modes of dispossession with new organizational capacities and biological richness.

II

NG10 brings together academics and practitioners to engage concepts of fallow in speculative and creative ways. The texts collected here help to build the analytical potential of the term, suggest possible strategies for its practice, and also probe its limits. To provide coherence, this volume is organized into the following four thematic groupings: the concept of fallow in modernity; rhythms and processes of fallowing in the capitalist built environment; conditions of fallowness in relation to constructed boundaries between human and nonhuman nature; and lastly, spatiotemporal scales of fallowness that create alternative means for social interaction and organization.

The first series of texts explores concepts of fallow in modernity by bringing into focus how the meaning of the word is tied to a broader political economy and evolves in relation to dynamics of land enclosure and land use under capitalism. A historical analysis by **Matthew Gandy** considers fallow as an evolving set of concrete social-ecological relations, highlighting the conceptual shift from ecological restoration to a fix for overproduction under the pressure of capitalism. **Álvaro**

Sevilla-Buitrago uses processes of enclosure in England and the United States to show how the practice of fallowing was eventually replaced by an ideology of improvement that disparaged idleness and inactivity. Beyond the Euro-American context, **Jane M. Jacobs** and **Stephen Cairns** develop a comparative analysis of land use in Western and Asian economies that complicates our understanding of the logics of capitalist enclosure and highlights the need for context-sensitive analyses of fallow.

Pursuing the idea that fallowing has certain rhythmic qualities, the second group of essays engages how specific processes of creation and destruction in capitalist urbanization produce varied conditions of fallowness. Framing this discussion in rich theoretical terms, **Mazen Labban** mobilizes the ideas of Gilles Deleuze and Félix Guattari to articulate a powerful analysis of the built environment in a perpetual state of building up and dissolving along several simultaneous modes of circulation and wasting. **Nathan Sayre** notes the complex and contradictory relation between climate change and the devaluation of the built environment in the temporal scales of climate impacts. He argues that the spatial pattern of uneven geographical devaluation is magnified by a feedback loop attributable to the securitization and financialization of risk. Linking the speed of transportation systems to a specific spatial form of fallowness, **Benedikt Boucsein** and **Eirini Kasioumi** claim "noise landscapes"—those sites absorbing the externalities of air travel—as prime areas for designers to experiment with novel forms of social and ecological revalorization. In his case study of Detroit, **Michael R. J. Koscielniak** suggests *decline-as-urbanization* as a concept more attuned to the wide-ranging processes of dispossession and uneven development than can be found in certain inherited frameworks of urbanization. **Wade Shepard** contextualizes the ongoing development of Cyberjaya, Malaysia, within a broader cohort of Asian cities undergoing rounds of speculative urban development, where boosters navigate the fraught process of building tabula rasa in projects that oscillate in potential from dizzying exuberance to next ghost city. Finally, in arguing that periods of rest or dormancy do not necessarily lead to recovery, regeneration, or future value through occupation, **Christopher Marcinkoski** identifies a limit of the fallow metaphor when analyzing contemporary land speculation in Africa.

A conversation with **Peter L. Galison** serves as an interlude, weaving together the thematic foci of NG10. In this wide-ranging discussion, Galison considers the deep temporality of nuclear waste storage as a paradigmatic problem of modernity, and the waste-wilderness as a complex landscape of temporary human occupation and novel ecological configuration.

The third set of texts explores the border between fallowness, wildness, and conservation. Here various authors highlight the dynamic—yet continually negotiated and socially constructed—boundaries that demarcate humans and nature, valued and valueless, productive and unproductive, and near and distant. Building on his influential studies of planetary ecology, **Erle Ellis** asks what fallow means in the Anthropocene and encourages us to consider grand land management projects to rebuild biodiversity and ecological value in light of ongoing human transformation of the biosphere. At a much smaller scale, **Jill Desimini** explores the threshold between fallow and wild, where the layered use values in overgrown spaces become productive opportunities for planners and designers. Taking a landscape conservation approach to postindustrial landscapes, **Caitlin DeSilvey** invites us to consider the hybrid quality of fallowed sites, where constructed boundaries between the built and unbuilt are thickened through purposeful human action or inaction.[16] **Benjamin R. Cohen** argues that beyond physical boundaries, creating and maintaining temporal separation is critical to fallowing operations, as it is the rhythmic spatiotemporal interlocking of activity and rest that holds generative capacity for designers and planners. Dissolving the binary boundary between waste and renewal, in his view of postindustrial landscapes, **Thomas Sieverts** proposes reading the "city as a special landscape," where permaculture forms the basis of a sustainable future. Lastly, **Nicole Bennett** analyzes the capacity of photography to collapse spatial and temporal boundaries of remote geographies through representational strategies of the Great Pacific Garbage Patch, as its depictions have evolved from stable and distant to dynamic and urgent, no longer contained by its isolation.

Whether uncovered through intimate and personal forms of knowledge production or emerging through more collective experimentation, the final group of texts explores the relationship between fallowness, social interaction, and organization at a variety of spatiotemporal scales. **Austin Zwick** confronts the transhistorical "othering" of Appalachia with a more complex reading of the region as caught between processes of economic restructuring and environmental degradation on one hand, and the desire to protect close social bonds and a connection to the land on the other. At the scale of the city, the interdisciplinary design practice **Urban-Think Tank** reconsiders the third dimension of buildings within the broader phenomenon of vertical sprawl—emptied towers that have been delinked from the market—as rich zones holding potential for alternative and flexible community planning practices, social relations, and forms of urbanity.[17] In an intimate narrative, **Keith Brower Brown** revisits the closed airport *Tempelhofer Feld* in Berlin, which holds a present yet distant memory that is recovered through storytelling (a neglected cultural practice revalorized here), to reveal a site vibrating with his family's history.

III

In agricultural practices, fallowing requires time to restore fertility; it is a key dimension. And time emerges as an important component of the structure and function of fallowness when extending the metaphor to the conditions explored in NG10. Recurring throughout the essays in this volume is the idea that fallowness—slowness or rest as a source of regenerative potential—is often discordant with broader processes of capitalist development. Under an ideology of improvement that guides land use decisions, there is no place for idle or inactive space. Other texts, however, view removing land from circulation as the ultimate expression of modernity. The question of time is raised in still another way here. Whether through rapid devaluation from environmental ruptures wrought by climate change, or the deep state of suspended animation necessitated by nuclear waste storage, the waste products of capitalist modernity play a significant role in both the form and duration of the devaluation-renewal dialectic at the heart of fallowing. In contrast, whether by conscious decision or benign neglect, fallowing has also been absorbed into the ideology of improvement which now incorporates unbuilding, wasting, and dispossession. Here it is essential to recognize that devaluation may (paradoxically) serve as an accumulation strategy. But it is equally important to note that alternative forms of social organization and ecological relations have been able to thrive in these same spaces of disinvestment. It is in these places—at moments in between devaluation and revaluation—where new boundaries can be drawn between humans and nature, and new social vectors initiated. This is the challenge for designers and planners.

As the varied contours that constitute the terrain of *fallow* come into focus, we see that it is neither wasted nor idle. Rather, fallow introduces a new epistemology that transcends binary schemes. It is gravid with potential; thick with accreted memory; layered with debris and toxins; governed by rule regimes and altered through legislation; and evolved through cultural attitudes toward nature and productivity. All of these characteristics play a role in its latency and future potential, as the spatiotemporal effects of fallowing are solidified within the political economy. We urge designers and planners to embrace fallowness and to insert themselves into its processes more thoughtfully, to explore new modes and methods of practice, and to chart a course for a more just future through this challenging contemporary condition.

1
Kimberley Kinder, *DIY Detroit: Making Do in a City without Services* (Minneapolis: University of Minnesota Press, 2016).

2
Andy Merrifield, *The New Urban Question* (London: Pluto Press, 2014), 32.

3
Daniel Abramson, *Obsolescence: An Architectural History* (Chicago: University of Chicago Press, 2016).

4
Kate Kennen and Niall Kirkwood, eds., *Phyto: Principles and Resources for Site Remediation and Landscape Design* (New York: Routledge, 2015), 5–6.

5
See the Rewilding Institute website for an overview of the rewilding concept: https://rewilding.org/about-tri/vision/. For a discussion of the economic dynamics leading to abandoned farmland in Europe and the potential for rewilding as a land management strategy there, see Laetitia M. Navarro and Henrique M. Pereira, "Rewilding Abandoned Landscapes in Europe," *Ecosystems* 15.6 (September 2012): 900; and Rachelle McKnight, "Rewilding the European Landscape: An Unconventional Approach to Land Management," *City Wild* 8 (Spring 2014).

6
Liz Koslov, "The Case for Retreat," *Public Culture* 28.8 (2016): 359–87.

7
For an extensive collection of references to how a lack of productivity is described negatively in the literature, see Manuela Mariani and Patrick Barron, eds., *Interstices at the Edge of the Pale* (New York: Routledge, 2014), 3–4.

8
Franz Oswald, Peter Baccini, and Mark Michaeli, *Netzstadt: Designing the Urban* (Basel: Birkhäuser, 2003), 23.

9
Roger Diener, Jacques Herzog, Marcel Meili, Pierre de Meuron, and Christian Schmid, *Switzerland: An Urban Portrait*, ed. ETH Studio Basel, Institut Stadt der Gegenwart (Basel: Birkhäuser, 2005). In particular, see "Book 3: Materials for an Urbanistic Project, Alpine Fallow Lands," 929–1006.

10
Manuela Mariani and Patrick Barron, *Terrian Vague: Interstices at the Edge of the Pale* (New York: Routledge, 2014).

11
See, for example, literatures on the Anthropocene, Capitalocene, and Planetary Urbanization.

12–13
Tony Weis, *The Ecological Hoofprint: The Global Burden of Industrial Livestock* (London: Zed Books, 2013), 54.

14
Tony Weis, *The Global Food Economy: The Battle for the Future of Farming* (London: Zed Books, 2007), 167.

15
Oxford English Dictionary, s.v. "fallow," http://www.oed.com/view/Entry/67874?result=5&rskey=laIcvT&.

16
"Unbuilding: Process and Preservation" is excerpted from Caitlin DeSilvey, *Curated Decay: Heritage beyond Saving* (Minneapolis: University of Minnesota Press, 2017). Copyright 2017 by the Regents of the University of Minnesota. Used by permission of the University of Minnesota Press.

17
This text builds on previous work on Torre David. See the Urban-Think Tank website, http://u-tt.com/project/torre-david; and Alfredo Brillembourg and Hubert Klumpner, eds., *Torre David: Informal Vertical Communities* (Zurich: Lars Müller Publishers, 2013).

FAL

MC

LLOV

ODE

WA
RNI

ND
TY

An Excursion through Fallow Lands

MATTHEW GANDY

There is something intriguing about spaces that appear to be marginal, unproductive, or difficult to define. The edges of modernity not only encompass ostensibly unusable sites—such as narrow strips of land that run parallel to infrastructural networks—but also a variety of locales that defy simple forms of categorization or control. Such spaces challenge existing aesthetic categories and modes of interpretation: these are not cultural landscapes in the conventional sense of aesthetic contemplation, and certainly not designed spaces that owe their character to precise forms of human intentionality. The presence of a fallow field lies in tension with the seeming immediacy of productive landscapes, and in particular, with land as a specific kind of material resource that has bolstered the expansionist dynamics of modernity. In this essay I consider the meaning of "fallow lands" not so much as a metaphor, but rather as a series of concrete relations: the idea of fallow is explored as a specific set of socioecological assemblages that have recently acquired a heightened degree of cultural resonance.

The idea of land is closely tied up with questions of designation and demarcation. Individual spaces, plots, or fields lie at the intersection of law, geography, and the biophysical dynamics of matter. Unlike terms such as "wasteland" or "brownfield," an emphasis on "fallowing" points to an active process of "letting alone," or to a suspension of use in which a parcel of land is temporarily "rested" so that its long-term fertility or viability can be assured. Of course, the very idea of rest, and of the resting of space in particular—letting the earth sleep—counters the accelerative and all-encompassing momentum of late modernity.[1]

Abandoned olive groves in Catalonia, last cultivated in the 1970s, 2009. Courtesy Matthew Gandy.

The idea of fallow land has an ambiguous relation to both conceptions of "wild nature" in the cultural imagination and to more intensively modified fragments of nature such as parks or gardens. Though connected to various notions of the commons, the presence of fallow land tends to be associated with a more clearly defined set of claims over its future use, or at least relatively unambiguous patterns of ownership. Whereas wastelands are frequently associated with the "unusable," fallow land does not typically denote a degree of irreversible devalorization or even contamination. (Nuclear wastelands would not typically be referred to as "fallow" since their state does not result from a temporary interruption in use, but rather from an irrevocable alteration in their material characteristics.) If the wasteland tends to be defined by various forms of absence, as Vittoria di Palma suggests, then arguably fallow lands denote a mere suspension of future promise before fecundity is restored.[2]

The English word "fallow" is deeply immersed in the idea of a "working landscape," to use Raymond Williams's formulation, and denotes a parcel of land that has been deliberately set aside so that it can recover its agricultural productivity.[3] The idea of fallowing land also connects with early observations of the destructive effects on soil wrought by agricultural overexploitation: the absence of fallowing and the abandonment of pre-capitalist agricultural practices was a key element in the classic account of metabolic rift first developed by Justus von Liebig and later elaborated by Karl Marx.[4] The idea of "resting the earth" denotes a temporal frame at variance with the exigencies of capital; there is a "slowness" to fallow land that correlates to biochemical cycles indifferent to human intentionality. And the idea of fallow clearly predates the advent of modern enclosure in a European context, and relates to an array of cultural interactions with nature beyond Eurocentric conceptions of landscape.

The English word "fallow" has complex, and to some degree contradictory, etymological roots denoting both the act of ploughing as well as the practice of leaving fields undisturbed. "I saw far off the weedy fallows smile," writes William Cowper in a poem from 1785, "With verdure not unprofitable."[5] Cowper's observations were made in the pre-chemical age, when parcels of land were set aside in order to recover their fertility, principally by encouraging specific types of plants to grow that could fix nitrogen in the soil. Under pre-capitalist agriculture the use of fallow tied rural communities to intricate modalities of time and place. The English word "fallow" is of Germanic origin, being derived from the Old English *fealh* or *felch* that is related to the Old Frisian *fallach*, the Dutch *valge*, and the Old High German *felga*.[6] There may also be a chromatic dimension to the etymology of fallow landscapes derived from the sandy appearance of fallow fields: there are similarities, for instance, between the Old High German *falo*, meaning "pale"; the Latin verb *pallēre*, indicating "to be pale" or "to fade"; and the Greek φαιός (*polios*) meaning "light" or "gray."[7]

More recently, the practice of fallowing has been used in relation to the temporary suspension of agricultural activity in response to overproduction.[8] In the European Union (EU), significant quantities of agricultural land were removed from production between 1988 and 2008 as part of so-called set-aside schemes: although sometimes couched in ecological terms to protect biodiversity, this centrally coordinated use of fallowing is integrally linked to the exigencies of capitalist agriculture and the power of agricultural interests within the institutional apparatus of the EU. These specific measures to create fallow landscapes illustrate an underlying ambiguity in the sphere of biopolitics at the interface of food production and biodiversity: there is a tension between different strands of intervention to secure life as a commodity, and as a strategic concern within conservation biology.[9]

The presence of fallow lands in formerly productive landscapes has also emerged as an outcome of uncoordinated agricultural abandonment and demographic decline. In these cases the relationship between fallowing and socioeconomic marginalization lies closer to the dynamics of landscape change observed in the post-Fordist emptying out of urban and industrial regions. In vegetation zones with relatively low or intermittent precipitation, the production of fallow lands through neglect rather than by design can have deleterious consequences. In the case of southern Europe, for example, there is now an increased risk of fire produced by the twin effects of neoliberal austerity and the decline in traditional forms of land management: cutbacks

1
See Jonathan Crary, *24/7: Late Capitalism and the Ends of Sleep* (London: Verso, 2013), and Byung-Chul Han, *Müdigkeitsgesellschaft* (Berlin: Matthes and Seitz, 2010).

2
Vittoria Di Palma, *Wasteland: A History* (New Haven, CT: Yale University Press, 2014).

3
Raymond Williams, *The Country and the City* (London: Chatto and Windus, 1973).

4
See Matthew Gandy, "Cities in Deep Time: Biodiversity, Metabolic Rift, and the Urban Question," *City* 22.1 (2018): 96–105.

5
William Cowper, *The Task: A Poem* (London: Cassell & Co., 1899 [1785]).

6
Oxford English Dictionary, s.v. "fallow," http://www.oed.com.i.ezproxy.nypl.org/view/Entry/67870?rskey=3v0Yn6&result=1&isAdvanced=false#eid.

Urban wasteland awaiting development, Chausseestrasse, Berlin, 2006. Courtesy Matthew Gandy.

in fire emergency services and the build-up of dry vegetation have proved to be a deadly combination.[10]

Outside the Anglo-American realm, in Germany, the word *Brache* is widely used to denote fallow land. The term *Brache* also has agricultural origins and is etymologically related to the Dutch *braak*, the English *brake*, and the Danish *brak*, with roots in the act of "breaking" the soil through ploughing. Unlike the English sense of fallow, however, the German *Brache* has acquired a much wider range of meanings and cultural connotations. In particular, *Brache* is used in relation to a variety of urban and industrial areas that have been neglected or abandoned. In Berlin, the proliferation of *Brachen* at different moments in the city's history, especially in the immediate postwar years and in the wake of geopolitical division, has become a recognizable if now rapidly receding feature of the metropolitan landscape. These temporary or transitional voids now form part of a rich debate over the future of urban space, as a diversity of vernacular cultural and scientific appropriations clash with more narrowly utilitarian conceptions of urban space as little more than a patchwork of investment opportunities. The term *Brache* is now embedded in the German cultural imagination as denoting a space of possibility and alternative pathways.[11]

We should be cautious, however, in relying too heavily on etymological nuance as a determining thread in our analysis. The use of specific words in relation to place, space, and landscape can generate associations independently from the specific sites to which they refer.[12] The Derridean term *différance* points to an inherent fluidity in the association between words and material artifacts. More specifically, Derrida's emphasis on absence and "spectrality" marks a significant departure from the bounded corporeal presence in Husserlian phenomenology. A fallow landscape is of necessity an interim space, a sphere of detachment and interruption. Although it may be experienced in the here and now, it is necessarily connected to other discourses and temporalities. There is a peculiarly intense degree of absence associated with fallow landscapes and their connections to other spaces, thoughts, and subjects.[13]

Fallow lands are now a focus of intense cultural and scientific attention. The evolving biophysical dynamics of these "slow spaces" are indicative of distinctive ecological sequences. The temporal dimensions to fallow lands exemplify Gilles Clément's articulation of the "garden in movement" as an endless source of aesthetic and botanical fascination.[14] Indeed, the aesthetics of biophysical spontaneity has become increasingly influential in landscape design. The meaning and purpose of urban design today is in a state of flux: on the one hand, there is a neoliberal impetus towards making public space serve the interests of capital, with new parks acting as a catalyst for real estate speculation and other strategic objectives; and on the other, there is a diversification of expertise with new possibilities for cultural and aesthetic experimentation. And there is an uneasy transition between the noninterventionist dynamics of fallow lands and their eventual incorporation into various forms of "staged" nonintervention as part of a strategy towards their partial retention in the landscape.

The contemporary resonance of fallow lands is derived from a series of dynamic cultural elements: the evolution of language itself, for which marginal spaces have generated a diverse array of terms; the interplay between words, meanings, and human experience, including the multiple lineages of collective memory; and naturally, the material traces of human activity inscribed into the landscape, marked by successive oscillations between use and "nonuse." This is not to suggest that our terminologies are merely arbitrary; on the contrary, it is to locate words and meanings in their precise cultural and historical contexts.

7
Merriam-Webster Dictionary, s.v. "fallow," https://www.merriam-webster.com/dictionary/fallow.

8
The capitalist use of "fallow" measures in response to overproduction can also be applied to other commodities like housing. For example, see Matthias Bernt, "Partnerships for Demolition: The Governance of Urban Renewal in East Germany's Shrinking Cities," *International Journal of Urban and Regional Research* 33.3 (2009): 754–69.

9
See Roberto Esposito, *Bíos: Biopolitics and Philosophy*, trans. Timothy Campbell (Minneapolis: University of Minnesota Press, 2008).

10
See Marien González-Hidalgo, Iago Otero, and Giorgos Kallis, "Seeing Beyond the Smoke: The Political Ecology of Fire in Horta de Sant Joan (Catalonia)," *Environment and Planning A* 46 (2014): 1014–1103.

11
Dieter D. Genske and Susanne Hauser, *Die Brache als Chance: Ein Transdisziplinärer Dialog Über Verbrauchte Flächen* (Berlin: Springer, 2013).

12
Kevin Raaphorst, Ingrid Duchhart, Wim van der Knaap, Gerda Roeleveld, and Adri van den Brink, "The Semiotics of Landscape Design Communication: Towards a Critical Visual Research Approach in Landscape Architecture," *Landscape Research* 42.1 (2017): 120–133.

13
See Nikolai Roskamm, *Die unbesetzte Stadt: Postfundamentalistiches Denken and das urbanistische Feld* (Basel: Birkhäuser, 2017); and John Wylie, "Landscape, Absence and the Geographies of Love," *Transactions of the Institute of British Geographers* 34.3 (2009): 275–89.

14
See Matthew Gandy, "Entropy by Design: Gilles Clément, Parc Henri Matisse and the Limits to Avant-Garde Urbanism," *International Journal of Urban and Regional Research* 37.1 (2013): 259–78.

Antinomies of Space-Time Value: Fallowness, Planning, Speculation

ÁLVARO SEVILLA-BUITRAGO

The production of space is at the same time its valorization.
–Elmar Altvater[1]

Fallowness. The condition of a resource or productive force set aside to accumulate potential value to be extracted or realized afterward.

History

In England, until the wave of enclosures that enabled the Industrial Revolution, the main agricultural regions used an open field system that facilitated the coexistence of subsistence farming, production for the market, and various modalities of commoning. Within these local and collectively planned arrangements, fallow land was considered "commonable" land. Private property that was left untilled could be pastured in common so that nutrients from cattle manure improved soil capacity and structure.[2] This complex design superimposed ownership and possession of land, making it possible for smallholders to augment potential yield value while simultaneously securing immediate use values that benefited all commoners, complementing their livelihoods and partially resolving their reproduction outside the market.[3] Together with common land and common rights, this system—which kept one-third to one-half of all parish territory under communal regime for centuries—disappeared with the parliamentary enclosure campaigns that swept the English Midlands in the 18th and 19th centuries. Subsequent property regimes were simpler and exclusive. Under the banner of modernization, large landholders and a new generation of agriculturists and surveyors disseminated an ideology of "improvement" that gradually abandoned fallowing or replaced it with a fodder crop system to maximize soil productivity and accelerate the turnover time of capital.[4] Improvers couldn't stand idleness, regardless of whether it referred to a quality of land or to poor commoners "wasting" productive time by contemplating their grazing livestock instead of embracing wage discipline as day laborers. The myth of productivity and efficiency, however, was misleading. By the 1840s intensive farming had leeched the soil of its nutrients in several regions and agricultural yields were gradually decreasing. To replenish lost soil capacity a new international trade in natural fertilizer—guano—arose, whereby Britain deprived communities in poor nations of traditional sources of phosphate and nitrogen, causing severe environmental degradation at the periphery of the world-economy.[5] At the same time much of the enclosed land was seized with a speculative aim or simply to accumulate property and secure social status—in such cases the land remained untilled for decades or was directly incorporated by booming industrial towns to absorb urban development.[6]

During the 19th century, the crisis of social reproduction caused by the separation of smallholders and propertyless commoners from the land deepened in big cities, which had become home to legions of the dispossessed. Under laissez-faire capitalism, urbanization was the lubricant for novel forms of accumulation that combined the acceleration of productive cycles and the hyper-exploitation of labor power and space in dense working-class neighborhoods with a new mode of fallowing: land speculation in programmed town extensions, where building lots were intentionally left vacant for decades until their value reached an inflated level. Against this background, informal alternatives developed that prioritized immediate spatial use value over artificially delayed exchange value. Empty parcels on the outskirts of cities such as Berlin and New York were occupied by garden colonies and shantytowns: rural underworlds where squatters and unruly proletarians created a sense of community and self-managed natures at the margins of the bourgeois vision of the new periphery and normalized citizenship.[7] Towards the last third of the 19th century, however, growing social conflict and intensified reproduction crises sparked a wave of urban reformism that introduced yet another iteration of fallowness. Parks, schools, adequate housing, and increased leisure time were understood as realms in which to restore and cultivate the value latent in workers' bodies and minds, and in their offspring. These novel spatial arenas would reshape municipal governance and urbanization. A mode of programmed waiting as opposed to mere speculation, the dawn of planning heralded a new shift in the dialectic of fallowing, by attempting to sustainably regulate human value creation through space, in time. However, ecological resources in general were not considered in the same light. To name only the most salient and ambitious scheme at the time, there were no idle or fallow spaces in Ebenezer Howard's Garden City concept, which instead sought to maximize functionality, through territory saturated with activity.[8]

In the early 20th century reform movements ushered in a progressive era that created welfare formations in core capitalist countries as a governmentalization of fallowing through, among others, the rationalization of economic development and state absorption of the externalities of a relentlessly expanding industrial world. Marked by a violent process of modernization and intermittent crises, Germany was an especially interesting laboratory in this regard. Innovative state mediation of national social and economic life sparked debate on the productive or unproductive character of public investment, with different alliances of capital and civil society defending antagonistic value schemes with specific articulations of the urbanization process.[9] At the turn of the century, Frankfurt mayor Franz Adickes promoted a strategy to amass municipal land for future development, quintupling public property on the city's outskirts.[10] Other large cities soon adopted the same scheme. Set aside for decades, these land reserves enabled the implementation of famous public facilities and social housing programs during the Weimar Republic in Frankfurt, Berlin, and Hamburg. Politicians and technicians were explicit about the role of this social infrastructure in

1
Elmar Altvater, "Ecological and Economic Modalities of Time and Space," *Capitalism Nature Socialism* 1 (1989): 59–70.

2
Joan Thirsk, "The Common Fields," *Past & Present* 29 (1964): 3–25, 3.

3
Álvaro Sevilla-Buitrago, "Territory and the Governmentalisation of Social Reproduction: Parliamentary Enclosure and Spatial Rationalities in the Transition from Feudalism to Capitalism," *Journal of Historical Geography* 38 (2012): 209–19.

4
Gregory Clark, "Too Much Revolution: Agriculture in the Industrial Revolution, 1700–1860," in *The British Industrial Revolution: An Economic Perspective*, ed. Joel Mokyr (Boulder, CO: Westview Press, 1999), 212.

5
Brett Clark and John Bellamy Foster, "Ecological Imperialism and the Global Metabolic Rift: Unequal Exchange and the Guano/Nitrates Trade," *International Journal of Comparative Sociology* 50 (2009): 311–34.

6
Álvaro Sevilla-Buitrago, "Urbs in Rure: Historical Enclosure and the Extended Urbanization of the Countryside," in *Implosions/Explosions: Towards a Study of Planetary Urbanization*, ed. Neil Brenner (Berlin: Jovis, 2013), 236–59.

7
Roy Rosenzweig and Elizabeth Blackmar, *The Park and the People: A History of Central Park* (Ithaca, NY: Cornell University Press, 1992), 64–73; Mark Hobbs, "'Farmers on Notice': The Threat Faced by Weimar Berlin's Garden Colonies in the Face of the City's *Neues Bauen* Housing Program," *Urban History* 39 (2012): 263–84.

8
Ebenezer Howard, *Garden Cities of To-Morrow* (London: Sonnenschein, 1902), 25–26, diagram 2.

9
David Abraham, "Conflicts within German Industry and the Collapse of the Weimar Republic," *Past & Present* 88 (1980): 88–128.

10
Jan Abt and Alexander Ruhe, *Das neue Frankfurt. Der soziale Wohnungsbau in Frankfurt am Main und sein Architekt E*

securing the reproduction of a high-quality workforce, then considered the country's main asset at a time of increased international competition. This form of human-resource fallowing required the "subtraction" of workers from the factory during the years of childhood, as well as during hours of leisure time spent in city parks, sports facilities, or at home. Progressive municipal schemes, however, were hindered by the national bloc of heavy industry and conservative parties and authorities, including the Reichsbank, which considered them unproductive expenditures. These agencies argued that public investment instead be used for immediately valuable endeavors such as ad hoc subsidies for industrial capital.[11]

Although more modest in ambition, early federal initiatives devised by Franklin D. Roosevelt's "brain trust" of advisors in New Deal America met similar opposition that blocked some of the boldest attempts to expand public services and implement regional planning across the nation, including projects like the Greenbelt Town program.[12] Here, however, another example can be found of the growing schism between the cultivation and extraction of human and nonhuman value under capitalism. A quintessential form of urban fallowing, the concept of using greenbelts of farmland and parks to structure metropolitan development was at odds with another aspect of New Deal resettlement programs. In distressed regions, rural planning initiatives by state agencies like the Tennessee Valley Authority and the Subsistence Homesteads Division of the US federal government promoted chemical fertilizers in campaigns to increase agricultural output and accelerate value cycles.[13] The rift between social and environmental reproduction schemes was artificially enlarged as a result of the tensions of industrial expansion.

Postwar Keynesian arrangements consolidated previous modes of fallowing labor power while securing unprecedented growth rates in industrial farming and manufacturing. By the 1960s, however, this system was already fraught with problems at various levels across the core capitalist countries. On one hand, behind the facade of social policy and welfare programs, capital established a new hegemony around its own agenda in the sphere of valorization. Conventional unions gradually focused on wage struggles, increasing workers' share in value creation only to realize it as purchasing power. At the same time, some population groups in advanced capitalist countries—including students and young metropolitan proletarians—refused the condition of fallowed labor power in a challenge to dominant schemes of reproduction. In Italy, where these forms of resistance were linked to both working-class protests and urban social movements, the rejection of work and consumerism nurtured the revitalization of qualitative value based on self-management, or what Antonio Negri and other activists termed "self-valorization."[14] This "use-value movement," to borrow Franco Piperno's phrase,[15] saw the emergence of a "revolutionary historical subject" and the "passage from wage struggle to the struggle over appropriation." According to Negri this shift would eventually "break capital's margins of valorization" by reconquering new "space[s] for workers' valorization."[16] In the ensuing decades a wave of autonomous social centers and liberated spaces spread across abandoned sites in Italy and elsewhere.[17] These movements productively repurposed fallowness by transforming transitory sites into prefigurative territories, interrupting the conventional real estate value system to allow for alternative, collectively organized use values.

In recent years, expanding and accelerating value chains have triggered new mutations in fallowing regimes. While none of the aforementioned processes were exclusive to core capitalist countries, the current trend towards planetary urbanization has not only produced a worldwide explosion of the urban fabric, but also of accumulation strategies linked to the secondary circuit of capital and the financialization of real estate markets.[18] Land grabbing and the acquisition of devalued property by vulture funds illustrate the prominent role of global corporate landlords and real estate investment trusts in the emergence of a new frontier of fallowing.[19] Today, as at the dawn of agrarian capitalism, many of these transactions are purely speculative. Large tracts of land seized in Africa and Latin America remain idle after the expulsion of local populations, while social housing units snapped up by foreign investors in distressed countries such as Greece, Ireland, or Spain lie empty after evictions. But unlike earlier forms of

11
Ben Lieberman, "Luxury or Public Investment? Productivity and Planning for Weimar Recovery," *Central European History* 26 (1993): 195–213.

12
Joseph L. Arnold, *The New Deal in the Suburbs: A History of the Greenbelt Town Program 1935–1954* (Columbus: Ohio State University Press, 1971).

13
Darrell A. Russel and Gerald G. Williams, "History of Chemical Fertilizer Development," *Soil Science Society of America Journal* 41 (1977): 260–65; Walter William Wilcox, *Planning a Subsistence Homestead* (Washington, DC: US Dept. of Agriculture, 1934), 9.

14
Antonio Negri, *Books for Burning: Between Civil War and Democracy in 1970s Italy* (London: Verso, 2005), 180–230; Nanni Balestrini and Primo Moroni, *L'orda d'oro: 1968–1977: la grande ondata rivoluzionaria e creativa, politica ed esistenziale* (Roma: Feltrinelli, 1997). For an architectural approach to the Autonomia movement, see Pier Vittorio Aureli, *The Project of Autonomy: Politics and Architecture within and against Capitalism* (New York: Princeton Architectural Press, 2008).

15
Franco Piperno, "Autonomia possibile, valore d'uso, lavoro non-operaio," *Metropoli* 1 (February 1978), pre-print.

16
Negri, *Books for Burning*, 18, 60.

17
Alexander Vasudevan, *The Autonomous City: A History of Urban Squatting* (London: Verso Books, 2017), see especially 150–83 for the case of Italy; see also Bart van der Steen, Ask Karzeff, and Leendert van Hoogenhuijze, eds., *The City Is Ours: Squatting and Autonomous Movements in Europe from the 1970s to the Present* (Oakland: PM Press, 2014).

18
Neil Brenner, "Theses on Urbanization," *Public Culture* 25 (2013): 85–114; Kevin Fox Gotham, "Creating Liquidity out of Spatial Fixity: The Secondary Circuit of Capital and the Subprime Mortgage Crisis," *International Journal of Urban and Regional Research* 33 (2009): 355–71; Neil Smith, "New Globalism, New Urbanism: Gentrification as Global Urban Strategy," *Antipode* 34 (2002): 427–50.

speculation, today these dormant spaces are incorporated as underlying assets in real estate derivatives and hedge funds to leverage ongoing or expected food, raw material, and energy crises, or to inflate prospective building and housing capacities that do not match the reality of lackluster local economies.[20] Under such conditions of deepened financialization, virtual use values transform into marketable values almost instantaneously, making fallowing immediately profitable. The same goes for reproductive realms beyond the built environment, as in the case of the privatization and equitization of welfare services like health care and education, or the penetration of financial logic into everyday life and the household.[21] The current trend to commodify or financialize spheres of fallowing paradoxically renders them instantly lucrative. Futures—use-value futures—are seen as merely triggering accumulation in virtual circuits and their actual realization risks becoming a residual feature. In this situation urbanization again assumes the form of an infrastructural apparatus to extract value on a planetary scale, and planning—once a regulatory framework to fallow both space and labor power—is simply eclipsed in the context of unprecedented crises of reproduction.

Theory

Fallowness is one of many configurations of labor power, space, and time engineered to generate value. The variety of these configurations can articulate productive, reproductive, and regulatory strategies in complex and often contradictory arrangements. Fallow resources are productive forces purposefully left idle to increase their value-added capacity and profitability in the future, but they can also support more sustainable socioecological and economic orders by rationalizing production flows to prevent excess and "avoid surplus."[22] In other words, these practices express the dialectical tension between speculation and planning. This ambivalence is also embedded in valorization struggles between antagonistic economic blocs and grassroots initiatives striving to build alternative worlds based on forms of counter-value.

Such valorization struggles around fallowness comprise three fundamental dilemmas: a) an ontological conflict over what defines value, what contains or generates value, and what is or is not productive; b) an operative conflict over the goals of valorization, the tension between qualitative and quantitative value, or between use and exchange value; c) a temporal conflict over the proper moment in which to realize value, and the programming of circuits of production, consumption, and reproduction. Under capitalism, regimes of accumulation rely on different arrangements around these three axes to maintain and expand its system; thus diverse formations of fallowness emerge giving such regimes their historically specific contours. At the same time, this process is overdetermined by a broader dialectic of capitalist development with two contrasting structural features: a) the "annihilation of space by time" (or the "usurpation of space") as a result of the system's drive to remove all spatial, territorial, natural, and cultural impediments so as to minimize the circulation time of capital;[23] b) the ecological and reproductive limits that environments and socionatural formations impose on the expansion and intensification of capital accumulation.[24] This tension has been summarized by different theorists as a "contradiction between economy and ecology,"[25] a second (i.e., environmental and reproductive) contradiction of capitalism,[26] or a "metabolic rift"[27] indicating that the overall expansion of the capitalist system makes social and environmental reproduction incompatible.

The brief discussion above suggests that specific fallowing formations are the path-dependent, variable outcome of the interplay between valorization struggles and broader structural contradictions of capital, and thus cannot be subsumed under a singular interpretive key linking certain socionatural configurations with specific political agencies, productive agendas, and regulatory schemes. That is, different fallowing strategies can be pursued,

19
Joe Beswick et al., "Speculating on London's Housing Future: The Rise of Global Corporate Landlords in 'Post-Crisis' Urban Landscapes," *City* 20 (2016): 321–41; Saturnino M. Borras and Jennifer C. Franco, "Global Land Grabbing and Trajectories of Agrarian Change: A Preliminary Analysis," *Journal of Agrarian Change* 12 (2012): 34–59; Philip McMichael, "The Land Grab and Corporate Food Regime Restructuring," *Journal of Peasant Studies* 39 (2012): 681–701.

20
See, for example, Luigi Russi, *Hungry Capital: The Financialization of Food* (London: Zero Books, 2013); Manuel B. Aalbers, "The Financialization of Home and the Mortgage Market Crisis," *Competition & Change* 12 (2008): 148–66; Michael Byrne, "Entrepreneurial Urbanism after the Crisis: Ireland's 'Bad Bank' and the Redevelopment of Dublin's Docklands," *Antipode* 48 (2016): 899–918; Daniel Coq-Huelva, "Urbanization and Financialization in the Context of a Rescaling State: The Case of Spain," *Antipode* 45 (2013): 1213–31.

21
See, for example, Lena Lavinas, *The Takeover of Social Policy by Financialization: The Brazilian Paradox* (New York: Springer, 2017); Randy Martin, *Financialization of Daily Life* (Philadelphia: Temple University Press, 2002).

22
The Oxford English Dictionary emphasizes this aspect in the main entry for "fallow."

23
Altvater, "Ecological and Economic Modalities," 60; David Harvey, *The Urbanization of Capital* (Oxford: Blackwell, 1985), 35–45; Karl Marx, *Grundrisse*, trans. Martin Nicolaus (London: Penguin, 1973), 524, 539.

24
John Bellamy Foster, "Capitalism and Ecology: The Nature of the Contradiction," *Monthly Review* 54 (2002): 6–16; Jason W. Moore, "Environmental Crises and the Metabolic Rift in World-Historical Perspective," *Organization & Environment* 13 (2000): 123–157.

25
Altvater, "Ecological and Economic Modalities," 60.

26
James O'Connor, "Capitalism, Nature, Socialism: A Theoretical Introduction," *Capitalism Nature Socialism* 1 (1988): 11–38.

27
John Bellamy Foster, "Marx's Theory of Metabolic Rift: Classical Foundations for Environmental Sociology," *American Journal of Sociology* 105 (1999): 366–405.

defended, and attacked by both the elite and the oppressed, with different goals. Throughout history, fallow land, fallow space, and fallow labor—much like wastelands, abandoned architectures, and surplus populations—have been framed by different social blocs as either idle or profitable in the long run, as barren or productive, as an unacceptable limit on collective prosperity, a balanced approach to resource exploitation, or merely an asset in larger value compounds regardless of actual use. Agrarian, industrial, and financial formations of capitalism—and the diverse expressions thereof—use different configurations and representations of space, time, and labor, and different inflections of fallowness, to generate, rationalize, or expand value chains according to the needs and expectations of historically specific capital and class compositions. Rather than attempting to trace a single genealogy for value allocation, distribution, and appropriation in time and space, the challenge for a politics of design is to elucidate the agency regulating these processes, and to evaluate their potential impact on urbanization and other forms of spatial production. Although the trajectories of fallowing cannot necessarily be determined in advance, the brief overview above suggests certain structural regularities, which I delineate here as a preliminary, tentative synthesis.

In a "double movement" similar to that theorized by economic historian Karl Polanyi, the historical fluctuation between production- and reproduction-oriented regimes of fallowness seems to ebb and flow between the commodification of land and labor, and protection against its excesses.[28] In terms of the structural patterns described above, this fluctuation expresses the ongoing tension between the usurpation of space and the attempt to address the metabolic rift and reproductive crises. States usually play a prominent role in both scenarios, but their regulatory apparatuses are more obviously present in the latter, as welfare agencies. During the earliest stages of original accumulation and industrial capitalism in the 19th century, the fallowing of land and labor was either marginalized or cast as part of a purely speculative scheme, in both cases bringing about severe environmental and social reproduction crises. Towards the end of the 19th century these conflicts animated state responses in the form of social policy and planning to secure social order, reduce environmental problems, and rationalize urbanization processes. The ensuing period of Fordist arrangements gradually incorporated a number of key externalities in the reproduction of the industrial system as a means of fallowing human resources, such as housing, urban public facilities, and education. At the same time, the fallowing of nonhuman resources rapidly declined as industrial fertilizers, mechanization, and other techniques to accelerate value extraction eclipsed natural methods of restoring ecological capacities. Thus social and environmental reproduction were increasingly and artificially decoupled as the contradiction between economy and ecology deepened and the metabolic rift grew larger. With the onset of neoliberalism in the late 1970s many prior fallowing schemes were put under pressure and became vulnerable, including both natural and social reserves, and core welfare agencies such as public education and health care, social housing, and urban planning. In the realm of urbanization a new global logic has recently emerged that combines long-term investment in lands in remote territories and the speculative seizure of depreciated real estate in core urban areas, generating massive waves of displacement and dispossession across the world.

These conditions suggest that capitalism has had some success in its enduring attempt to eliminate dormancy and schedule diverse layers of accumulation across different markets to secure steady revenue flows. Through trading futures, fallowness is rendered immediately productive: exchange value is realized before prospective use values are generated, and virtual profits are engineered to replace wealth stored slowly over time by nonmarket agencies. But by accelerating the aptitude of certain spaces and resources to create value beyond their restorative capacities, these forms of artificial "fertilization" fuel new crises of reproduction, both socially and environmentally.

Against this longue-durée trend we can trace an alternative tradition of struggles to remove communities and ecosystems from the capitalist imperative for instant profitability and quantitative value. In commoning space and time, these experiences preserve use values either through a kind of combatant fallowing or by appropriating state fallows to establish platforms for alternative worlds. This tradition can be found among those who refuse to abandon common land or to give up common rights that render their households partially independent from wage labor, and in Luddite struggles against the "fertilization" of manufacturing with machine technologies. It is found in Paul Lafargue's plea for laziness, in working-class sabotage and wildcat strike actions to seize control of the shop floor from Taylorist management.[29] It is also in the Surrealists' praise of flânerie and sleep as productive activity, and in the calls of both the Situationist International and Henri Lefebvre to subvert the normalization of everyday life through revolutionary festivals.[30] It is the refusal of work and the operaist demand for self-management in Italy, the ethos of punk, the wave of autonomous spaces thriving in thousands of occupied social centers in late-20th-century Europe, and the Invisible Committee's recent appeal to embrace the "now" as an urgent political ontology.[31] By

28
Karl Polanyi, *The Great Transformation* (New York: Farrar & Rinehart, 1944).

29
Paul Lafargue, *Le droit à la paresse* (Paris: Oriol, 1883).

30
Association Fédérative Générale des Etudiants de Strasbourg, *De la misère en milieu étudiant* (Strasbourg: Union Nationale des Étudiants de France, 1966), 28; Henri Lefebvre, *Writings on Cities* (Oxford: Blackwell, 1996), 168.

breeding qualitative values, these self-valorization struggles are also formidable incubators of political hope for developing counter-territorialization and alter-urbanization strategies,[32] initiatives in which communities and collectives craft alternative modes of coexistence with others and with ecosystems that may destabilize capitalism.

Design

Any form of fallowing is a project: a certain articulation of design and politics to organize space in time. Fallowing connects a particular configuration of sociomaterial orders—a specific allocation or restriction of access to resources—to a concept of production and its distribution as future wealth. But how should designers react to the ambivalence of fallowing, and its increasing commodification? What formations of fallowness should activist planning pursue and engage? Is it possible to mediate dormancy, vacancy, and productivity so as to reorganize landscapes, environments, and urbanisms in a progressive fashion? History suggests hybrid regimes that superimpose different territorialities and temporalities are more versatile and resilient—they can support unexpected forms of grassroots appropriation and provide a more robust ground to overcome endemic social and environmental contradictions. It is necessary, therefore, to devise schemes to combine institutionally endorsed forms of egalitarian and ecological reproduction with an open infrastructure to cultivate qualitative use values from the bottom up.

Planning cannot simply be reduced to a powerless, aestheticizing exercise of identification and administration of rent gaps over time. At minimum, to establish a "regime of rest" opposed to contemporary forms of speculation and accelerated accumulation, planning ought to regain its capacity to mediate and rationalize capital's temporalities, inhibiting its inclination to annihilate use value with exchange value. Fallowness must be reappropriated as a regulatory category based on restoration, dilation, and slowness, to promote the enrichment of space by time. Planning's fundamentally social-reproductive function should be reactivated, to bring back its unrealized drive to synchronize the economy with the pace of environmental recuperation and the cultivation of both individuals and communities. But these forms of state building are only a (reformist) beginning. Public apparatuses should be devised to create conditions of possibility for alternative praxes that escape institutional closure in imaginative, autonomous ways. Design can help prevent the functionalist ossification of fallow realms by developing a more delicate understanding of the dormant potentialities of current spatial configurations. State apparatuses, public services, and urban infrastructures can be reinvented as open-ended machines to reserve spaces that other polities can subsequently transform. Grassroots collectives could take advantage of such state-run mechanisms to inhibit exchange value encroachments and prevent surplus, to forge new forms of commoning use values *hic et nunc*. Through the juxtaposition of state rest regimes and the self-valorization of idle space, fallowing may reveal a prefigurative potential as a transitory territoriality that allows the construction of alternative worlds in the meantime.

31
Comité Invisible, *Maintenant* (Paris: Fabrique, 2017).

32
Neil Brenner, *Critique of Urbanization: Selected Essays* (Basel: Birkhäuser, 2017), 284–85.

Fallow: A Comparative Reflection

STEPHEN CAIRNS &
JANE M. JACOBS

It is some four years since we wrote *Buildings Must Die: A Perverse View of Architecture* (2014),[1] a book inquiring into the oft-ignored end condition of buildings and what that means for architecture as a profession, invested as it is in the natalism of design. The matter of time lies deep within that problematic, and affects how the fortunes of buildings change in relation to a general economy of value, determined by the intersection of market, functional utility, material viability, and symbolic worth. We wanted to bring into view the many instances in which buildings move towards, or come to an end—and to generate a terminal literacy with respect to this process. We did so not because we wanted to will buildings away before their time, but in order to attune architects (and others) to the alternative possibilities offered by such processes; possibilities that include reuse, misuse, political appropriation, ruin aestheticization, life-cycle design, planned destruction, resistance, and more. The concept of "fallow," which is the focus of this issue, resonates well with that project and further expands the terms by which to engage with alternative productivities of the built environment.

Built environments are obdurate and tend to yield their social and economic value in overly prescribed ways. But every now and then a building's social purpose (such as its use or meaning) can fall out of sync with the form itself. When that happens a building is in place but out of time, as urban designer Kevin Lynch has described.[2] Responding to such a circumstance is no simple matter. Unlike an appliance or a frock, a building that is no longer useful or fit for purpose cannot be easily thrown away. This is because there is often a lot invested in built forms, as well as the land upon which they are built. As Marxist geographer David Harvey reiterates in his extended inquiry into the political economy of urbanization, buildings and infrastructure "imprison" value by fixing capital in a place, in materials, and in specific uses and social relations (such as production and reproduction).[3] This in turn creates a central spatial tension within capitalism. As he put it, "capitalist development has to negotiate a knife-edge path between preserving the values of past capital investments in the built environment and destroying these investments in order to open up fresh room for accumulation."[4] This accounts for capitalism's drive towards "perpetual perishing."[5]

The cycles of investment associated with the built environment occur through a circuit that Harvey, following Henri Lefebvre, refers to as the secondary circuit of capital. Capital generally switches into this secondary circuit only when there is surplus value in the primary circuit of commodity production. And of course, that switching can only happen if certain other things are in place. Most evidently, there must be a formalized property market that creates the land commodity. Secondly, there must be instruments of "fictitious capital" (credit systems, debt financing, insurance) to support the often slow, long, and big character of such investment. Thirdly, the assistance of the state is often required to mediate or expedite what often become large-scale and long-term transactions. Finally, investment in this circuit is not always made to create new use value. An investment can be made in a property commodity that itself creates the desired economic return. Indeed, in many land markets today it can perversely make better economic sense to own a property and leave it unburdened by use. In one sense this could be seen to generate a condition of fallowness, given that the prescribed use of the site is in abeyance. But in another sense such property is still "in use": holding, accruing, or shedding value as a commodity.

It may well be an economic fallacy to imagine that a built environment that is also property can ever be in a truly fallow state—for property is always active, through appreciation or depreciation of value. Yet buildings do become socially fallow, meaning they stop realizing their prescribed use value as, say, a factory or a house. When this happens a gap is created: a building that stops realizing its prescribed use value is suspended in time as it (or usually, the land beneath it) awaits a new cycle of investment through development. This temporal gap results in many different kinds of transitional states of varying duration. There might be slow abandonment and decay, there might be instant demolition and the emergence of a vacant brownfield site. There have been many terms used to describe such phases of devaluation: "blight," "abandonment," and more romantically, "urban ruins." Thinking of unused land and buildings in this way sits firmly within the categorical binary of the capitalist city, wherein enclosed land not in productive use can be cast back into the category of waste. Yet there are other ways to think about such spaces and cycles, as well as other ways to act in relation to them. The term "fallow" offers a suggestive alternative framework. In an agricultural setting, fallow land is deliberately left free of cropping activity to enable the recovery of its soil structure and fertility. Translating this term to lived built environments allows for a productive reconceptualization of those temporal and spatial gaps generated by capitalism's cycles. Describing such social and economic "gaps" as periods of fallow opens up alternate imaginaries of productivity for land and buildings that are normally precluded: squatting, guerrilla gardening, urban exploration, "demolition" art, pop-up enterprises. In other words, thinking of such spaces as fallow, and so released from the long and costly cycles of city-building-as-usual, delivers opportunities for what urban designer Ali Madanipour has called a "temporary urbanism."[6]

Madanipour and others often refer to such urbanisms as "interventions," a term that carries with it the idea of intervening in a current state of affairs, but also that of interrupting, implying an occurrence situated between existing things. The term also evokes how such urbanisms run according to a different time scale. Rather than obdurate, they are more likely to be ephemeral. Although the general outcome of such interventions is to disrupt "the settled habits of society,"[7] the motivation for urban experimentalists is diverse. There are the self-consciously political, though most would admit that insurgent effects often remain "small-scale and place-specific."[8] Those who have documented the political potential of do-it-yourself urbanisms also lament that the market is often not far behind, able to capitalize on the aesthetic and social "capital" (a community garden here, an atmosphere of liveliness there) generated by such interventions.[9] As Madanipour suggests, such interventions work in and through the spatial and temporal opportunities delivered by capitalism's cycles of creative destruction. Such fleeting disruptions inject alternative architectural and urban imaginaries, nudge us towards different futures, and may even restructure circumstances such that an idea that begins as a pop-up transforms into a fixture. But for the most part they are temporary and often localized by-products of the rhythms of advanced capitalism. To admit that fact does not mean city building must succumb to the hegemonic

1
Stephen Cairns and Jane M. Jacobs, *Buildings Must Die: A Perverse View of Architecture* (Cambridge, MA: MIT Press, 2014).

2
Kevin Lynch, *What Time Is This Place?* (Cambridge, MA: MIT Press, 1976).

3
David Harvey, "The Geography of Capitalist Accumulation: A Reconstruction of the Marxian Theory," *Antipode* 7.2 (September 1975): 9–21.

4
Harvey, "Capitalist Accumulation," 10.

5
Harvey, "Capitalist Accumulation," 12.

6
Ali Madanipour, *Cities in Time: Temporary Urbanism and the Future of the City* (London: Bloomsbury Academic, 2017).

7
Madanipour, *Cities in Time*, 11.

8
Megan Heim LaFrombois, *Reframing the Reclaiming of Urban Space: A Feminist Exploration into Do-It-Yourself Urbanism in Chicago* (Lanham: Lexington Books, 2018).

9
Gordon C. C. Douglas, "Do-It-Yourself Urban Design: The Social Practice of Informal 'Improvement' through Unauthorized Alteration," *City & Community* 13.1 (March 2014): 19.

imaginary of an inevitable capitalism with an unvarying logic that a postcapitalist politics can only resist or think beyond.[10] Indeed, it may focus greater attention on the cyclical interruptions in those logics so that the (ephemeral) foundations of other futures may be laid, and alternative value gleaned.

Land banks, Clementi, Singapore.
Courtesy Jane M. Jacobs and Stephen Cairns.

Resituating the Fallow

We were based in Europe when we began writing *Buildings Must Die*, and the cities around us presented many forgotten bits or sites of disinvestment that had become experiments in alternative futures. This reflection is written from Asia, living in and surrounded by cities where "fallow" spaces present themselves in entirely different ways, and development proceeds through entanglements of incrementalism and bold aspiration. One example of "fallow" in this context is the state-run land banking system of Singapore, which hoards land assets acquired or manufactured (through reclamation) to variously maximize public good or market revenue.[11] Land banks in Singapore are left entirely empty, marked with signs that invite casual use by "everyone," yet reminding those users that it is "STATE LAND." The lack of any designed investment (a bench, a playground) communicates clearly that the land is intended for other purposes. This "fallow" land is so tightly scripted into future plans that any use that could generate awkward attachments is dissuaded. Of course, as sociologist Chua Beng Huat notes, the state-capitalist model of Singaporean development is a poor proxy for other Asian cities, where the spatial and temporal logics of development wrestle with other challenges.[12]

In an essay on the "great cities of India" from 1962, Claude Lévi-Strauss famously stressed the need for alternate thinking when encountering the Asian city, specifically in relation to Calcutta.[13] There he observed that although much of the Asian city could be viewed, by the Western eye, as "a kind of wasteland . . . a kind of blight," such a condition was really the "ultimate expression of urban living."[14] Despite the dubious caricatures of "Asiatic cruelty" described in the same essay, his analysis ultimately makes a claim for the radically "other" logic of Asian cities at that time. In such impoverished and overcrowded cities, Lévi-Strauss noted, everywhere and anywhere could "acquire a kind of domestic status"; every street, gutter, cul-de-sac, and spare inch was used for living, working, sleeping. As he observed, Asian urban life was not simply "outside the limits," but had no "limit on its spread." In Lévi-Strauss's Asian city, all spaces that could "fit in" a little more life or activity were called upon to do so. This "Asian city" ideal type did not, in short, feature enclosures where temporally and spatially bounded investment occasionally gave way to a period of fallowness before the anticipated next investment cycle. Instead, the "Asian city" supported a continuous and everywhere general economy of investment and disinvestment, with all its borrowing and sharing, stealing and giving, anointing and defacing.

Today, due to the new literature on noncapitalist economic activity, we might read Lévi-Strauss's essay as registering an alternative urban commons; relied upon by the poor and vested more in currency of use than ownership.[15] This has not been the dominant assessment of circumstances in Third World cities. Developmentalist models of modernization viewed such dissipated conditions of "making do" as hindering the full and proper transition from Third World to First, even describing them as instances of economic "involution," wherein the "economic pie" is steadily divided into minute pieces by an "incredible volume of *ad hoc* acts of exchange," thus producing a society of "just-enoughs" and "not-quite-enoughs."[16] When anthropologist Clifford Geertz—who first used the term "involution"—discussed low-productivity and labor-intensive economic activities in relation to the urbanization of

10
J. K. Gibson-Graham, "Diverse Economies: Performative Practices for 'Other Worlds'," *Progress in Human Geography* 32.5 (October 2008): 613–32.

11
Anne Haila, *Urban Land Rent: Singapore as a Property State* (Chichester: John Wiley & Sons, 2016).

12
Chua Beng Huat, "Singapore as Model," in *Worlding Cities: Asian Experiments and the Art of Being Global*, eds. Ananya Roy and Ong Aihwa (Malden, MA: Wiley-Blackwell, 2011).

13
Claude Lévi-Strauss, "Crowds," *New Left Review* 15 (May–June 1962): 3–6.

14
Lévi-Strauss, "Crowds," 3.

15
Vinay Gidwani and Amita Baviskar, "Urban Commons," *Economic and Political Weekly* 46.50 (2011): 42–43.

16
Clifford Geertz, *Peddlers and Princes: Social Change and Economic Modernization in Two Indonesian Towns* (Chicago: University of Chicago Press, 1963). Geertz's thesis and the causal mechanisms he proposed have been widely challenged, with many scholars pointing to the ways in which households operate in self-interested as opposed to corporatist or egalitarian fashion with respect to crops. (See Jonathan Rigg, "Redefining the Village and Rural Life: Lessons from Southeast Asia," *Geographical Journal* 160 [1994]: 123–35; J. M. Hardjono, *Land, Labor, and Livelihood in a West Java Village* [Yogyakarta: Gadjah Mada University Press, 1987.]) Setting aside the nuances of these debates, the idea of "shared poverty" has become part of "everyday discourse" with "profound influence" on policy making and scholarship in Indonesia (Benjamin White, "Agricultural Involution and Its Critics: 20 Years after Clifford Geertz" [The Hague: ARD Seminars Institute of Social Sciences, 1983], 1).

Land bank, Clementi, Singapore. Courtesy Jane M. Jacobs and Stephen Cairns.

Marunda, East Jakarta. Courtesy Jane M. Jacobs and Stephen Cairns.

Indonesian cities, he positioned them as part of a residual "bazaar-peasant" economy at odds with the exchanges of the emergent, "firm"-based capitalist economy.[17] The geographer Terry McGee later described how capitalist logics in Third World cities often depend upon coexistent "noncapitalist egalitarianism" which supplements the inadequacies of the market and the state, essentially self-solving such intractable challenges as housing and service supply.[18] Yet as urbanist Ananya Roy's genealogy of informality shows, undercapitalization is persistently framed as a problem.[19] Economist Hernando de Soto has even gone so far as to describe informal settlements as comprising "dead" or "defective" assets.[20] Furthermore, value is as much a worry today for the activist reformer seeking to use instruments like property and credit to bring greater security to informal settlements, as it is for the ambitious property developer eager to evict a settlement to make way for a shopping mall.

Although nowadays convergent, the spatial and temporal logic of development in the Third World city still contrasts with the rhythmic production of fallowness in First World cities. In the first instance, there are distinct differences with respect to the logics of enclosure (property) and cyclicity (investment) necessary for capitalist development. For example, in contemporary Jakarta both the temporality and spatiality of development operate across hybridized systems which leave little room for the emergence of fallow states. Urban historian Abidin Kusno argues that the "temporality of the informal" is "simultaneously within and outside the time of capitalist development."[21] This is evident in the durable ephemerality of the *kampung* settlement, made possible through an incremental mode of construction that accommodates limited and sporadic household income. The materials used for individual buildings within a *kampung* are themselves rarely very permanent, as the buildings are subjected to incessant, if minor, home improvement: clay floors harden with use and may later be poured in concrete or tiled; timber structures built from gleaned materials rot and are replaced; woven bamboo cladding is rewoven, repaired, and often swapped with timber planks, brick, or concrete block and plaster walls; thatch roofs are constantly tended and in time may be traded for clay tile, or later, corrugated iron sheeting. The work of building, consolidating, and improving one's home in the *kampung* does not often require entering into the scale and temporality demanded by market-linked credit and mortgage systems.[22] Rather, it proceeds collaboratively, through complex micro-economies of recycling, skill-sharing, and borrowing, what geographers Helga Leitner and Eric Sheppard describe as "practices of communing that exceed capitalist social relations."[23] Such work is often supported by the cultural value of "gotong royong," which literally means "to share a burden." Yet as sociologist AbdouMaliq Simone cautions, "collective resourcefulness" does not eradicate individuated interest, aspiration, or corruption.[24]

Waduk Pluit, North Jakarta.
Courtesy Jane M. Jacobs and Stephen Cairns.

Informal *kampungs* are not only shaped by distinct temporalities of development, but also often underwritten by hybrid property rights models that disrupt pathways to exclusivist enclosure. Jakarta has an unusually flexible land tenure system that allows for the incremental acquisition of rights along a continuum from fully informal to fully formal. Although the intent of the law is that all land be registered through the national land agency or Badan Pertanahan Nasional (BPN), the majority of it remains unregistered.[25] Further complexity arises from the fact that the registration status of land does not necessarily determine whether or not it is occupied. Indeed, institutional lag has compelled the Indonesian government to allow the occupation and development of unregistered land, and to support its formalization through municipally managed tax and service regimes. Thus, at one end of Jakarta's tenure

17
Geertz, *Peddlers and Princes*, 28.

18
W. R. Armstrong and T. G. McGee, "Revolutionary Change and the Third World City: A Theory of Urban Involution," *Civilizations* 18.3 (1968): 353–78.

19
Ananya Roy, "Slumdog Cities: Rethinking Subaltern Urbanism," *International Journal of Urban and Regional Research* 35.2 (March 2011): 223–38.

20
See Timothy Mitchell, "The Properties of Markets: Informal Housing and Capitalism's Mystery" (Cultural Political Economy Working Paper Series, Working Paper 2, Institute for Advanced Studies in Social and Management Sciences, Lancaster, UK, 2004).

21
Abidin Kusno, *After the New Order: Space, Politics, and Jakarta* (Honolulu: University of Hawai'i Press, 2014), 175.

22
See AbdouMaliq Simone, *Jakarta: Drawing the City Near* (Minneapolis: University of Minnesota Press, 2014).

23
Helga Leitner and Eric Sheppard, "From *Kampungs* to Condos? Contested Accumulations through Displacement in Jakarta," *Environment and Planning A* 50.2 (March 2018): 440.

24
AbdouMaliq Simone, "'We Are Here Alone': The Ironic Potentials and Vulnerabilities of Mixed (Up) Districts in Central Jakarta," *International Journal of Urban and Regional Research* 38.4 (July 2014): 1509.

25
Michael Leaf, "Land Regulation and Housing Development in Jakarta, Indonesia: From the 'Big Village' to the 'Modern City,'" (PhD diss., University of California, Berkeley, 1992).

continuum is the occupation of unregistered land, unsupported by local documentation. A more common case is the occupation of unregistered land with rights of exploitation and use recognized and formalized through taxation and other arrangements administered by municipal offices, or *kelurahan*. This condition is sometimes referred to as "informally registered land"; it is an institutionalized informality.[26] At the other extreme is occupation with formal rights over registered land. In some instances, the tenure continuum is crossed by forms of customary (*adat*) rights. Yet at the heart of the hybrid system is the incomplete governmental project of land registration. Touted as the key mechanism for eliminating the problem of "land dualism," it nevertheless offers few incentives to formally register. Besides convoluted administrative procedures and high certification costs, there are tangible advantages to enjoy by occupying unregistered land, including the exemption from complying with certain planning and building regulations.[27]

Conceptually and empirically, this hybrid general economy of dwelling complicates capitalist logics of enclosure. To support large-scale development initiatives in Jakarta, the municipal authority established an *ijin lokasi*, or land permit system.[28] A developer awarded an *ijin lokasi* earns the exclusive rights to purchase land from unregistered users. As such, large-scale land permitting effectively becomes a mechanism for "transferring lands from the informal popular sector to the formal private sector."[29] As Leitner and Sheppard document, this can proceed by incremental acquisition of land from voluntarily sellers, through to forced evictions of settlements designated "illegal."[30] The displacements that precede the "conversion" of "informally settled spaces of an urban commons into privatized, commodifiable land assets" are achieved by diverse means in a process that might be described as flexible enclosure.[31]

The logics of urbanism in a city like Jakarta demonstrate that fallow space and time is a contingently produced surplus, one that struggles to manifest in the fleeting opportunities that may exist between an incrementally assembled commons of informal settlement and the consolidated aspirations of capitalist development. The extended, hybridized transactional logic of the Third World city raises the question: in which cities, under what urban circumstances does the condition of fallow arise, and which agents are enabled to make use of it? In other words, we must always remember to ask what exactly enables the production of the fallow, and to what ends.

26
Kusno, *After the New Order*.

27
Mercy Corps, "Summary of Land Tenure Research Findings in Jakarta," *Urban Bulletin* 2 (2008).

28
Gavin Shatkin, *Cities for Profit: The Real Estate Turn in Asia's Urban Politics* (Ithaca: Cornell University Press, 2017).

29
Leaf, "Land Regulation," 127–28, as cited in Shatkin, *Cities for Profit*, 113.

30
Leitner and Sheppard, "*Kampungs* to Condos."

31
Leitner and Sheppard, "*Kampungs* to Condos," 437.

RHYT

U

FALLO
HMS O
URBAN

W AND
CAPIT
ZATION

ALIST

N

Rhythms of Wasting/Unbuilding the Built Environment

MAZEN LABBAN

The Urban Stratum: Lithosphere, Technosphere, Detritusphere

Urbanization is stratification. Stratification, according to Deleuze and Guattari, is a process of continual creation, the actualization of apparently and relatively stable entities.[1] It takes place between the earth—the realm of all virtual potentialities, consisting of unformed, unorganized, unstable matters flowing in all directions—and existing strata, the residua of past stratifications, as well as between existing strata. Strata are momentary interruptions of processes of continuous change; they tend to stability but they are also vulnerable to destratification (dismantling or change) and are available for stratification on other levels. Strata are formed within and alongside exterior milieus (environment, medium), from which they capture flows of materials and energy, and they occur "at least in pairs," one stratum serving as substratum for another. Every stratum therefore is multiple, comprising several strata. There is no hierarchy or fixed order among the strata, but rather a great mobility.[2] Any stratum can serve as substratum for another, becoming an "integral part" of it, bound up with it, as the exterior milieu that furnishes the material for the substantial elements and compounds that constitute its interior milieu. Exterior milieus are not exterior *to* the stratum but constitute an exterior *of* the stratum. They belong to the stratum as much as the stratum's interior (or intermediate) milieus. Both exterior and interior milieus are relative and can exchange places; they exist only through their exchanges, "only by virtue of the stratum responsible for the relation between them."[3] Milieus are "block[s] of space-time constituted by the regular repetition of a component."[4] They are more than environments in the narrow sense; a milieu is the medium (substance) that traverses things as much as surrounds them; it is what a thing is in the middle of, in the process of doing, experiencing. Things continually pass between milieus, each with its own cadence, but milieus also pass into each other, communicating constantly with each other, one milieu serving as the milieu of another, or establishing itself on top of it, or dissipating into it, or being constituted in it, or colliding with it. Whereas within a milieu the repetition of the component is an identical recurrence over a regular division of time, the relation between milieus is expressed in rhythm: unequal, asymmetrical, immeasurable repetition marked by difference. Rhythm arises from the communication between milieus; it occurs in between milieus.[5] Things have rhythm not in their milieus but in their passage between milieus, or when they come into being. Rhythm thus pertains to interstratic movements and to stratification.

Urbanization is a process of stratification that interrupts material flows, captures materials and energy from diverse milieus, and expresses them in quasi-stable layers upon the earth. The built environment is one residuum of urbanization, a stratum that is itself composed of several strata. The urban environment is irreducible to a physical mass, but at the physical, inorganic level it is composed of three principal strata: lithosphere, technosphere, detritusphere. In a narrow sense the built environment coincides with the technosphere, the physical environment created or modified by socio-technological agency. The built environment, however, cannot exclude the lithosphere; they are not exterior to each other. The built environment encompasses the material processes involved in both building and unbuilding it, the material structures and infrastructures involved in its production and reproduction—infrastructures of extraction, transportation and communication; the means of production and social reproduction (i.e., the production of commodities and the production of life and society); and various modes of waste circulation and accumulation: slag heaps, scrap yards, landfills, incinerators, "garbage slums," abandoned structures and infrastructures: infrastructures of waste and wasted infrastructures. The technosphere is bound up with the strata from which it captures materials and the strata on which it deposits materials. It is bound up with the lithosphere and with what I call the detritusphere. Detritus connotes debris, residuum, remainder, ruin; as well as transference, things transferred, deposited or sedimented—that is, stratification and the residua of stratification. The sphere in detritusphere is not figurative; rather, it refers to the geometrical shape that (imprecisely) describes the planet. Just as the lithosphere is a layer of the earth in its entirety, the detritusphere is a material stratum that encircles the planet in its entirety, with layers composed of solid, gaseous, and liquid residues of processes of production and reproduction. The detritusphere is a layer of the earth sedimented by processes of urbanization, a residuum of urbanization as much as the technosphere, yet irreducible to a zone of the technosphere. Both lithosphere and detritusphere are exterior milieus of the technosphere, which in turn serves as substratum and milieu for the other strata. The three strata do not exist in any fixed order or hierarchy; they are mobile in relationship to each other and in relationship with each other; they continually change order, pass into each other; they are bound up with each other, integral to one another.

Lithosphere, technosphere, detritusphere: three strata, same materials, different organization. Diverse materials move across and between the strata, binding them to each other. Take, for example, industrial metals: iron and steel, aluminum, and copper. These have been crucial for urbanization since they enter all forms of structures and infrastructures, and a wide range of industrial and consumer products essential for modern urban ways of life. The movement of materials such as metal cuts through and across geological and technological strata—all three strata are always both—and holds them together. Urbanization qua stratification is actualized in the interruption of metal flows beginning, so to speak, with the geological formation of metals in the earth's crust, their mobilization from mineral ores and their flow through extraction, milling, smelting, refining; fabrication and manufacturing; consumption in various modes; disposal, landfilling, recycling, dissipation. But there is never really a beginning or end: material flows are always *au milieu*, in the middle, in the midst of milieus and moving between milieus that have their own cadences (periodic repetition) and that communicate with each other, passing into each other. Their movement is an act of stratification, it has rhythm. Urbanization maps the movement of materials that constitute the built environment across the strata. It is always *au milieu*. It has neither beginning nor end (in space and time) and it moves in all directions between the strata. Its movement is rhythmic.

Urbanization does not end with the actualization of the discrete components of the technosphere—those are, as the built environment as a whole, in a perpetual process of maintenance, modification, and demolition, partial or complete. The built environment is an arrangement of disparate elements that tends towards stability, even permanence, at the same time that it tends towards rearrangement and renewed creation. It is in a perpetual state of simultaneous building, rebuilding, and unbuilding, of becoming and becoming waste. By becoming-waste of the built environment I mean the movement of formed materials into the detritusphere—a double movement since the becoming-waste of the built environment is the same process of its becoming-mine, the passing

1 Gilles Deleuze and Félix Guattari, *A Thousand Plateaus*, trans. Brian Massumi (Minneapolis: University of Minnesota Press, 1987).

2 Ibid., 502.

3 Ibid., 49.

4 Ibid., 313.

5 Ibid., 314.

of the technosphere (and detritusphere) into the lithosphere. A double movement, or two aspects of the same movement:

> (A) *The built environment becoming waste:* The movement of formed materials from the technosphere (and the lithosphere) to the detritusphere does not always involve a change in location or form: construction and demolition materials can leave their location and accumulate in specialized places; but infrastructure and other components of the built environment can become obsolete in situ, become waste without being demolished. They move between strata without changing location or form.

> (B) *The built environment becoming mine*: The movement from the technosphere and the detritusphere to the lithosphere: the stratification of an anthropogenic lithosphere, or the reconstitution of the lithosphere with an anthropogenic layer, or zone. Here also this may or may not involve movement in space or change of form. Moreover, this movement does not predicate on the first: the built environment can become mine without becoming waste.

The reproduction of the built environment is never simple repetition: it produces difference and in this sense it is rhythmic. Construction, maintenance, replacement, renovation, demolition, and reconstruction have their cadences and repeat periodically, but their repetition does not produce the same technosphere. And it produces more than the technosphere: it sediments the detritusphere and reconstitutes the lithosphere. Urbanization, the stratification of the built environment, is a geological process not only because it entails the excavation of the planet, but because it also produces the built environment as a geological formation. I have dealt with the becoming-mine of the built environment elsewhere, so here the focus will be on the becoming-waste of the built environment—the sliding of the technosphere into the detritusphere.[6]

Becoming-Waste of the Built Environment

Urbanization, regardless of its sociohistorical form, is above all a process of building; but it is as much a process of unbuilding. Contra Mumford, unbuilding is not limited to mining in the strict sense, and it is not necessarily a destructive process discontinuous with the earth.[7] Unbuilding entails dismantling the built environment in the process of its consumption and reproduction, and in this sense it is also creative, productive of the built environment. If stratification is a thickening upon the body of the earth,[8] building and unbuilding are two aspects of the same process of urbanization qua stratification. Insofar as urbanization is capitalist urbanization, the dominant, if not exclusive, thickening agent is the circulation of capital—the drive of capital to reproduce itself on an expanded scale.

Urbanization, in its aspects as building and unbuilding, is both a productive and a wasting process. It is wasteful as a productive process and productive as a wasting process. Urbanization produces waste in various forms: from the wasting of mines and mining sites, and much of the spaces mediating those and urban agglomerations, to the production of prodigious amounts of construction and demolition waste and increasing volumes of consumer and commercial waste associated with urban lifestyles. The primary waste product of capitalist urbanization, however, is the built environment itself. David Harvey's dictum captures the inherently destructive nature of the urban process under capitalism: capital builds physical landscapes appropriate to the conditions of its reproduction at a particular moment, only to destroy them subsequently to reestablish the necessary conditions of its reproduction.[9] Wasting the built environment, however, does not necessarily entail the destruction of physical landscapes. The landscapes of capitalism are littered with what archaeologists of the contemporary past call "modern ruins": "a modern ruin landscape of closed shopping malls, abandoned military sites, industrial wastelands, derelict amusement parks, empty apartment houses…"[10] Modern ruins are the material expression of cycles of industrialization and deindustrialization, investment and disinvestment in the built environment. They are often abandoned, sometimes demolished to make space for more profitable investments, or rebuilt or rehabilitated when their use becomes profitable once again. Like destruction, which is a mode of rapid or instant ruination, ruination is only one mode of wasting, and wasting the built environment does not necessarily entail ruination.

6
Mazen Labban, "Deterritorializing Extraction: Bioaccumulation and the Planetary Mine." *Annals of the Association of American Geographers* 104.3 (2014): 560–76.

7
Lewis Mumford, *The City in History: Its Origins, Its Transformations, and Its Prospects* (New York: Harcourt Brace Jovanovich, 1961), 450ff.

8
Deleuze and Guattari, *A Thousand Plateaus*, 70.

9
David Harvey, *The Urban Experience* (Baltimore: Johns Hopkins University Press, 1989), 83.

10
Þóra Pétursdóttir and Bjørnar Olsen, "An Archaeology of Ruins," in *Ruin Memories: Materiality, Aesthetics, and the Archaeology of the Recent Past*, eds. Bjørnar Olsen and Þóra Pétursdóttir (Oxon: Routledge, 2014), 3.

To understand how capitalist urbanization wastes the built environment we must clarify a concept of wasting specific to the capitalist mode of production. By waste I mean that which is irretrievably lost. In this sense only that which is immaterial can be wasted, even if it is recoverable: time, labor, value, form. Matter and materials (formed matters) are indestructible and therefore they cannot be wasted. They can lose their form or function (use-form), or both (e.g., burnt coal, demolished structures), but this loss is an alteration, a change of form rather than an absolute loss. In a sense their form and use-form are wasted, but the material itself is not. The form and use-form of the materials that constitute the built environment are the product of labor. By wasting the built environment, therefore, I mean wasting the labor consumed in its production, reproduction, and maintenance as a composite of formed material elements, regardless of whether this involves destruction or ruination, loss of form or use-form.

This is a specifically capitalist mode of wasting which arises from the dual nature of the labor process under capitalism as concrete, useful activity and abstract, value-creating activity; and the dual nature of the product of labor as material use-form and value. Commodities produced under capitalist conditions of production lead two separate lives, an economic life and a physical life. Their economic life may expire before their physical life. They may become functionally or aesthetically obsolete, or they may lose their value, before their complete consumption, the slow or instant destruction of their material form in use. More to the point, commodities appear as waste regardless of whether they are consumed. Under capitalism, wasted time is not opposed to productive time. On the contrary, it is productive labor, the labor consumed in producing surplus value, that is a waste of time—labor expressed as surpluses of commodities that will obsolesce or lose their value before they have been consumed. And just as every minute of the working day is part surplus labor, every individual commodity, and not only the aggregate mass of commodities, contains surplus value. Every commodity is therefore already part waste. This mode of wasting is immanent to the capitalist mode of production. It cannot be eliminated with some technical fix or change in culture or habit. Waste is produced even before the immediate process of wasting in the production or consumption of commodities begins because the valorization process, the production of surplus value, is itself a wasting process—a wasting of human material and social capacities.[11]

Specifically capitalist wasting has two mutually reinforcing forms: overproduction and devaluation. Waste first appears as an accumulation of commodity surpluses. Because capitalist production proceeds without regard to social needs or effective demand, a portion of the social product always appears as an excess of commodities that cannot realize the value they represent. The value that commodities represent is not a stable quantity because of the technological and aesthetic dynamism of the capitalist mode of production and consumption. Commodities are therefore vulnerable to devaluation—a waste of the living and dead labor spent on their production. Competition between capital and labor for the extraction of surplus value and competition among capitalists for its realization and appropriation leads, on one hand, to the acceleration of genuine technological change in the production and circulation of commodities and, on the other, to the incessant drive to create false newness, superficial improvements in commodities to encourage their replacement. The first tendency leads to the accelerated obsolescence, and thus devaluation, of the means of production (and circulation), while the second leads to, and depends on, the progressive obsolescence of consumer products. Insofar as the built environment, at once means of production and consumption, is the product of capitalist urbanization, it is subject to the same tendencies of overproduction, obsolescence, and devaluation, hence the wasting of the (dead and living) labor consumed in its production and reproduction.

Landscapes of Surplus, Surplus Landscapes: Overproduction of the Built Environment

In *Monopoly Capital*, Paul Baran and Paul Sweezy argued that the modern capitalist economy is beset by the tendency to generate an ever-increasing "economic surplus"—idle money capital, commodity gluts, underutilized production capacity, and unemployment—without creating the outlets necessary for its utilization.[12] The problem for capital is the disposal of the surplus to avoid stagnation, either by its consumption, reinvestment, or wasting. Consumption alone is insufficient to absorb the surplus because of the relative limits on "society's power of consumption,"[13] while reinvestment exacerbates the problem because it leads to growth in underutilized surpluses. Wasting therefore appears as the most effective, though momentary, mechanism for absorbing the surplus under monopoly capitalism: expenditures on unproductive, wasteful, and destructive activities. The diversity of the wasteful application of capital and labor capacities has exploded to dizzying extent in the 50 years since Baran and

11
Labban, "Deterritorializing Extraction," 573.

12
Paul A. Baran and Paul M. Sweezy, *Monopoly Capital: An Essay on the American Economic and Social Order* (New York: Monthly Review Press, 1966).

13
Karl Marx, *Capital*, vol. 3, trans. David Fernbach (London: Penguin, 1981).

Sweezy made their argument about the contradictions of monopoly capital, yet some of the forms they identified remain salient: financialization (including speculative investment in real estate), urbanization (direct investment in the built environment), expenditure on the "sales effort" to stimulate consumer demand, and expenditures on civilian government and militarism.

All forms of surplus disposal involve investment in the built environment, directly and indirectly, and therefore they can be considered lineaments of urbanization. Expenditure on the sales effort has produced landscapes of department stores, shopping malls, and outlets, and has transformed urban landscapes into advertising space. Government investment in public works and transportation and energy infrastructure—as long as it does not threaten private interest—has contributed more directly to the urban process. The same for militarism. We do not usually think of military expenditures as a vehicle of urbanization, but militarism is as productive as it is destructive of physical landscapes, in times of peace as in wartime. Expenditure on militaries across the world has sedimented a planetary layer of wastelands comprising not only the debris of wars scattered across the planet and abandoned surpluses of equipments that were never used or became obsolete because new generations of weapons with more destructive power replaced them. It has also produced a landscape of military bases and infrastructures that have required continuous maintenance (wasteful expenditure of social labor) even after they had been decommissioned, and in some cases even if they had never been used—veritable monuments to wastefulness—until eventually abandoned, scrapped, demolished, or refitted for other purposes.

Regardless of its sociohistorical form, urbanization has always involved the mobilization of economic surpluses.[14] Under capitalism, however, urbanization becomes internal to the circulation of capital and subservient to its logic, and thus caught up with recurrent crises of overaccumulation. Investments in the built environment and speculation in real estate may provide a momentary solution to those crises in the form of spatial and temporal displacement of surplus capital, but they do not resolve the contradictions that inexorably lead to crises of overaccumulation. Instead, they displace the tendency towards overaccumulation onto the built environment. The absorption of the economic surplus is transformed into a "pervasive tendency" toward the production of surpluses in the built environment.[15] Social labor is doubly wasted, spent on the production of surplus landscapes which render the built environment more vulnerable to devaluation.

Devaluation of the Built Environment

The devaluation of the built environment permeates the capitalist mode of production because the built environment constitutes a large part of the means of production (fixed capital) and social reproduction. All labor processes, except in some aspects of transportation, are tied down to particular places for the duration of a production period. During that period, no matter how long or short, production involves localized means of production—those "held fast in their place once they enter the production process" and those that are "produced from the start in this static form . . . fixed in location, with their roots in the soil"—that have lifespans of several production periods, often several years or decades.[16] The lifespan of the means of production is the period during which their value returns to the capitalist in the form of money, their turnover time. It varies with their type, material, and function in the production process. (Social reproduction also consists of activities tied down to particular places, for certain durations, that depend on the use of means of consumption of varying lifespans. The means of consumption, however, are not employed as capital and therefore do not have a turnover time, although they do have determinate functional and aesthetic lifespans.) Reducing the turnover time of the means of production accelerates the return of their value to their owner. Competition among capitalists therefore compels them to reduce the turnover time of fixed capital, hence to accelerate its depreciation. The pressure is exacerbated by what Marx calls "moral depreciation," whereby fixed capital loses its value regardless of actual wear and tear, either because instruments of the same sort are produced more cheaply or because better instruments enter into competition with it.[17] The means of production are made "prematurely obsolete" regardless of their physical lifespan and are even replaced before their economic lifespan is exhausted.[18] (On the consumption side, the sales effort of competing capitalists has the same effect on consumer products: decline in lifespans due to accelerated obsolescence of quality, function, and desirability.)

The vulnerability of the built environment to devaluation is more acute than in the case of other means of production because of its relative immobility and durability.[19] Although fixity in space does not in itself confer the character of fixed capital on the means of production, it places certain constraints on the circulation of value they represent because a large part of the capital fixed in the built environment cannot be moved without

14
Harvey, *Urban Experience*, 53.

15
Harvey, *Urban Experience*, 70.

16
Karl Marx, *Capital*, vol. 2, trans. David Fernbach (London: Penguin, 1978), 248.

17
Karl Marx, *Capital*, vol. 1, trans. Ben Fowkes (London: Penguin, 1976, 528); Marx, *Capital*, vol. 2, 264.

18
Harvey, *Urban Experience*, 191.

19
David Harvey, *The Limits to Capital* (London: Verso, 1982), 224ff.

its material form being destroyed, hence its value also destroyed. Moreover, the commodities constituting the built environment tend to have longer amortization periods compared to other means of production and reproduction, partly because of their relatively higher durability. *Ceteris paribus* the degree of fixity increases with the durability of the means of production.[20] The more durable, the longer the period during which fixed capital remains fixed in the means of production, the more vulnerable it is to devaluation and moral depreciation.

The problem of the devaluation of the built environment is complicated by the nature of that peculiar commodity and by the elasticity of the concept of durability. The built environment is a "complex composite commodity comprising innumerable different elements—roads, canals, docks and harbors, factories, warehouses, sewers, public offices, schools and hospitals, houses, offices, shops, etc."; it is "long-lived, difficult to alter, spatially immobile . . ."[21] The elements of the built environment are themselves composed of innumerable components of wide material diversity and varying mobility, alterability, and durability. They wear out at different rates; they require varying degrees and different types of maintenance. The built environment as a whole may be long-lived, difficult to alter, and spatially immobile, as Harvey sees it; as a complex composite, however, it is not. Some elements forming the components of the built environment are shorter-lived than others; some elements more easily alterable than others; some more spatially immobile (as is the built environment as a whole), others more mobile; some are completely replaceable, others less so; some can be destroyed or taken out of use while the ensemble continues to function as a whole, others cannot; and so on.

The built environment is a complex composite of complex composites of complex composites . . . of elements that wear out and depreciate according to varying rhythms. This partly derives from the material nature of the composite elements that constitute the built environment; but it also derives from what Michael Thompson calls the "social malleability of objects."[22] Objects do not have the qualities they do because of their inherent physical properties; even though those properties present some limits, objects have the qualities they do as a result of a "social process of endowment." As Marx observes, calculating the average lifespan of fixed capital assumes it undergoes a certain degree of maintenance to keep it in working order; but it also undergoes maintenance according to an expected average lifespan, after which it is replaced in its entirety.[23] Similarly, the physical structures that constitute the built environment are built with expected lifespans according to which they receive "reasonable maintenance," the latter deemed reasonable according to the expected lifespan of that structure.[24] As the lifespan of a structure declines, its value also declines until—on reaching its allotted lifespan—its value declines to virtually nothing. Individual components of the built environment may lose their value regardless of their own durability or decline in their own lifespan. The value of physical structures, Rachel Weber argues, is "context-dependent," it is "held hostage by the vagaries of proximity and its relationship to other properties."[25] Thus, individual components of the built environment are devalued because the zone of the built environment in which they are located is devalued, or because their relative location loses its competitive advantage. They can become obsolete because of rezoning, or go out of fashion because the extension of transportation networks makes other areas more attractive. They may be designated as obsolete and intentionally devalued by their owners to justify demolition and replacement with more profitable structures because of appreciation in real estate values, regardless of actual condition or functionality (also, depreciation means a lower tax bill). Conversely, components of the built environment may gain value for the opposite reasons, regardless of their own material conditions.

The devaluation of the built environment does not necessarily entail its destruction or ruination. Devalued physical structures and infrastructures can languish for years or decades in what Thompson calls the "rubbish category," as valueless waste with zero expected lifespan, abandoned to the forces of nature, vandals, and local junk dealers who strip them of useful or tradable materials, elements, and fixtures. From this "region of flexibility" they can become negatively valued and eventually demolished to make space for more profitable development; or they can become durable again, with an expected lifespan and henceforth renovated and maintained. Thus, at any one point, certain components of the built environment exist as valueless waste, potentially moving in either direction. In one sense the built environment is always becoming waste, in another, it is always already waste.

20
Marx, *Capital*, vol. 2, 240.

21
Harvey, *Urban Experience*, 74.

22
Michael Thompson, *Rubbish Theory: The Creation and Destruction of Value* (Oxford: Oxford University Press, 1979), 50.

23
Marx, *Capital*, vol. 2, 253.

24
Thompson, *Rubbish Theory*, 37–38.

25
Rachel Weber, "Extracting Value from the City: Neoliberalism and Urban Redevelopment," *Antipode* 34.3 (2002): 521–22.

Rhythms of Wasting

The rhythms of wasting the built environment are the rhythms of the becoming of the detritusphere, the sliding of the technosphere into the detritusphere. It is at once an inter-stratic movement and an act of stratification congruent with the (value) circulation of the built environment which, keep in mind, does not necessarily involve movement in space (change of location). It would seem odd to explicate the movement of material things by the circulation of value rather than their circulation in physical space, but the latter does not tell us anything about the devaluation of fixed capital—the becoming-waste of the built environment—which effects the stratification of the detritusphere.

The built environment becomes waste according to varying, simultaneous rhythms determined by the modes of circulation of fixed capital and fluid capital. The difference between the two modes of circulation arises from the different ways in which value circulates through the objective means of production, the form by which they give up their value to the product. Fluid capital—capital in the form of ancillary and raw materials—gives up all its value during a period of production and is entirely consumed in the process of forming the product, that is, it also gives up its material form in the process regardless of whether it enters the product itself.[26] In contrast, fixed capital—capital fixed in the instruments of production—gives up only a portion of its value during a period of production, in proportion to its wearing out. The remainder of its value remains fixed in its material form, which it retains as the means of production are consumed gradually, over several periods of production, until they are worn out and have to be replaced or reproduced. Even when they are worn out and all their value is (presumably) transferred to the product, the instruments of production retain their independent material form:

> Just as during their lifetime, that is to say during the labour process, they retain their shape independently of the product, so too after their death. The mortal remains of machines, tools, workshops etc., always continue to lead an existence distinct from that of the product they helped to turn out.[27]

Hence the persistence of valueless means of production throughout the built environment, including components of the built environment. (The same goes for the means of reproduction, the means of producing human beings, life, and society. Those elements cannot be treated as capital since they are not employed in the production of capital, but they behave in the same manner in terms of their material consumption during periods of reproduction. Some wear out gradually over longer periods of time, maintained throughout the process until they are replaced entirely, preserving their material forms as they are consumed, even after their death. Others are consumed all at once, their material form entirely transformed or rendered useless; they are discarded and must be replaced in kind at the beginning of the process.)

The "material bearers" of fixed and fluid capital are consumed over varying periods. The means of production embodying fixed capital are consumed over longer periods and their replacement is repeated over longer temporal intervals and less frequently than the replacement of the means of production bearing fluid capital. Yet the means of production constituting fixed capital, and their different parts, are also consumed over varying periods and replaced according to varying frequencies because they have different lifespans, including the more durable means of reproduction. They wear out at varying speeds depending on the materials from which they are made; on their actual use (wear and tear), which in turn depends on their function or position in the production process; and on their relative exposure to "the destructive power of natural processes."[28] All means of production and reproduction have average lifespans after which they must be replaced in their entirety, but during their lifetime their parts are worn out unevenly and must be replaced for the whole thing to keep functioning, allowing—or requiring—"partial or periodic replacement."[29] The boundaries between maintenance, repair, renewal, and replacement are not always sharp—maintaining or repairing machines, generators, buildings, infrastructures, and so on, often implies renewing or replacing some parts such that the means of production and social reproduction are in a state of perpetual partial reproduction. This is especially the case with larger, more durable structures and infrastructures which would incur tremendous costs to replace as a whole. These appear durable, even permanent, because they are in a "constant state of rejuvenescence."[30] Their wear and tear is imperceptible and slow, spread over longer periods; they are continuously reproduced in "infinitesimal magnitude," reproduced piecemeal such that in time some are almost replaced in their entirety without ever having been replaced as a whole, all at once.

26
Raw materials enter the product physically, reappearing in a transformed manner in the material form of the product. The material form of ancillaries "vanishes" in the process without reappearing in the product. The same material can function as both: for example, gas burned in the generation of electricity to make plastics, in contrast to the gas used as raw material to make plastics. Marx is mistaken to write that ancillary materials vanish in the production process: "The coal burnt under the boiler vanishes without leaving a trace" (Marx, *Capital*, vol. 1, 311). Would that it were true. We know that that coal is transformed into carbon dioxide and water, among other things, and lingers in the environment for long periods, with devastating consequences.

27
Marx, *Capital*, vol. 1, 311.

28
Marx, *Capital*, vol. 1, 289.

29
Marx, *Capital*, vol. 2, 250.

30
Dionysius Lardner, *Railway Economy: A Treatise on the New Art of Transport, Its Management, Prospects and Relations* (New York: Harper & Brothers, 1850) as quoted in Marx, *Capital*, vol. 2, 259.

The same could be said about the built environment as a whole, the totality of material objects supporting production and social reproduction. The built environment is in a perpetual state of wasting and rejuvenescence, renewed becoming and becoming-waste. The built environment wastes according to various rhythms tracing the circulation of fixed and fluid capital. Since we are no longer exclusively in the sphere of production, however, we can no longer use the categories of fixed and fluid capital to elucidate the stratification of the detritusphere, though we can retain the modal distinction between the two forms of circulation. I propose, instead, two categories that correspond to two qualitatively different rhythms defining the wasting of the built environment, the one determined by the mode of circulation of fixed capital, the other by that of fluid capital: *gradual-immediate wasting* and *instant-mediate wasting.*

Gradual-immediate wasting may seem paradoxical since immediate is a synonym of instantaneous, the opposite of gradual. The two aspects of this category, however, correspond to two different things: the gradual aspect involves the mode of wasting, the immediate aspect describes the relationship to the object of wasting, the built environment. The same for instant-mediate wasting: the instantaneous aspect involves the mode of wasting, the mediate (indirect) aspect the relationship to the object of wasting, the built environment. Gradual-immediate wasting is the wasting over longer periods of time of objects that appear durable, even permanent. As I have argued above, the primary forms of wasting the built environment are overproduction and devaluation; but here we must include abandonment, demolition, dismantling, and the disposal of objects that have become prematurely obsolete, or that have been deliberately obsoleted. These include all manner of structures and infrastructures directly employed in or supporting the production and circulation of commodities, as well as those supporting social reproduction. More or less durable objects are rarely wasted in their entirety, or all at once, in a single event (in the event they are, their wasting would be instant-mediate). The process of their wasting is largely imperceptible, punctuated by intervals of repair and maintenance such that after a certain period they are replaced entirely without ever being discarded all at once. Indeed, their durability presupposes periodic maintenance, repair, and partial replacement.

In instant-mediate wasting the immediate object of wasting moves from the technosphere to the detritusphere in its entirety and all at once, in a single event—but not the ultimate indirect object of wasting, the built environment. It is a mode of wasting the structures and infrastructures that constitute the built environment, mediated by the immediate wasting of the objects whose production and existence are supported by those structures and infrastructures. Instantaneity does not refer to the absolute duration of the wasting event but to its mode and cadence, single use being a limit. The overproduction, devaluation, and destruction of surpluses of consumables—non-durable goods that give up their form when they are used and must be replaced in kind at more or less regular, recurring intervals—fall in this category, as well as the overproduction, devaluation, and premature obsoleting of consumer durables such as electronics, household appliances, automobiles, and so on. (Consumer durables are hardly consumed instantaneously and, no matter that they are manufactured to make repairs more expensive than replacement, thus rendering them more disposable, they may undergo maintenance and partial replacement over the course of their lifetime; but they are periodically discarded and replaced in their entirety.) The same for the immediate, instantaneous wasting of components of the built environment. The demolition or disposal or abandonment of structures and infrastructures made prematurely obsolete is an immediate wasting of the labor consumed in their production that mediates the wasting of (the labor consumed in the production of) the physical structures and infrastructures supporting the production of their elements and components and the means of production employed in their construction. The wasting of any component of the built environment involves the wasting of the built environment that supports the production of its constituent elements, its construction, and maintenance.

• • •

The built environment is in a perpetual state of building and unbuilding, becoming and becoming-waste, directly or indirectly, gradually or instantaneously, such that over long periods of time large parts of the built environment are replaced without having been discarded in their entirety. Harvey's quip that "instant throwaway cities are hardly feasible no matter how hard the folk in Los Angeles try" is true only in the sense that Los Angeles has not been thrown away instantly, *in toto*.[31] But what does the built environment of Los Angeles or any urban agglomeration consist of? Where does it begin, where does it end? Should it not include the planetary infrastructure upon which the existence of Los Angeles depends: mines, refineries, transportation networks stretched over the planet? Hardly any city is ever discarded all at once, as a whole—leaving aside those destroyed by wars and natural disasters—but all cities and the built environment that supports them, and of which they constitute but one relatively stable component, are thrown away gradually, piecemeal, continually, and imperceptibly over long periods, directly or indirectly. It does not suffice to measure urbanization by the "entries

31
Harvey, *Urban Experience*, 77.

32
Harvey, *Urban Experience*, 75.

of construction materials into the city," as Harvey would have it.[32] It is also necessary to take into account the exit of construction and demolition materials from the city (one-third of the waste stream of Los Angeles consists of construction and demolition materials) or, more precisely, the movement of materials within the built environment of which any city is only one component.

Most components of the built environment are localized, but not the processes that bring the built environment into being. Urbanization has become planetary, as Neil Brenner argues, but the urbanization of the planet is not simply urbanization at the scale of the planet.[33] The planet is at once the exterior milieu (environment and medium) of urbanization qua stratification, integral to it, bound up with it, and serving as its substratum; it is an agent in the process as well as its expression and residuum. Urbanization qua stratification is the continual, renewed creation of the planet. Materials do not enter or exit the built environment inasmuch as they do not enter or exit the planet; they can only circulate within it, between its strata. And this polyrhythmic movement, a movement that is always in the middle, is an essential aspect of the urban process. The becoming of the built environment, its becoming-waste and its becoming-mine—the simultaneous stratification of the technosphere, detritusphere, lithosphere in the movement of materials between them—are aspects of the same process of urbanization as a thickening upon the body of the earth.

Unbuilding the built environment is not synonymous with its wasting. Like building, unbuilding sets in motion the circulation of materials within the built environment. Materials are not wasted, even when components of the built environment are dismantled or demolished. Most materials are retrievable, and are often retrieved, reused, and recycled. What is wasted is the labor consumed in the production of those components and, as I have argued above, this form of wasting does not necessarily entail the unbuilding or destruction of the built environment. The wasting of the built environment is the wasting of the living and dead labor consumed in its production, labor wasted when the built environment and the commodities whose production it supports are produced in excess, when they are rendered obsolete and devalued. Some of this labor is recovered. Devalued components of the built environment are not necessarily destroyed. They are often abandoned in one form or another, the labor embodied in them languishing in the detritusphere, to be lost or recovered depending on whether they are demolished or revalued. Or they are dismantled, their parts reentering the built environment intact as elements of construction, or they reenter manufacturing processes as raw materials to be formed again into new construction elements. Whether they retain their form in reuse or lose it in recycling, part of the labor embodied in them is preserved, recovered. The preservation or recovery of that labor, however, absorbs more labor, and insofar as that labor is consumed in the production of surplus value—surpluses of commodities vulnerable to the threat of devaluation—it will be wasted again.

Materials can circulate indefinitely, changing form or not, and the apparent infinite recyclability of materials such as metals—unique in that they have infinite recyclable properties—forms the basis of the delirious drive of capital to close the materials loop, to create a circular economy that produces zero waste. This delirium is nothing but the expression of the desire of capital to perpetuate the conditions of its reproduction, desire reflected in the material flow analysis charts of industrial ecology: closed systems with no outside, where nothing is lost, which can repeat indefinitely. The capitalist mode of production, however, thrives on the production of waste. Capital might succeed in closing the materials loop, but it cannot eliminate the one condition of its reproduction, the wasting of social labor in the production of surplus value and the devaluation of commodities. Materials can recycle indefinitely, but capitalist urbanization cannot; the reproduction of the built environment under capitalism cannot repeat without producing difference, and in the rhythm-repetition of its wasting, something else must come into being.

Acknowledgments

This essay is a fragment of a larger project presented in a seminar at the Urban Theory Lab at the Harvard University Graduate School of Design. I am grateful to the seminar participants for their insightful and generous criticisms, and to Michael Chieffalo and Julia Smachylo for inviting this contribution.

33
Neil Brenner, "Theses on Urbanization," *Public Culture* 25.1 (2013): 85–114.

Point Versus Non-Point Climate Impacts and the Profit Potential of Uneven Geographical Devaluation

NATHAN F. SAYRE

> The concept of dormant capital, capital lying fallow, can only refer to its barren existence in one of these aspects [as fixed or circulating], and it is a condition of capital that part of it always lies fallow. . . . During crises—after the moment of panic—during the standstill of industry, money is immobilized in the hands of bankers, billbrokers, etc.; and, just as the stag cries out for fresh water, money cries out for a field of employment where it may be realized as capital.
> –Karl Marx[1]

As of April 2018, the concentration of carbon dioxide in the earth's atmosphere stood at 410 parts per million (ppm), 46 percent above preindustrial levels. That figure is nearly halfway to 560 ppm, or the doubled level of preindustrial atmospheric carbon dioxide that scientists have proposed as a rough upper limit for what human civilization can withstand. Nearly three-quarters of the increase (95 of 130 ppm) has occurred in the six decades since Charles David Keeling began making his famous measurements atop the Mauna Loa volcano. At the current global annual rate of 10 gigatons (Gt) emitted, reaching the upper limit is only six decades away. Meanwhile, the six warmest years in recorded history have all occurred since 2010.[2]

In an earlier paper I argued that "global warming is going to devalue our current built environment," and that the question was "not whether widespread devaluation will occur, but how: by the effects of climate change, or by intentional, deliberate policies."[3] If devaluation by rising temperatures and sea levels, increasingly intense floods, droughts and heat waves, widespread crop failure, wildfires, and so on was otherwise inevitable, then there was no reason not to enact policies that would proactively dismantle and replace fossil fuel–dependent infrastructures and practices. This, I argued, was "a logic that everyone should be able to understand, regardless of political or ideological leanings."

Although growing numbers of activists and social movements have embraced the premise that "we must leave as much fossil fuel in the ground as possible, for as long as possible,"[4] it is nonetheless clear, eight years later, that my logic was either flawed, unpersuasive, or both. The biophysical effects of global warming have indeed grown more conspicuous, and more quickly than projected, and the threats posed to cities, agriculture, and infrastructures of all kinds are well documented.[5] But the capitalized value of the built environment in the US remains robust, having "recovered" from the Great Recession alongside the stock market and gross domestic product.[6] Similarly, the rate of global greenhouse gas emissions has not slowed, and it is still driven far more by capital accumulation (i.e., economic growth) than by diplomatic accords or regulations. In the US, political responses have been contradictory: the military and most executive branch agencies of government have candidly documented the current impacts and future threats that climate change poses to the nation and the world, but many elected officials and the Republican Party in particular persist in denying the issue categorically. The most farsighted and comprehensive policy efforts to mitigate and adapt to climate change have been forged at municipal, state, and regional scales, where jurisdictional authority is high but potential influence is limited.[7]

Research and events since 2010 have shown that the relationship between climate change and devaluation is more complex and contradictory than my earlier article stated. Here I argue that climate change impacts on the built environment have qualitatively different relationships to devaluation depending on the temporal scales at which they occur. In cases where the status quo ("business as usual") means slow, incremental degradation—with any more severe impacts occurring decades in the future—capital is effectively indifferent or blind to the problem. For investors, CEOs, and economists, everything depends on the discount rate one uses to determine the net present value of future events, and their discount rate is simply too high.[8] On the other hand, capital can comprehend abrupt change—whether physical destruction in a flood or a wildfire, or devaluation via policy changes or economic implosion. For purposes of accumulation, violent destruction may be preferable to proactive transition to a non-fossil-fuel-based built environment, since the latter would result in enormous (and uninsured) "stranded assets" on the balance sheets of some of capital's most powerful players.

Point Versus Non-Point Climate Impacts

In a recent book, David Harvey distinguishes between "(1) the physical *destruction* and degradation of use values, (2) the forced monetary *depreciation* of exchange values and (3) a concomitant *devaluation* of values as the only 'rational' way to overcome the irrationality of over-accumulation. . . . Each of the forms involved—use value, exchange value and value—is subject to a specific form of negation and one form does not automatically imply the other."[9]

Harvey does not distinguish between destruction and degradation as mechanisms of devaluation, however, and his only example is the damage inflicted on human bodies by exploitative labor conditions and contaminated

1
Karl Marx, *Grundrisse: Foundations of the Critique of Political Economy*, trans. Martin Nicolaus (London: Penguin, 1993), 621.

2
NOAA National Centers for Environmental Information, *State of the Climate: Global Climate Report for Annual 2017*, January 2018, https://www.ncdc.noaa.gov/sotc/global/201713.

3
Nathan F. Sayre, "Climate Change, Scale, and Devaluation: The Challenge of Our Built Environment," *Washington and Lee Journal of Energy, Climate, and Environment* 1.1 (2010): 104, https://scholarlycommons.law.wlu.edu/jece/vol1/iss1/7.

4
Sayre, "Climate Change," 84 (emphasis in original). However, I do not claim any credit for persuading activists of the same. See Naomi Klein, *This Changes Everything: Capitalism vs. the Climate* (New York: Simon & Schuster, 2014).

5
For a comprehensive summary of the scholarly literature for the US, see Jerry M. Melillo, Terese Richmond, and Gary W. Yohe, eds., *Climate Change Impacts in the United States: The Third National Climate Assessment* (Washington, DC: US Global Change Research Program, 2014): 841, https://nca2014.globalchange.gov/report.

6
Outstanding aggregate mortgage debt as of the fourth quarter of 2017 totaled $14.903 trillion, surpassing its previous peak of $14.795 trillion in the 3rd quarter of 2008. See Board of Governors of the Federal Reserve System (US), *Mortgage Debt Outstanding*, All holders [MDOAH], retrieved from FRED, Federal Reserve Bank of St. Louis, https://fred.stlouisfed.org/series/MDOAH. The US municipal bond market was worth $3.9 trillion as of March 2018, up from $2.7 trillion at the end of 2008. See Municipal Securities Rulemaking Board, *Muni Facts* (March 2018), www.msrb.org/msrb1/pdfs/MSRB-Muni-Facts.pdf; *Municipal Finance, before the Committee on Financial Services*, House of Representatives, 111th Cong. (2009), https://www.federalreserve.gov/newsevents/testimony/wilcox20090521a.htm.

7
Fifty-eight percent of US cities are actively making adaptation plans. See Susan L. Cutter, William Solecki, Nancy Bragado, JoAnn Carmin, Michail Fragkias, Matthias Ruth, and Thomas J. Wilbanks, "Urban Systems, Infrastructure, and Vulnerability," in Melillo, Richmond, and Yohe, eds. *Climate Change Impacts in the United States*, 287, 288.

8
Nicholas H. Stern, *The Economics of Climate Change: The Stern Review* (Cambridge: Cambridge University Press, 2007). That a fixed investment will be valueless 50 or 100 years from now is, from the point of view of capital, to be expected even without any climate change impacts.

9
David Harvey, *Marx, Capital, and the Madness of Economic Reason* (New York: Oxford University Press, 2018), 86 (emphasis in original).

environments. The implication is that both destruction and degradation produce "a concomitant devaluation" because of the necessary dependence of value on use value. My earlier paper made the same assumption. But what if *how* use value is lost—abruptly or incrementally—determines whether it negates value, at least in the case of the built environment?

Specifying (and perhaps modifying) Harvey's terms, I propose that destruction results from what could be termed "point sources" of climate impacts (or point impacts): discrete events that are abrupt, devastating, and conspicuous.[10] Hurricane Sandy inflicted an estimated $65 billion in damages in New York City alone, for example.[11] The cost of wildfire suppression in the US has increased 541 percent since the mid-1980s, from an average of $376 million to $2.032 billion per year.[12] Impacts of this type occur at specifiable points in time, although they are also determined (both physically and probabilistically) by ongoing "background" conditions that change only slowly, such as sea surface temperatures and the moisture content of trees. Their infrequent and extreme character is why, generally, point impacts are difficult to attribute (in the causal, scientific sense) to climate change per se.

By contrast, degradation results from "non-point sources" of climate impacts (or non-point impacts): changes that are slow, incremental, and often under-recognized. Thawing permafrost now costs the state of Alaska an extra $10 million per year to maintain its roadways, for instance, and a projected 2,400 miles of major roads and highways in the Gulf Coast region will be inundated by 2100 due to sea-level rise.[13] Heat-related production losses in the livestock sector exceeded $1 billion in 2011, and increasingly frequent heavy rainfall events are shortening the planting season in Iowa and prompting farmers there to install additional drainage infrastructure at a cost of $500 per acre.[14] Degradation is keyed to drivers and processes that scientists understand well (such as the greenhouse effect and the hydrologic cycle) and can therefore be attributed to climate change with greater confidence, even if the precise rate of change—and thus the timeline for more severe or cumulative impacts—remains difficult to predict.

Of course, there are climate impacts that complicate this distinction. Drought, for example, is a protracted event with a beginning, duration, and endpoint that may be difficult to specify. In relation to devaluation, however, the difference between destruction and degradation does not hinge solely on an impact's material attributes; rather, it concerns whether and how physical change translates into economic change. Precisely because of its temporal ambiguity, drought functions as a non-point impact until some entity (usually a government agency) declares an "official" emergency that triggers relief payments; thereafter, the drought functions as a point impact. But most other non-point impacts lack any such temporal definition (physical or discursive) whereby their economic consequences can be identified and transacted. A hotter-than-usual summer may diminish crop yields or increase the cost of air conditioning for the owner of a building, but these effects are difficult or impossible for the farmer, the building owner, or scientists to attribute to climate change as distinct from normal variability. Similarly, non-point impacts are unlikely to devalue underlying capital assets in ways that are distinguishable from the normal rate of amortization, "wear and tear," or background market variability. Thus, much as government agencies have difficulty regulating non-point sources of pollution, capital struggles to find traction in accounting for (let alone confronting) non-point climate impacts.

Securitizing Risk, Profiting from Destruction

The example of drought articulates a dynamic zone where the relations mediating capital, climate, and the built environment are subject to ongoing change and struggle. Because these relations are historically and geographically conditioned, they are at least potentially contingent and path dependent. It happens, for example, that the impacts of drought on agricultural producers in the US are subject to government disaster relief programs. Flood insurance is also largely provided through (or subsidized by) the federal government, whereas private insurance policies protect homeowners and businesses against losses resulting from other "natural" disasters. These are institutional arrangements inherited from before the era of climate change, when such disasters could still be unproblematically considered "acts of God." The fact that non-point climate impacts are not subject to insurance is also an accident of history, albeit a readily understandable one.

The insurance sector performs essential roles in structuring and making visible the value embedded in the

10
In borrowing the terminology employed for regulating pollution sources, I am intentionally transposing from the spatial to the temporal dimension. Point sources of pollution are spatially discrete, whereas non-point sources are spatially diffuse and thus difficult to locate. Point climate impacts are temporally discrete, whereas non-point climate impacts are temporally diffuse.

11
Cutter et al., *Climate Change Impacts*, 287.

12
For federal government agencies only, in unadjusted dollars, comparing the six-year periods 1985–1990 and 2012–2017. The average annual number of wildfires in the US has actually declined 10 percent from 1985 to 2017, but the average size has increased 244 percent and the costs of suppression per acre have increased 246 percent. Calculated by the author using data available here: *Federal Firefighting Costs* (Suppression Only) (Boise, ID: National Interagency Fire Center, 2018), https://www.nifc.gov/fireInfo/fireInfo_documents/SuppCosts.pdf.

13
Henry G. Schwartz, Michael Meyer, Cynthia J. Burbank, Michael Kuby, Clinton Oster, John Posey, and Edmond J. Russo et al., "Transportation," in Melillo, Richmond, and Yohe, eds. *Climate Change Impacts*, 130–49, 132, 135.

14
Jerry Hatfield, Gene Takle, Richard Grotjahn, Patrick Holden, R. Cesar Izaurralde, Terry Mader, and Elizabeth Marshall et al.,"Agriculture," in Melillo, Richmond, and Yohe, eds. *Climate Change Impacts*, 150–74.

built environment in capitalist society. Naively stated, insurance is designed to prevent the devaluation of an insured's invested capital, by providing an equivalent amount of money (exchange value) to replace the lost (use) value. In practice, of course, the replacement capital has to come from someone, and when claims come due insurers and the insured often struggle over the losses each party must absorb. After all, insurers seek to profit from the business of selling their "anti-devaluation" service. One of the ways they protect themselves from insolvency when disaster strikes is by purchasing their own insurance, known as reinsurance, to cover the cost of payouts from a single event above some negotiated threshold.

In a series of remarkable articles, geographer Leigh Johnson has described how the reinsurance industry responds to climate change. What she has found effectively turns the logic of my earlier argument inside out. Rather than steering capital away from built environments imperiled by climate change, and into others so as to reduce overall risk exposure (as would be expected, given structural market incentives), reinsurers have instead innovated ways to turn both the risks and the damages of point impacts into profit opportunities.

At the center of Johnson's tale is the simple yet decisive fact that reinsurance policies are renegotiated annually. For this reason, reinsurers such as Munich Re and Swiss Re effectively use the same discount rate as bankers, CEOs, and economists, assessing their decisions as a function of liabilities, assets, and the probabilities of various disasters over the coming 12-month period.[15] If major disasters deplete reserves built up during periods of calm, they also serve to enable (or compel) premium increases in subsequent years. The profitability of reinsurance crucially depends on these post-disaster increases. Thus, there is a structural "contradiction between the value-preserving purpose of the insurance form and the devaluation of real property necessary to sustain accumulation within the industry."[16] The potential of climate change to increase the frequency and intensity of disastrous events such as hurricanes, then, is both cloud and silver lining; for reinsurers, "external, ecological sources of devaluation . . . —if 'managed' properly—could repeatedly reset conditions for profitable accumulation."[17]

In an insidious further twist, the reinsurance industry has been financialized in the past decade or so, giving reinsurers access to the vast capital stocks of global banks, hedge funds, and institutional investors, who in return can tap into the nearly $2 trillion in annual revenue flows generated by non-life-insurance premiums.[18] Rather than mergers or simple equity, the mechanisms linking reinsurance to finance capital are so-called catastrophe bonds, which are securitized in much the same fashion as the infamous mortgage-backed securities that helped precipitate the Great Recession.[19] As Johnson writes, securitized catastrophe risk "allows mobile capital on a search for yield to reframe spatial liabilities as tradable assets."[20]

Subjecting point climate impacts to the logics and mechanisms of finance capital has profoundly perverse ramifications. These catastrophe bonds, or "cat bonds," are attractive to (certain kinds of) investors both because they are unaffected by other forces bearing on the behavior of financial markets,[21] and because the very high risks—hundreds of billions of dollars for a massive earthquake or hurricane in large, wealthy urban areas, for example—serve to justify correspondingly high returns. Not surprisingly, then, catastrophe bonds select for "high-paying peak peril regions": places and types of fixed investments that combine high exposure (the probability of a disaster multiplied by the economic value of the exposed assets) with high capacity to pay the associated premiums.[22] Finally, high rates of return can be sustained only if, from time to time, actual disasters trigger policy claims and large payouts that remind primary insurers of the need for reinsurance. "Without continuing catastrophic damages, returns for investors fall because premium rates generally decrease and (re)insurance firms draw on internal capital or are able to access other reinsurers' capital cheaply."[23] Because these "services are only necessary insofar as the physical world continues to generate devaluation events," the industry depends "on cyclical catastrophic external devaluations."[24]

15
Leigh Johnson, "Catastrophic Fixes: Cyclical Devaluation and Accumulation through Climate Change Impacts," *Environment and Planning A* 47 (2015): 2503–21. Proponents of market-led solutions to global warming ought to consider changing this banal detail with legislation that would force reinsurers to write fixed-rate policies of 25–50 years in duration. Such a step would be far more effective for internalizing the costs of climate change than schemes to quantify "natural capital" by pricing "ecosystem services."

16
Johnson, "Catastrophic Fixes," 2504.

17
Johnson, "Catastrophic Fixes," 2513.

18
Johnson, "Catastrophic Fixes," 2505.

19
Leigh Johnson, "Geographies of Securitized Catastrophe Risk and the Implications of Climate Change," *Economic Geography* 90 (2014): 155–85.

20
Johnson, "Securitized Catastrophe Risk," 155.

21
Catastrophe bonds are not so much counter cyclical as *acyclical*; in industry lingo, they have "zero beta" due to their "ontological disconnection from the behavior of financial markets." Johnson, "Securitized Catastrophe Risk," 173.

22
Johnson, "Securitized Catastrophe Risk," 181.

23
Johnson, "Securitized Catastrophe Risk," 167.

24
Johnson, "Catastrophic Fixes," 2510, 2517.

25
Model projections of climate change impacts on agriculture are illustrative: through 2050 there is little effect from the emissions scenario employed, with the most grievous global-scale impacts set to occur around 2080. Martin L. Parry, Cynthia Rosenzweig, Ana Iglesias, Matthew Livermore, and Günther Fischer, "Effects of Climate Change on Global Food Production under SRES Emissions and Socioeconomic Scenarios," *Global Environmental Change* 14.1 (April 2004): 53–67.

Conclusion: Recurrent Destruction and Uneven Geographical Devaluation

The distinction between point and non-point climate impacts acquires significance in light of Johnson's findings. The most profound threats that climate change poses to humanity—those scientists associate with the doubling of atmospheric carbon dioxide—are non-point impacts whose consequences assume apocalyptic proportions only in the longer run: rising sea levels, ocean acidification, and temperature increases that disrupt agricultural production, for example.[25] But such slow, prolonged degradation is effectively indistinguishable, from capital's point of view, from the expected amortization of any fixed investment, regardless of the climate. As Johnson points out, if a firm's insurance policy permits it to rebuild in a different location, then having an existing factory or similar fixed investment (one that has already been amortized in whole or in part) destroyed by a point impact is actually desirable, especially if non-point impacts are gradually undermining the plant's viability.[26] In this view, catastrophic destruction liberates capital from its "fallow" condition, letting it loose in money form to seek out new opportunities for accumulation.

What is emerging, in other words, is a set of institutional arrangements that selectively decouple the biophysical effects of climate change from the devaluation of capital. The resulting geographies are likely to cleave along lines of wealth and ownership, with private capital relatively insulated and the public sector disproportionately burdened. The fact that point impacts can be insured—buffering the primary insured's capital while creating profit opportunities for reinsurers and finance capital—means that destruction may not negate value for private capital, even if it wreaks short-term havoc on human lives and the use values on which they depend. In contrast, public infrastructural investments in transportation, energy, water provision, and so on generally lack insurance against destruction and in any case are often more seriously threatened by non-point degradation.[27] These disparities are likely to grow as catastrophe bonds "make more capital available for rebuilding and new underwriting in areas where high concentrations of value are becoming even more vulnerable to extreme events. . . . In this context, if a series of major catastrophes then prompted investors to retreat, the state would find itself as insurer of last resort for a built environment that had ironically become *less* adapted to climate extremes."[28]

Thus, the "concomitant devaluation" that in theory should accompany the destruction or degradation of use values is far from guaranteed in the case of climate change and the built environment today. Abrupt destruction by point impacts may not negate value at all, at least not for private capital, and gradual degradation by non-point impacts may effectively disappear into the background noise of business as usual. The aggregate picture is patently absurd from a use value perspective, not to mention unethical. It would be far more rational to decouple the built environment from fossil fuels rather than pretend it can be decoupled from the effects of climate change. But that would require another kind of point impact altogether: the abrupt writing off of assets that would be "stranded" by a wholesale shift to non-fossil-fuel energy sources. Consider, for perspective, the relative magnitudes at stake. The estimated value of all US transportation facilities in 2010 was $4.1 trillion.[29] A lot of money, to be sure, but not much at all compared to the $27 trillion in fossil fuel reserves that the world's major oil companies have "booked" to satisfy investors of their long-term profitability.[30] These are reserves that have not yet been extracted, values capitalized but not yet realized and thus purely notional assets. But for capital, such devaluation without destruction or degradation would be an outcome far worse than countless real catastrophes.

26
Johnson, "Catastrophic Fixes," 2513.

27
Take, for example, the 13 major US airports that have at least one runway fewer than 12 feet above sea level—already within reach of a moderate storm surge and highly vulnerable to sea-level rise over the longer term. See Schwartz et al., *Climate Change Impacts*, 134.

28
Johnson, "Securitized Catastrophe Risk," 181. Furthermore, Johnson foresees what she calls "splintering protectionism: a patchwork of high-risk, high-reward areas where insurance is available only to those with the ability to pay rising premiums, leaving the state to manage the retreat and relocation of less remunerative properties and populations" (Johnson,"Catastrophic Fixes," 2503).

29
Schwartz et al., *Climate Change Impacts*, 131.

30
Klein, *This Changes Everything*, 148.

Noise Landscapes: Fallow Lands of Global Mobility

BENEDIKT BOUCSEIN & EIRINI KASIOUMI

Since 1945, humankind has entered the era of "Great Acceleration": a time of unprecedented growth in human activity on a global scale, reflected in metrics like material consumption, global trade, transportation, telecommunications, natural resource extraction, and energy use. The increased scope and intensity of this activity is such that it has begun to alter the earth system, producing phenomena like the atmospheric concentration of greenhouse gases responsible for global warming. Observing such changes led Nobel Laureate Paul Crutzen to coin the now widely used term "Anthropocene" in the early 2000s.[1]

The Great Acceleration is at the root of the major ecological, urbanistic, and cultural challenges of our time, in which ecosystems, food chains, and the climate are severely out of balance. Several indicators point towards a critical system overload.[2] And the "imperial lifestyle" developed in this period transfers the negative externalities of material processes associated with human activity onto other regions, countries, and continents. As more and more countries adopt the same lifestyle, its unsustainable character becomes apparent.[3] This means that the end of the Great Acceleration may be drawing near, raising the question of how to secure the best possible future for humankind in whatever period follows. Here we argue that an enlightened spatial view of the impact of human action on the one hand, connected to an urbanistic agency aimed at introducing resilience into urban systems on the other, are paramount.

Fallow lands are central to this discussion, as we contend that the anthropogenic activity of the Great Acceleration is the systemic source of the phenomena discussed above. Ever shorter economic cycles trigger the need for an ever-expanding terrain to support the control-and-command centers of the global economy. This terrain often has widespread fallow sectors.[4]

Among the most emblematic sites of anthropogenic activity are those linked to the global mobility of people and goods. Since the Industrial Revolution, transport infrastructures have tended to produce a polarization between nodes, or points of maximum connectivity; and impact spaces, or areas that support node functionality by absorbing externalities like discontinuity and nuisance. Today this phenomenon is best exemplified by air travel and the growth of airports, considered by geographers as the last in a series of transport revolutions.[5] During the past decades, the expansion of air transport infrastructure has produced the vast impact spaces that we call "Noise Landscapes."[6] Apart from the obvious reference to aircraft noise, Noise Landscapes more broadly encompass the spaces that incur the externalities of airport operation. Often seen as marginal or residual, yet possessing dormant potential for revalorization, they are emblematic fallow lands of global mobility.

Examining the space surrounding several major airports in Europe allows the further characterization of Noise Landscapes as negotiated territories, where anthropogenic conflicts are highlighted. The complex negotiation mechanisms that take place there can be viewed as test cases for the coming decades, during which conflicts may increase as the effects of cultural practices including global mobility can no longer be externalized onto the future, or onto other geographical regions elsewhere. Engaging with Noise Landscapes thus allows an empirical approach to the substantial question: What role can urbanism play in a future in which the boundless acceleration of recent decades will be reversed, either voluntarily or involuntarily? Can spaces like Noise Landscapes provide any answers?[7]

Fallow Lands of Unprecedented Size

Traffic infrastructure and urban development have always been closely intertwined. Each permutation of the modern city has transpired in relation to new mobilization modes, and their infrastructures have been essential to how cities function. Thus, the spatial effect of airports on their surroundings since the second half of the 20th century has often been compared to that of railways in the 19th century. The analogy has mostly focused on their "pull" effect. As train stations became new centers in 19th century cities, so too have airports increasingly attracted a variety of not only aviation-related functions, leading observers in the late 1990s and early 2000s to discuss the emergent "aerotropolis" in North America[8] and "airport city" in Europe.[9] Since then, more attention has been given to the types of interaction between airports and cities. But this research does not often transcend basic truisms—such as the economic importance of airports in the context of globalization, or their increasing connectivity to urban surroundings—that typically affirm growth and acceleration, the very factors at the basis of contemporary environmental issues, which will not be alleviated by more efficient means of transport.[10]

The analogy between airports and railways can be further nuanced by considering the notion of fallow lands in connection with the impact spaces of transport infrastructures. Since railways were first introduced to industrializing cities in the 19th century, the demand for approach lines and supporting infrastructure created the separation of large tracts of land from the urban fabric.[11] In the post-industrial period, these fallow lands have often been the initiation point of important urban renewal schemes. Centrally located sites once regarded as undesirable became hotspots of urban development and integral parts of the city. It can thus be speculated that residual areas in the vicinity of airports will see similar transformations in the future.

The fallow condition around airports is caused by two major factors: interruptions on the ground due to connective infrastructures, and airplane emissions. Noise is the most noticeable and the most contentious emission. The European Environment Agency (EEA) estimates that five million people in Europe are regularly exposed to "high annoyance" noise levels caused by airplanes.[12] And many more are exposed to noise irregularly. The affected areas are very large: the noise carpets of arriving and departing airplanes stretch into their respective metropolitan areas for

1
Crutzen proposed the Anthropocene as a new human-dominated geological epoch for the earth, succeeding the Holocene. See Paul J. Crutzen, "Geology of Mankind: The Anthropocene," *Nature* 415 (January 2002): 23.

2
Will Steffen, Wendy J. Broadgate, Lisa Deutsch, Owen Gaffney, and Cornelia Ludwig, "The Trajectory of the Anthropocene: The Great Acceleration," *The Anthropocene Review* 2.1 (April 2015): 81–98.

3
Ulrich Brand and Markus Wissen, *Imperiale Lebensweise Zur Ausbeutung Von Mensch Und Natur Im Globalen Kapitalismus* (Munich: Oekom, 2017).

4
In this sense, fallow lands include ore mines, large infrastructural facilities, and the surrounding areas of traffic infrastructures like highways, as documented by Edward Burtynsky. See Lori Pauli, *Manufactured Landscapes: The Photographs of Edward Burtynsky* (Ottawa: National Gallery of Canada; New Haven: Yale University Press, 2003).

5
Jean-Paul Rodrigue, Claude Comtois, and Brian Slack, *The Geography of Transport Systems*, 2nd ed. (London: Routledge, 2009).

6
This paper builds on ideas introduced in Benedikt Boucsein, Kees Christiaanse, Eirini Kasioumi, and Christian Salewski, *The Noise Landscape: A Spatial Exploration of Airports and Cities* (Rotterdam: nai010 publishers, 2017).

7
The impact of mobility in the contemporary world is rightly associated with climate change. In that respect, airports embody the carbon economy. Air travel accounts for 2% of carbon dioxide emissions worldwide, and due to other harmful non-carbon dioxide emissions the cumulative effect is between 4% and 9% of the total climate change impact of human activity. If aviation continues to grow at the current rate, even given technological advancement that ratio will reach 15% by 2050. For example, see Joyce E. Penner, David H. Lister, David J. Griggs, David J. Dokken, and Mack McFarland, *Aviation and the Global Atmosphere: A Special Report of the Intergovernmental Panel on Climate Change* (Cambridge: Cambridge University Press, 1999); Vera Paradee, *Up in the Air: How Airplane Carbon Pollution Jeopardizes Global Climate Goals* (Tucson, AZ: Center for Biological Diversity, 2015).

several kilometers. The spatial contours corresponding to the high noise level zones of hub airports are often equal in size to the urban areas they serve. Inevitably, delineating exposed terrain based on noise contours defined by weighted decibel values is an approximation that does not entirely capture the actual experience of noise. However, noise contours are important for urbanism, as they constitute the basis for development restrictions, especially concerning residential uses.

Unraveling Patterns in Noise Landscapes

In *The Noise Landscape: A Spatial Exploration of Airports and Cities* (with Kees Christiaanse and Christian Salewski, 2017), we investigated the conditions encountered in this new type of urbanized landscape through case studies of eight European airports: London Heathrow, Paris Charles de Gaulle, Amsterdam Schiphol, Frankfurt, Madrid Barajas, Munich, Paris Orly, and Zurich. For this investigation, we used the 55 dB(A) noise level contour to frame our observations of the spatial qualities of those areas near the node that are routinely regarded as marginal or residual.

The M50 motorway cutting into the landscape near the Madrid-Barajas airport. While this particular infrastructure seems to anticipate future demand rather than cater to current needs, large-scale interruptions on the ground caused by multiple airport access lines are common, and prototypical for Noise Landscapes. Courtesy Joris Jehle.

Combining photographic documentation with historical accounts and both economic and regulation data, we noted that Noise Landscapes often seem to have been forgotten by mainstream urban planning action: land values are low with only sporadic exceptions; they are traversed by myriad infrastructures serving the airport; the least profitable and most provisional of the node's economic offshoot activities are found there. Even Noise Landscapes close to their respective cities exhibit fallow conditions, in the form of inconsequential agricultural land located at the urban fringe, the predominance of infrastructural lines, and the maintenance of a "terrain vague" condition often host to logistics warehouses and low-grade office buildings, or sites with "unwanted uses" such as scrapyards, recycling facilities, adult entertainment clubs, and so on. The "backyard condition" of these uses is in direct contradiction to the status of hub airports as important centers of the global economy and their key locations in respective metropolitan areas.

A decrepit building in the Noise Landscape of Paris Orly offers cheap Japanese cuisine. It exemplifies the food services available to the few residents and large workforce in the area, and the temporary character of the architecture here, as in many other European Noise Landscapes. Courtesy Eirini Kasioumi.

Although Noise Landscapes are not typically regarded as spaces with a shared urbanistic condition, several specific patterns point towards the emergence of a typological paradigm. These patterns reflect the presence of the airport, global flows of goods and capital, logics of ground-based infrastructure, spatial policy, and the choices of individual actors in the free market. The nine categories of these patterns are as follows:

1 *Technocratic operational logics.* The logics and constraints that pertain not only to the operation of the airport, but also to motorways, railway lines, and other infrastructures, often of a very technical nature, strongly influence the spatial development of Noise Landscapes.

2 *Complex policy frameworks.* As Noise Landscapes cover a large territory, crossing municipal and sometimes

8
John D. Kasarda, "Aerotropolis: Airport-Driven Urban Development," in *ULI on the Future: Cities in the 21st Century* (Washington, DC: Urban Land Institute, 2000), 32–41.

9
Mathis Güller and Michael Güller, *From Airport to Airport City* (Barcelona: Editorial Gustavo Gili, 2003).

10
David Metz, *The Limits to Travel: How Far Will You Go?* (London: Earthscan, 2008).

11
John R. Kellett, *The Impact of Railways on Victorian Cities* (London: Routledge & Kegan Paul, 1969).

12
High annoyance is generally agreed to correspond to noise above 55 dB(A) Lden (A-weighted decibels, day-evening-night equivalent).

LAND USES

- urban fabric
- industry and landfill
- transport and infrastructure
- urban green
- agriculture
- forest and vegetation
- water

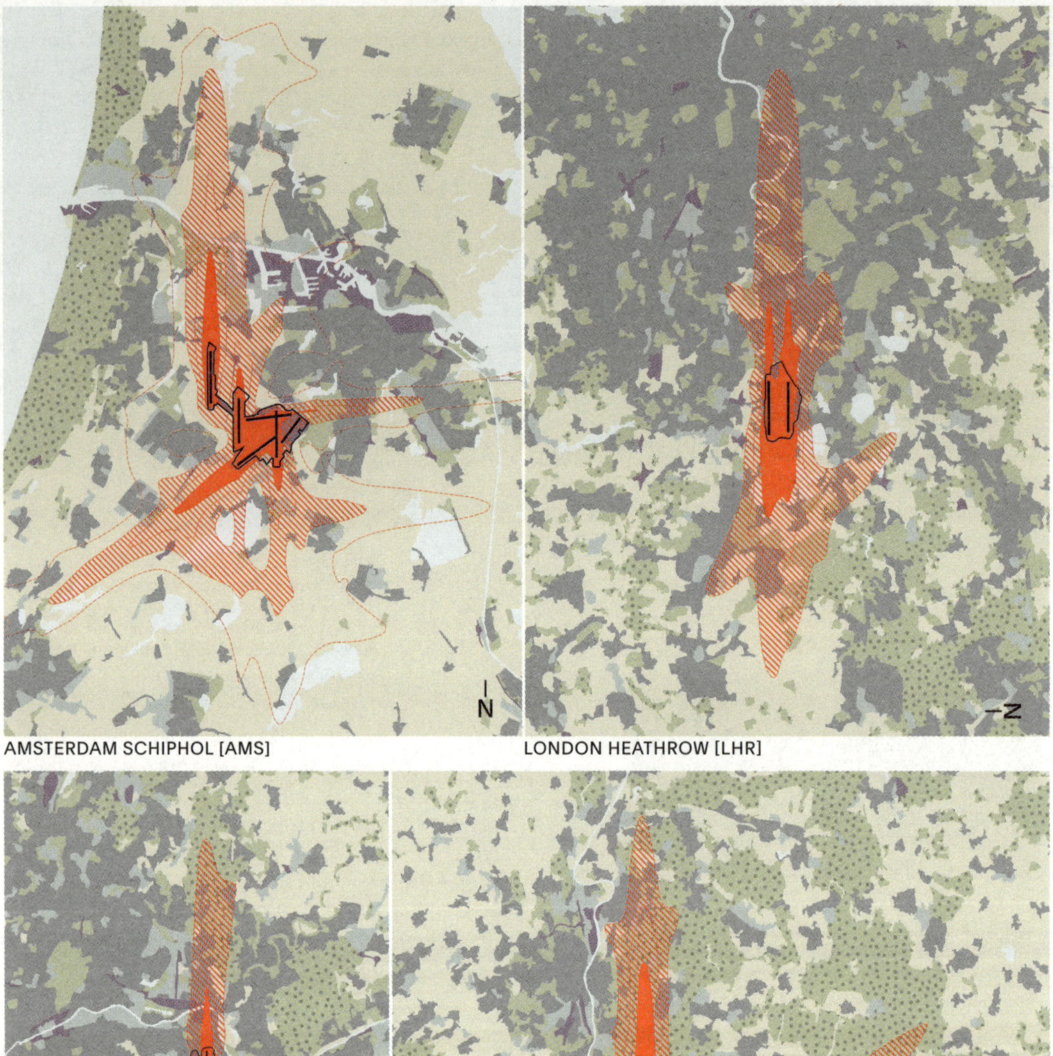

The Noise Landscapes of eight major European airports show distinct spatial conditions (urban, suburban, agriculture, park, etc.) that are differently combined in each case. Image based on information provided by Provincie Noord-Holland, DGAC Direction générale de l'aviation civile, Flughafen Zürich AG, AENA Aeropuertos Españoles y Navegación Aérea, CAA Civil Aviation Authority, EEA European Environmental Agency; edited by Studio Joost Grootens.

L_{den} CONTOUR BANDS

55–65 dB

65+ dB

0 5 km

MADRID BARAJAS [MAD]

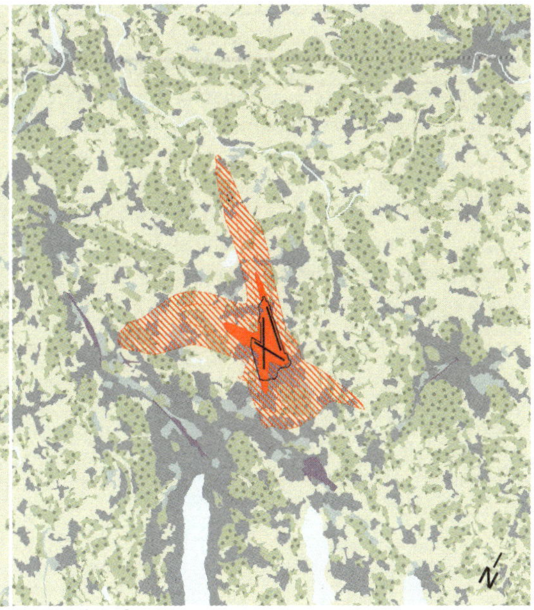

ZURICH [ZRH]

PARIS CHARLES DE GAULLE [CDG]

MUNICH [MUC]

even national boundaries, their governance depends on a great number of actors including political bodies and strong corporations like airports and airlines, which can create a web of often-conflicting policies and regulations.

3 *Interrupted urban structure.* The traffic network around hub airports is oriented to ease access to certain specific locations and not necessarily the immediate surroundings. Sites topographically near the terminal may be topologically very far away from it, whereas other nodes in the network can be reached within minutes.[13]

4 *Heterogeneous image.* Noise Landscapes exhibit abrupt changes of scale and function: logistics firms beside horse racing tracks or small residential sectors, large tracts of open land bordering elaborate business parks with manicured landscapes, six-line motorways adjacent to small footpaths.[14]

5 *Unplanned mixed use.* The heterogeneity of the Noise Landscape is reflected in the irregularity of land use—for purposes often of metropolitan necessity, but deemed undesirable—that would likely be located elsewhere if not for the noise.

6 *Recreational landscape.* Open tracts of land are an advantageous "side-effect" of noise regulations. They are increasingly used for leisure by facilities such as golf clubs, amusement parks, and sailing clubs, and for louder recreational spaces like racing tracks.

7 *Temporary architecture.* Noise Landscapes are characterized by two extremes: a few elaborately designed buildings, usually airport terminals and certain adjacent office buildings; and the remaining urban structure, seldom designed with architectural quality in mind, and more often seen as adjustable or replaceable.

8 *Distinct movement patterns.* Apart from arriving and departing airplanes, Noise Landscapes host three types of movement that seldom overlap: target-oriented passenger movement between the hub airport and areas outside the noise contour; movement relating to airport services within the noise contour; and the movement of everyday commuters, inhabitants, and workers.

9 *Polarized modality.* Whereas access to European airports is increasingly multimodal, often offering combinations of car, bus, local and regional rail access—as in Zurich and at Amsterdam Schiphol—many modalities remain exclusive, from the Heathrow Express line, to the projected CDG Express, to completely car-dependent business enclaves.

Emerging Large-Scale Urban Frameworks

These physical and functional characteristics of Noise Landscapes, and the processes that define them, testify to a unique urban potential. If we return to the question of urbanism's role in mobilizing the dormant fallow lands of global mobility, several answers can be found by examining processes already in motion. The overarching condition of noise, which creates a restrictive framework not conducive to the straightforward valorization of affected spaces, at the same time produces spatial reserves with a distinct role in their respective metropolitan areas.

The Noise Landscape of Amsterdam Schiphol is an example of how such a space can become a resource. Due to the airport's distinct runway layout, the noise-affected area is particularly large. While most parts of this Noise Landscape are unbuilt, they are certainly not empty. North of the Polderbaan, the most recently constructed runway, detailed mapping revealed the development of an "ecology of amusement parks." The large open space features expansive parks, racing tracks, sailing clubs, paintball arenas, and other noise-emitting sports activities. These uses would not exist, at least in such density, without the presence of the airport. This region and other parts of Schiphol's Noise Landscape already function as a park for the entire metropolitan region—in part highly regulated, and in part spontaneous appropriation. Different mechanisms are in play: national regulation reserving the area between Amsterdam and the neighboring city of Haarlem (which also steered the direction of airport expansion, however indirectly), regulations obliging the airport to compensate its surroundings with landscaping measures, and most importantly, restrictions to housing construction. Because of Dutch planning culture, there is also an unusually strong willingness among relevant actors to view the Noise Landscape as a common condition.

The Amsterdam case shows the potential for Noise Landscapes to transform into urbanistically, socially, and economically integrated parts of their respective metropolitan regions. The mobilization of this dormant potential can be observed in other cases as well. Surrounding Charles de Gaulle airport in Paris, the Arcadian character of the Plaine de France communities in the city's agricultural hinterlands has long contrasted the "big box" warehouses and distribution facilities mushrooming along road axes. Unable to expand due to noise-related regulations, physically detached from the center and lacking efficient transport connections, many communities in the area are in limbo. Recently, actors in the airport area have acquired an awareness of these issues that is reflected in urban project initiatives: the development of new types of clusters that combine functionalities

13
This urbanistic phenomenon has been described in Albert Pope, *Ladders* (New York: Princeton Architectural Press, 1996).

14
This chaotic and visually contrasting constellation of uses echoes what urban planner Thomas Sieverts has described as the *Zwischenstadt* (in-between city). See Thomas Sieverts, *Zwischenstadt: Zwischen Ort Und Welt, Raum Und Zeit, Stadt Und Land* (Braunschweig: Vieweg, 1997).

Large logistics centers and small industries are situated below the noise of approaching airplanes, here in the case of Frankfurt. Typically these areas are defined by large-grained urban grids, almost void of people, reserved for big machines and transport. And they often contain bigger infrastructures, such as oil harbors or kerosene tanks, needed for airport operations. Courtesy Joris Jehle.

possible under noise restrictions; new transport links, both "hard" and "soft"; and attempts to accentuate unknown natural assets. The Noise Landscape is already attracting new users, making its valorization as a functional and integrated sector of the metropolitan region a real possibility.

In that respect, the Frankfurt airport case is also significant. The Nazi government originally planned it as a critical part of a multimodal transit center for the German Reich, which still today contributes to its near perfect integration into its surroundings, in terms of flows of persons, goods, and resources related to airport operations like energy, water, and waste. At the same time, widespread protests against runway expansion later were important for the emergence of Germany's Green Party and for a shift towards greater democratic participation in national planning procedures for large infrastructures. Today the airport is integrated on several infrastructural levels, including a regional heating network. Furthermore, commercial zones are consciously developed in the Noise Landscape as distribution centers for the surrounding metropolitan area, and other noise-affected sectors constitute parts of a regional park surrounding the city of Frankfurt.

These cases demonstrate that Noise Landscapes have the potential to develop into large-scale urban frameworks that fulfill a specific role within a metropolitan area. Yet currently this process is mostly without overarching spatial strategies. Such strategies are important to implement, provided they do not contribute to the marketization of these areas or an attempt to incorporate them into the profit-oriented, inherently unsustainable airport infrastructure. Instead, Noise Landscapes should be promoted as the spaces of experimentation that they are already now—their special status can be leveraged to implement new solutions for the contemporary questions addressed at the beginning of this paper.

New Complexities of Interaction

The low density and dispersed functionality of most Noise Landscapes make them into fertile terrain for spatial experiments promoting alternative forms of revalorization. But what happens when affected areas are already densely inhabited? The case with the most affected residents inside the Noise Landscape by far, and Europe's largest airport in terms of passenger numbers, London Heathrow is an example of the increasingly complex interaction between airport and city in terms of measurement and mitigation.

This particular interaction between airport and urbanized surroundings dates to the 1960s, when a report published by the Wilson Committee, or the Committee on the Problem of Noise (established by the Ministry of Health), attempted to relate the experience of noise to urban space.[15] The first noise contours in the Wilson Report were drawn by hand, based on the subjective impressions of scientists in the field. Such primitive mapping techniques have since been replaced by more elaborate measurement and communication systems. The noise contours of large hub airports in Europe are now determined by a methodological mixture of measurements taken at fixed points on the ground and complex calculations.

The weak restrictive framework and laissez-faire approach to urbanization around London Heathrow have continued to subject generations of residents to high noise levels. Recently, attempts to resolve the situation have relied more on digital tools than physical intervention. The residents near London Heathrow have access to an internet platform where they can complain about a specific flight in real time once it has passed a certain point. And technological advances in navigation have made it possible for the airport to experiment with the flight paths of approaching airplanes, for example, concentrating them over certain areas instead of evenly spreading them out.[16]

Through increasingly technical capabilities on the ground, more such feedback systems can be anticipated in the future. The next decade will likely see even more complex interactions between traffic infrastructure and urban tissue, as negotiations around major airports occur on new levels, aided by 3-D geographic information system (GIS) simulations and data on past and projected noise levels in affected areas. The development of Noise Landscapes in this context correlates to current discourse on the configuration of "smart cities"—either as democratically authorized and community regulated means of advancement, or more frequently, as schemes that further the interests of authoritarian regimes or multinational corporations.[17] For example, increasingly precise noise data poses the question of how it is provided, interpreted, and stored—whether by airport authorities, concerned parties, or municipalities, often under financial strain—and if it is used to benefit the city or commercial interests.

The spatial view that urban design and architecture can offer is strongly needed in analyzing Noise Landscapes. Yet space is strangely absent from work on noise mitigation. Including space more proactively in the discussion of noise management would open up a host of possibilities: selective densification and de-densification; alternating functions in times of "repose" and high-volume

15
For more on the Heathrow case, see Peter Ortner's analysis in Boucsein et al., *The Noise Landscape*, "Metric as Mediator: Data-Driven Negotiations about Heathrow's Noise Landscape", 215–26.

16
This particular experiment failed, leading to irritations and protest on the ground, yet there is willingness to continue such experiments.

17
Daniel Araya, *Smart Cities as Democratic Ecologies* (Basingstoke: Palgrave Macmillan, 2015); Esteve Almirall, Jonathan Wareham, Carlo Ratti, Pilar Conesa, Francesca Bria, Anibal Gaviria, and Amy Edmondson, "Smart Cities at the Crossroads: New Tensions in City Transformation," *California Management Review* 59.1 (November 2016): 141–52.

traffic; flexible appropriation of noise corridors; and most importantly, participatory, fact-oriented communication about the negative externalities of our technologies—one step towards building a societal response to the challenges of the Great Acceleration.

The Spatial View as a Driver of Change

Noise Landscapes—the fallow lands of global mobility—are prototypical challenges and opportunities for architecture and urban design in the Anthropocene, an era of radical human influence on ecology and eventually geology at a global scale. As the Great Acceleration approaches its end, the scenarios of what will follow range from full-fledged ecological collapse, to partial societal breakdown with rising inequality, to the possibility that a combination of technology and reduced consumption will stabilize the world system.[18] To reach the last scenario, however, an unprecedented collective effort of humanity is necessary. The need for this effort, the existential character of the current situation, and the epochal change that lies ahead prompt the mobilization of urbanistic genius as well as the realization of the limits of our discipline: here the spatial view is paramount.

The devices of measurement, calculation, and mediation currently developing around major hub airports offer a glimpse of the tools that will be decisive for negotiated territories like Noise Landscapes in the post-acceleration era. Essentially, they are instruments through which the consequences of environmental damage are demonstrated and negotiated. In the age after the "end of the world,"[19] when the fallout from human action will no longer be absorbed by an exhausted world system, the measurement and calculation of cause and effect will be a central point of both politics and science. Noise Landscapes reveal these processes as inherently spatial; urbanism must engage with them to influence the built environment. This engagement will not necessarily take the form of direct influence on spatial outcomes typical of the discipline. Instead, it may empower communities by using real-time emissions and noise data to determine the use of outdoor space, for example, or by exerting pressure on the dispersion of flight paths based on time-sensitive spatial needs.

Nevertheless, a large-scale urban framework for fallow lands—already in progress near certain major airports, as discussed above—could be an important tool for spatial design in the post-acceleration economy. But the Noise Landscape should be framed as a productive spatial entity only on a case-by-case basis, after in-depth study of a particular site. For instance, Amsterdam's Noise Landscape could be transformed into a large metropolitan park with experimental pockets for mitigation and compensation. Elsewhere, entire areas could become carbon absorption engines with the help of technology, as in the case of the arid Noise Landscape of Madrid Barajas. In Noise Landscapes with *Zwischenstadt* characteristics,[20] flexible urban grids can be put in place to prepare the reception of alternative activities in the post-global mobility era.

Noise Landscapes are by definition spaces of exception, of extreme legal circumstance; but experimental ways of living can be practiced only in such exceptional places today. Thus the fallow condition of Noise Landscapes may be understood as its opposite, since Noise Landscapes are in fact already fertile spaces for both the used and the residual, the urban and nonurban, hosting differentiated forms that are no longer so clearly defined as in the pre-Anthropocene era.

The environments in which we dwell are now entirely man-made, but they have yet to become spatially legible. It will be a major challenge for urbanists to provide such legibility, and to actively intervene in its interpretation. Framing and naming Noise Landscapes as spaces of common interest, negotiation, and influence is a task for which the spatial viewpoint is crucial.[21] And what currently takes place in Noise Landscapes is only precursor to the role that urbanism will play in other environmental impact spaces, which will soon encompass the whole earth, when the distinction between culture and nature is obsolete.[22]

18
Jorgen Randers, *2052: A Global Forecast for the Next Forty Years* (White River Junction, VT: Chelsea Green, 2012).

19
Timothy Morton, *Hyperobjects: Philosophy and Ecology after the End of the World* (Minneapolis: University of Minnesota Press, 2013).

20
See note 14.

21
This theme has been addressed in relation to other spaces by practices including Territorial Agency and Forensic Architecture. See Lawrence Abu Hamdan, Nabil Ahmed, Maayan Amir, Hisham Ashkar & Emily Dische-Becker, Ryan Bishop, Jacob Burns, Howard Caygill et al., *Forensis: The Architecture of Public Truth*, ed. Forensic Architecture (Berlin: Sternberg Press, 2014).

22
Bruno Latour, *Facing Gaia: Eight Lectures on the New Climatic Regime* (Cambridge: Polity Press, 2017).

How to Placemake a Killing: Critical Encounters with Decline-as-Urbanization

M. ROMAN-JOHN KOSCIELNIAK

In November 2017, another overwrought paean to the ongoing revitalization of Detroit, Michigan, appeared in *The New York Times* travel section. In a series of ethnographic vignettes sewn together with the occasional incredulity, writer Reif Larsen argued that the fading city is now roaring back to life—perhaps even deserving of the sobriquet "the most exciting city in America." After a facile take on online mortgage mogul Dan Gilbert (the founder of Quicken Loans, Inc.), Larsen breathlessly claimed: "As capitalism returns to Detroit's downtown in all its feverish forms, you can see the city materialize before your eyes."

Larsen is not alone in his optimistic assessment of redevelopment in Detroit. In the brief period since state-appointed Emergency Manager Kevyn Orr actuarially restructured local government to avoid bankruptcy, public officials, nonprofit leaders, and real estate investors have declared Detroit ready for investment. Despite the local and national frisson over its revival, rumors of capitalism's recrudescence in the city have been greatly exaggerated. Decline does not imply the wandering or withering of capitalist urbanization, but rather concretizes capital's inclination to plunder and profit as a means of building cities.

This essay seeks to make sense of contemporary urbanization by challenging how decline is conceptualized and mobilized in policy, activism, and scholarship. I argue that critical planning and geography scholars must approach the processes and instruments of urban decline with a renewed sensitivity to dispossession and plunder. While customary analytical tools and approaches are adequate for comprehending power, profit, and property in rapidly growing cities and neighborhoods, they have been less effective at understanding extractive or non-gentrification processes. My objective here, and the aim of my broader research, is to prompt questions on the political-economic and material qualities of decline. Rather than narrate decline as emptiness, depreciation, or undervaluation, I engage it as a distinct process that is neither the inverse nor the enabler of growth. Decline is not de-urbanization, but an idiom of urbanization. Of particular interest here are arrangements of destructive accumulation supported by ruling class interests that are not reducible to redevelopment. Improving analytical approaches to decline means increasing sensitivity to a wider variety of dispossessions and exploitations that shape the metropolis.

The public perception of emptiness serves as an ideological battleground pitting capital against its critics. Popular imagery and the language of urban decline suggest real estate and industrial capitalists withdraw their investments and flee to cheaper yet more profitable ground in suburban and exurban greenfields. Capital masters fixity by expanding to different, devalorized geographies in which the potential for rents outweighs initial risks. Scholars allied with this approach often observe and politicize decline at the twilight and dawn of certain forms of land market exploitation. For the mainstream development community, abandoned buildings await investor courage, and vacant lots anticipate investor imagination. Rendered this way, decline is the interregnum of city building and the temporary end of urbanization.[1] This essay challenges the wisdom that declining cities are fallow grounds requiring new investment to enable city building and kick-start urbanization. Instead, it carves out a conceptual space for "decline-as-urbanization" that politicizes decline by arguing for refreshed attention to the constellations of profit and property that signal late-capitalist urbanization.

Interrogating Urban Decline

The typical scholarly approach to decline laments gentrification and portrays grassroots, working-class resistance to reinvestment-driven displacement. Scholars and activists inherit critiques of real estate capital and focus their analyses on neighborhood confrontations with the lack of affordable housing and campaigns to control capital. These approaches are marked improvements over prior rational economic analyses that depoliticized growth and decline as changing patterns of consumption in relation to urban lifestyle. Rather than a consumer choice, here decline is considered an artifact of a disinvestment phase that sets the preconditions for future speculation and profit: destroy now, make a killing later.

Within that cycle, decline has two dominant forms. First is the discursive weaponization of decline to justify neglect and marshal its stigma to displace extant residents. The second is the material production of decline as part of gentrification and the capitalization of land rents. However, neither is sufficient to address decline-as-urbanization.

1 Stigma and Decline Discourses

Institutions and real estate interests mobilize place-specific imagery of decline to justify interventions and attract new investment. Decline discourses gloss over the details of a neighborhood and become powerful tools in shaping visions of civic progress. Consequently, misrepresentations stigmatize neighborhoods and land uses. These visions marginalize inhabitants and distinguish between who and what belongs.[2] In this scenario, low-income people and people of color are discursively evicted from the future, their lives made expendable. Brick buildings covered in soot and graffiti are discursively dismantled, their masses made disposable. These dynamics play out in a variety of marketing campaigns that naturalize the features of decline—disorder, blight, poverty, crime—and market value analyses that associate such deleterious features with resident pathology, capital flight, or investor hesitation. In declining cities, the hyperbole of arson, murder, and general devastation facilitates consensus around intervention, regardless of the projected human or social toll.[3]

These stigmatizations drive changes in land value and land use. Casual observers will also be familiar with the routine use of decline to justify restructuring "obsolete" local industrial geography. Public and private leaders target centralized light industrial zones, arguing they require more intensive and productive mixed uses. The prevailing pop urbanist redevelopment agenda is inhospitable to warehousing and manufacturing, regardless of the necessary services these firms provide. Development agency documents deem these activities dead, antiquated, or unappealing (depoliticized explanations of decline). Legislators, urbanists, and investors push to reshape and rebuild these zones in favor of a specific (classed/racialized) kind of walkable, "livable" city.

While the subject is salient in many cities, the related discourse often reduces urban decline to a meme battle. Real estate interests and policy institutions wage a propaganda war against expendable zones and inhabitants. Activists return fire with imagery and narratives of the authentic neighborhood, its sui generis rhythms and details. The back-and-forth suggests real estate capital lacks accurate information or a counter-narrative for a place, while the "true story" emerging from the grassroots opposes the exchange value ethos of officials and rentiers.

1
Todd Swanstrom, "Is St. Louis Gentrifying?," *City Observatory*, August 14, 2018, http://cityobservatory.org/is-st-louis-gentrifying.

2
Loïc Wacquant, "Territorial Stigmatization in the Age of Advanced Marginality," *Thesis Eleven* 91.1 (2007): 66–77.

3
Jeff R. Crump, "The End of Public Housing as We Know It: Public Housing Policy, Labor Regulation and the US City," *International Journal of Urban and Regional Research*, 27.1 (2003): 179–87.

Despite the outcome of these skirmishes, research and activism run the risk of romanticizing community and marginalizing the political-economic relations that produce decline and deterioration. There is little doubt that correcting distortion is vital for neighborhood resistance to gentrification and dispossession. However, scholars and activists should balance rhetoric with critical attention to material resource distribution and infrastructure provision. Poor people are not only stigmatized discursively, they suffer financial exploitation and physical displacement. Deteriorated buildings are not only rendered obsolete in our imaginations, they are targeted for wrecking, mothballing, or rehabilitation.

2 Rent Gap, Capital Expansion, Decline

Beyond its discursive usage, critical urban scholars frequently theorize decline as a material stage along the way to profit in land markets. Capital resolves overaccumulation and its fixed/liquid contradiction by expanding geographically and producing markets and fixes with the potential for new financial windfalls that preserve power relations.[4] The urgency for stable returns pushes capital to buy in "stigmatized" working-class neighborhoods where initial rent income may be low but achievable rent income increases as the surrounding city grows.[5] In short: buy low now, and rent-lease-sell high later. In this view, submarkets heat up when prior decline from neglect enables healthy returns from newly created landscapes.

In cities with rapidly growing neighborhoods, private developers themselves purchase and fund the demolition or repair of existing structures, because a city's official enthusiasm for development often encourages the recycling of neighborhoods. Interventions in historic housing stock trigger increases in property value and rents, forcing lower-income residents from neighborhoods. Property owners observe unrealized rent gains and intimidate existing tenants to clear units for higher income residents and increased potential rents.[6] Policymakers and rentiers rationalize these casualties as the tolerable cost of urgent improvement.

Inevitably, the process of decline and growth continues across space. Even luxury development may be vulnerable to time and neglect. Fixed, built-environment investments are subject to deterioration and increasing repair costs. Over time, the rate of profit from rehabilitated properties or new construction slows. Consequently, capital tilts or flows to the next speculative opportunity.[7] Landlords extract from desperate tenants, defer building maintenance, and the geographical and social cycle begins anew. In this formulation, decline is a stage in the cycle of accumulation and profit through land markets. In total, these relationships are moments in an urbanization process rather than qualities of an urbanized object.

Researchers have mobilized robust evidence from a variety of cities and countries to support this rent gap thesis of decline and growth.[8] Analyses from many deteriorating and booming neighborhoods confirm that Neil Smith's "simple and obvious" insight is a powerful explanation of urban change.[9] Speculators and investors buy available properties with the goal of profiting from the rapid transformation of the built environment and its users. In declining cities, the rent gap also describes the movement of capital back into urban centers, and those neighborhoods flanked by entrepreneurial state institutions and investor-entrepreneurs. Nevertheless, the rent gap thesis does not adequately explain forms of urbanization and neighborhood change that do not culminate in gentrification—a form of change here termed "accumulation-by-destruction."

Scholarly literature on cities like Detroit has mistaken narrow zones of rapid reinvestment or resettlement as characteristic of the broader city.[10] At best, these critiques of gentrification make sense of specific redevelopment projects in core neighborhoods. But the same analyses often bemoan a "tale of two cities" that views peripheral neighborhoods as potential rents trapped in an ill-defined pre-gentrification stage of poverty and deterioration.[11] Exploitative class relations are often disregarded in narrating a story of adjacent but unequal submarkets. At worst, this scholarship grieves the loss of authenticity and use values to real estate capital and wealthy newcomers. Here, Detroit appears as the next quarry in an uninterrupted *planetary gentrification*. Although quick to focus on community-based responses to redevelopment, such work often posits urban change as the inevitable, self-evident staging of gentrification. Detractors and boosters of these processes each see vacancy, disrepair, and abandonment as preconditions for redevelopment (either as racialized class threat or rentier opportunity). Researchers and rentiers often share this interpretation of urban decline only to disagree on the virtue of development outcomes. Despite my

4 David Harvey, "The Geography of Capitalist Accumulation: A Reconstruction of the Marxian Theory," *Antipode* 2 (1975): 9–21.

5 Neil Smith, "Toward a Theory of Gentrification: A Back to the City Movement by Capital, Not People," *Journal of the American Planning Association* 45.4 (1979): 538–48.

6 Neil Smith, *The New Urban Frontier: Gentrification and the Revanchist City* (London: Routledge, 1996).

7 Daniel J. Hammel, "Reestablishing the Rent Gap: An Alternative View of Capitalized Land Rent," *Urban Studies* 36.8 (1999): 1283–93.

8 Loretta Lees, "Super-Gentrification: The Case of Brooklyn Heights, New York City," *Urban Studies* 40.12 (November 2003): 2487–2509.

9 Tom Slater, "Planetary Rent Gaps," *Antipode*, 49.1 (2015): 114–37.

10 Sara Safransky, "Greening the Urban Frontier: Race, Property, and Resettling in Detroit," *Geoforum* 56 (2014): 237–48.

11 Laura A. Reese, Jeanette Eckert, Gary Sands, and Igor Vojnovic, "'It's Safe to Come, We've Got Lattes': Development Disparities in Detroit," *Cities* 60 (2017): 367–77.

sympathies for movements challenging gentrification and colonization, it is vital for scholars to more closely examine the forms of political-economic power against which marginalized inhabitants must resist.

Critical urbanists have taken up the question of why certain neighborhoods realize rent gaps while others remain devalorized. As geographer Tom Slater writes, "The challenge remains enticing—to consider the disparity between potential and capitalized ground rent in the context of how dwellers at the bottom of the class structure are discredited and devalued because of the places with which they are associated."[12] Critics of gentrification suggest the substantial territorial stigma attached to the poorest neighborhoods prevents rentiers from profiting off prior decline. While a "highest and best use" may exist for these severely disinvested zones, racist and classist perceptions of disorderly neighborhoods nevertheless thwart developers from closing the rent gap. Conveniently, stigma here serves as an explanation for both the presence and absence of gentrification. But it does little to explain other forms of urban decline. However appealing the project of understanding the intricate relationship of rent to territorial stigma may be, it is essential to confront the range of activities profiting from neighborhood decline itself. To put it bluntly, we must examine how gentrification both enables and corrals analysis.

Notwithstanding its ubiquity, gentrification cannot be a turnkey explanation. The non-appearance of gentrification in the present should not be misinterpreted as a guarantee of future onset. In neighborhoods across the US, complexes of policy, finance, and real estate interests produce decline in ways that do not fit neatly into the rent gap thesis or the usual cycle of gentrification. When an explanation becomes axiomatic, it suggests we should sharpen our dialectical sensitivity to the conflicts and frictions actively urbanizing cities today. We need to understand forms of power that produce destruction beyond or outside of gentrification processes. Decline is not simply urban change, but part of an active construction of the urban. Asher Ghertner takes up this question in an analysis of Indian urbanization processes and suggests gentrification is not an automatic explanation for the wide variety of urban change.[13] A similar intervention is necessary to scrutinize American cities in which decline and destruction are the dominant expressions of urbanization. Scholarly investigations should arrive at gentrification as an explanation for land market conflicts instead of capitulating to gentrification's explanatory power and then unmasking the specific actors behind it as if following a recipe. The mobilizing power of gentrification as a working-class call to arms does not justify sidelining the processes of decline and destruction that wreck neighborhoods and ordinary lives in other ways.

Linking Demolition and Decline in Detroit

Constrained by austerity and retrenchment at imbricated scales of government, community and economic development interests strive to reenter the regional, national, or global mesh of private investment. Here the commonsense view is that declining cities are risky for capital because poverty, crime, or corruption thwart investor confidence in returns. For local leaders, demolition is one method to resuscitate interest and unlock development. Scholars in planning and geography often characterize demolition as the destructive enabling work of capital's return and neighborhood revitalization.[14]

Typically, blight removal amounts to the transaction cost of eliminating a physical barrier to new investment. Governments justify the allocation of public resources to demolition campaigns since these efforts establish the requisite condition—a flattened physical environment—for capital expansion away from the fixed investments of prior movements and land market exploitation. Leaders prescribe demolition to produce "undeveloped land"—to compete with investment at the periphery and the suburban frontier (rife with speculative residential projects).

By eradicating physical barriers to redevelopment, demolition loads the seesaw of capital towards disinvested neighborhoods that still contain attractive building shells or shovel-ready lots. In post-subprime-crisis cities, these completed and planned demolitions amount to the janitorial work of mopping up the evidence of predatory lending and subsequent mortgage and tax foreclosures. In most cases, city officials devise comprehensive policy agendas linking demolition to other forms of public intervention to create attractive (i.e., safe) zones for investment. Whether muscular policing, targeted infrastructural provision, subsidization, or concierge planning services, the city's objective is to produce frictionless, low-risk reentry for capital and the wealthier residents it accompanies.

My research interrogates the political economy and geography of demolition-dependent redevelopment in Detroit. By late 2013, an ensemble of public, private, and philanthropic leaders had engineered a local, regional, state,

12
Tom Slater, "Clarifying Neil Smith's Rent Gap Theory of Gentrification," *Tracce Urbane* 1.1 (2017): 83–101.

13
D. A. Ghertner, "India's Urban Revolution: Geographies of Displacement beyond Gentrification," *Environment and Planning A*, 46.7 (2014): 1554–71.

14
Emily Rosenman and Samuel Walker, "Tearing Down the City to Save It? 'Back-Door Regionalism' and the Demolition Coalition in Cleveland, Ohio," *Environment and Planning A*, 48.2 (2015): 273–91.

15
Jackie Calmes, "$300 Million in Detroit Aid, but No Bailout," *New York Times*, September 26, 2013, https://www.nytimes.com/2013/09/27/us/300-million-in-detroit-aid-but-no-bailout.html.

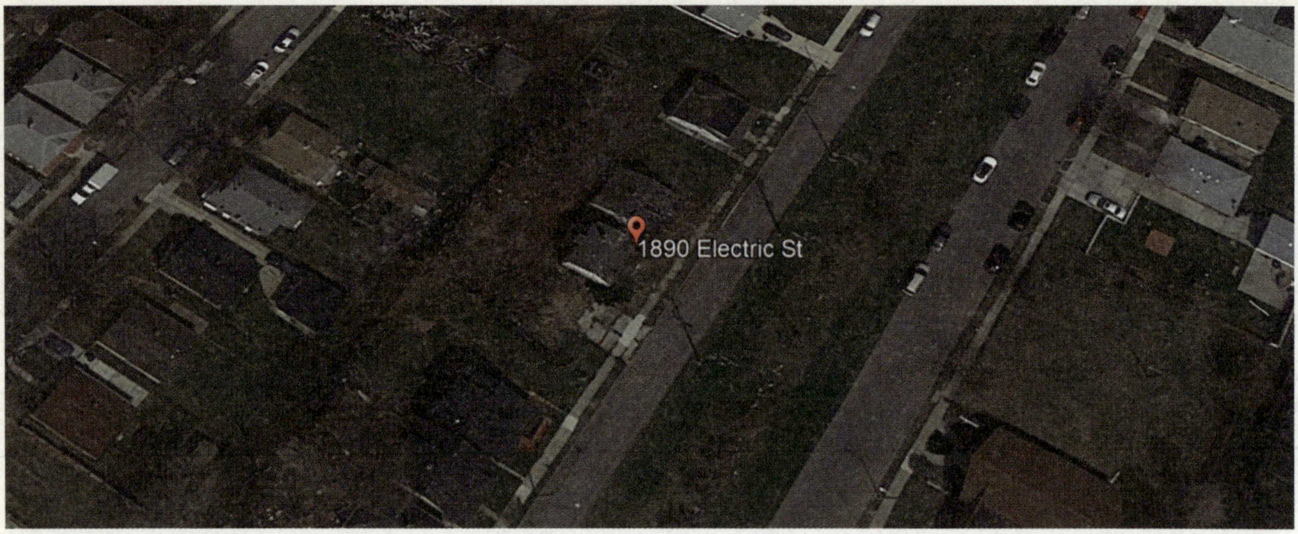

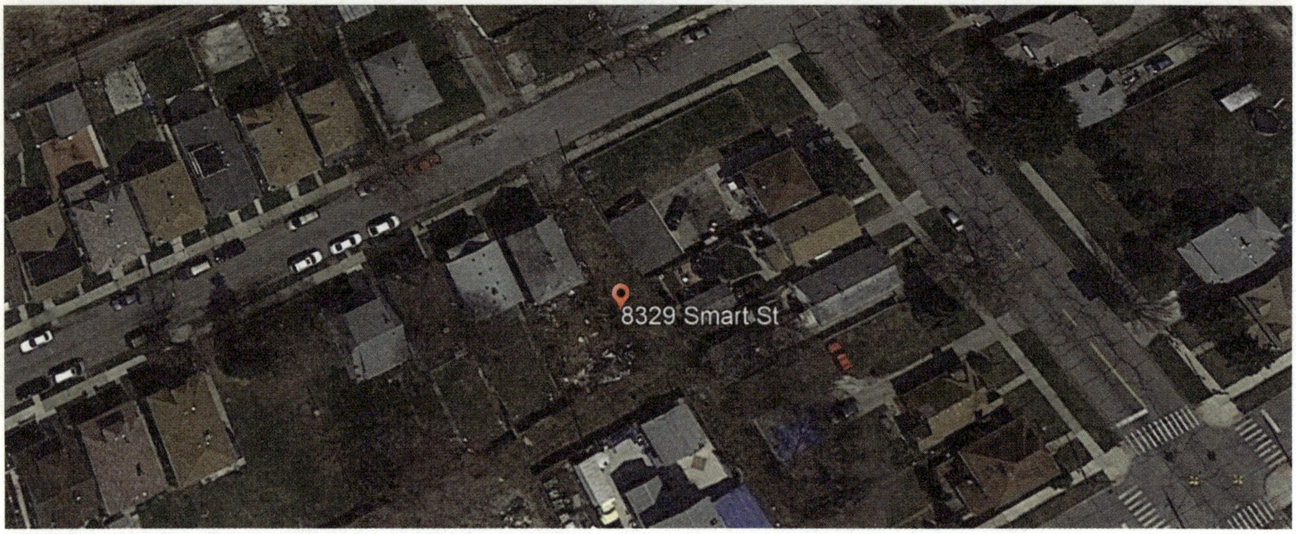

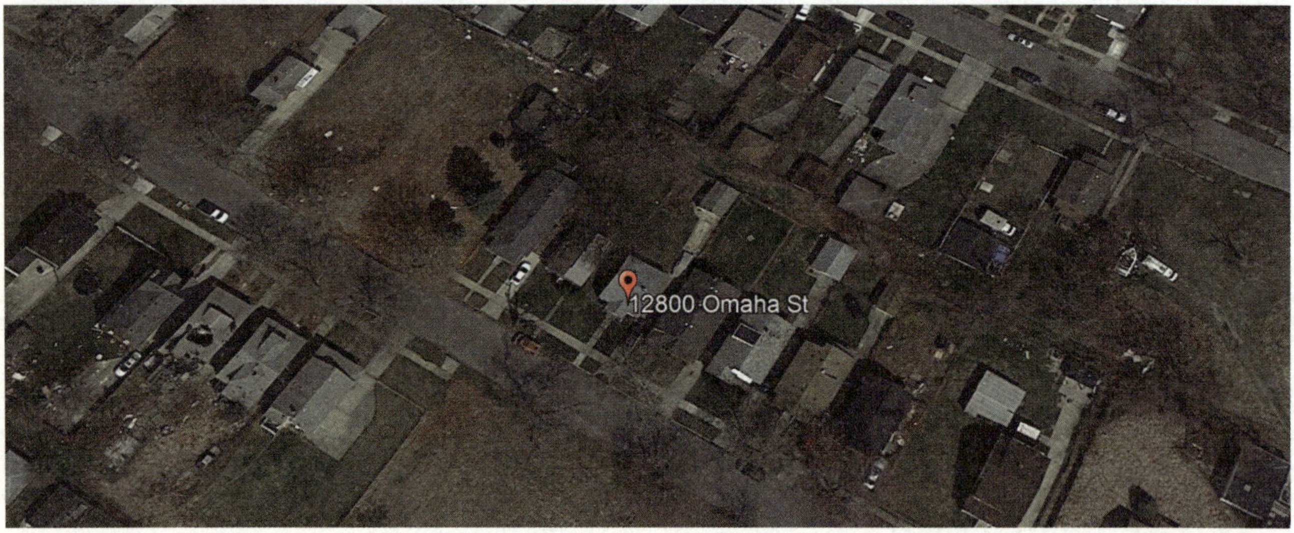

Before and after images of demolition sites. Top to bottom: 1890 Electric Street, 8329 Smart Street, 12800 Omaha Street. Courtesy Google Earth.

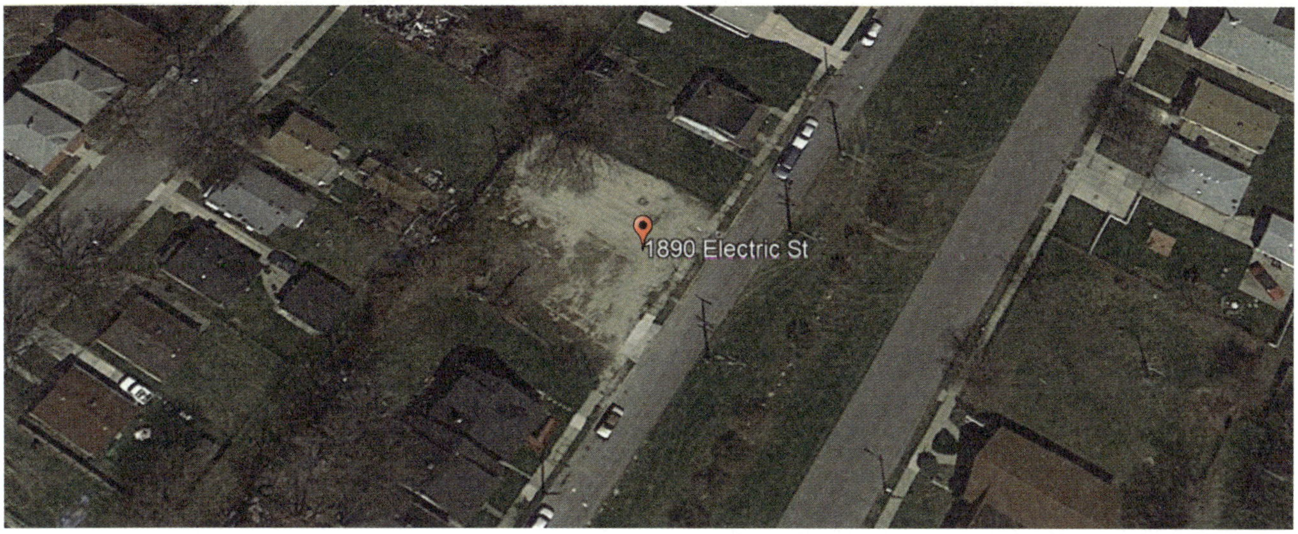
1890 Electric St

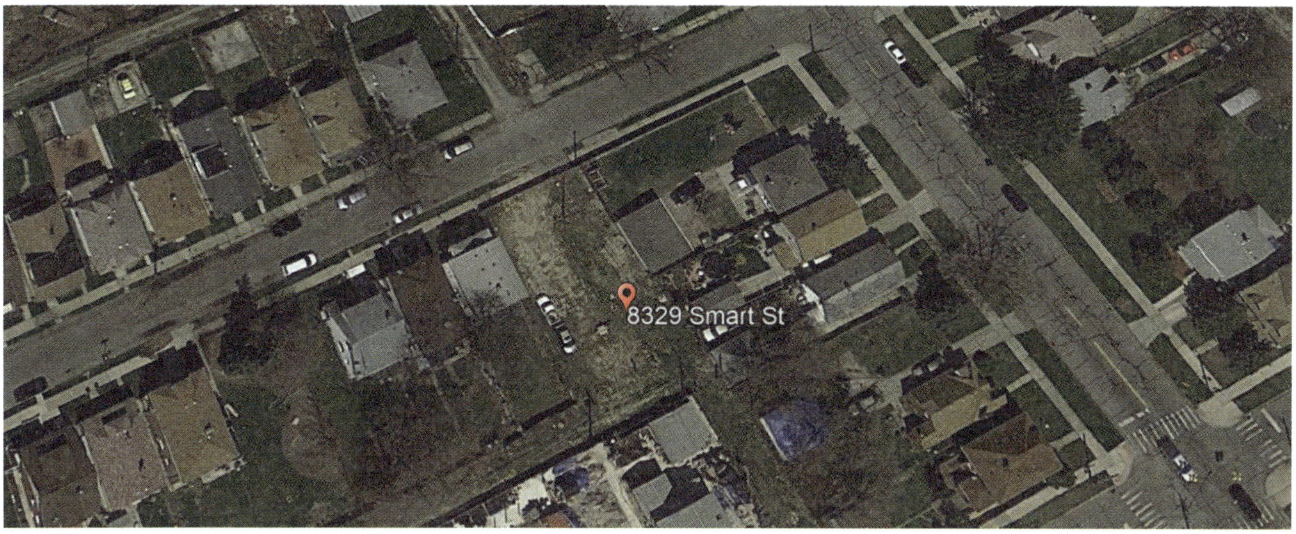
8329 Smart St

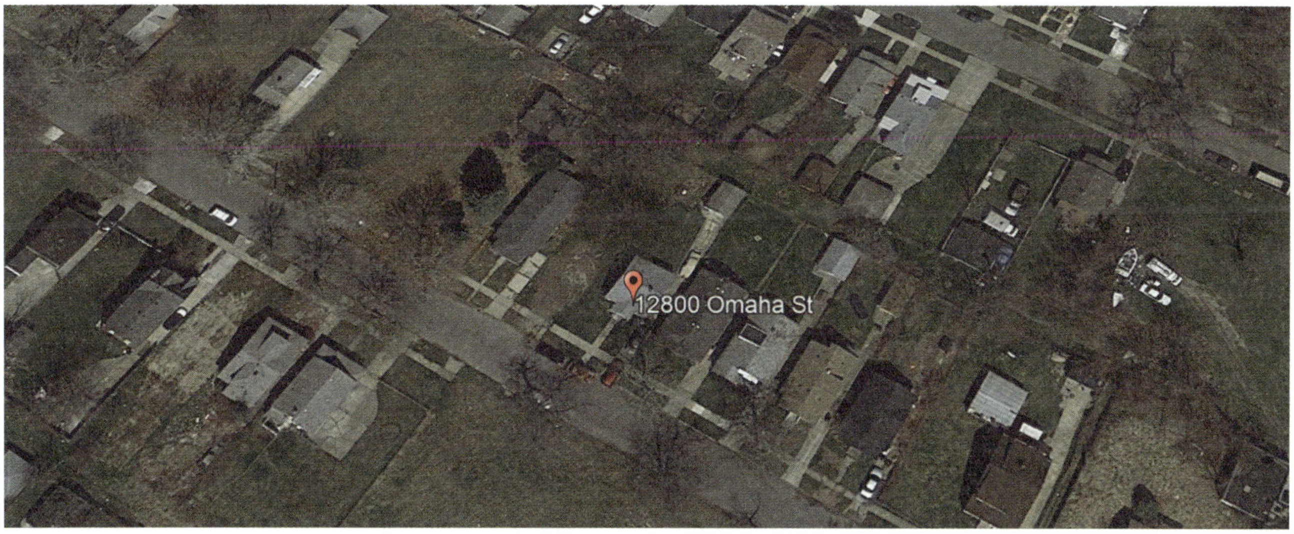
12800 Omaha St

and national consensus establishing blight removal as the essential tool for city revitalization.[15] After Governor Rick Snyder declared a financial emergency—stemming from decades of population decline, segregation, and housing exploitation—various movers-and-shakers sidelined structural factors and fomented a popular political climate in which widespread clearance was the only acceptable method to halt decline. On more than one occasion, civic leaders declared residential dereliction to be the nagging cause of Detroit's condition. Today, they term this "blight flight."[16]

Kevyn Orr used his considerable powers as emergency manager to unilaterally proclaim a "blight emergency" comparable to that of a natural disaster or civil unrest.[17] In May 2014, the Detroit Blight Removal Task Force (DBRTF) concluded Detroit contained tens of thousands of blighted or nearly blighted properties requiring immediate intervention.[18] The task force proposed a 10-year, $1 billion plan to remedy residential abandonment.[19] In the subsequent months, and with little debate, Detroit boosters, academic observers, and elected officials summarily concluded that demolition served two "public" purposes: 1) targeted removals steady housing values in stable neighborhoods; 2) widespread removals eliminate barriers to new investment in depopulated neighborhoods.[20]

In the last quarter of 2014, two quasi-governmental entities, the Detroit Building Authority (DBA) and Detroit Land Bank Authority (DLBA), collaborated with the mayor's office to launch the Detroit Demolition Project (DDP). DBA coordinated physical wrecking and DLBA managed the property and financial side, together striking at blighted housing in a citywide removal project largely financed by reassigned federal Hardest Hit Funds (HHF), the city's Quality of Life budget, escrowed fire insurance settlements, and private donations.

Early on, DDP administrators prioritized a colossal backfill program to complete demolitions. Backfill plays a key role in the city's belief that "the starting point for continuing to reinvigorate the market is the clearance of the decades-old signs of disinvestment in the area."[21] Basement foundations are ubiquitous in Detroit's single-family housing stock and ordinances require their removal to complete a demolition. Contractors create a cavity when removing basement foundations, which must be filled to grade with clean fill to accommodate a range of future uses. On average, each cavity needs 250 cubic yards of material. If public estimates are accurate, the DDP will eliminate approximately 50,000 residential structures. Its backfill program will thus need to identify and distribute 12.5 million cubic yards of material, in hundreds of thousands of truckloads. The demolitions constitute a megaproject—a blight removal offensive unprecedented in US history—but to execute it the DDP backfill program must circulate eight times the material displaced by constructing the Hoover Dam.

In September 2014, the DLBA requested proposals from firms to manage the backfill material monitoring and testing services.[22] A few weeks later, AKT Peerless and Greater Detroit Resource Recovery Authority were retained to administer the program. Within months, DLBA released a soil guidance document regulating laboratory analysis, backfill categories, and approval processes. The document formalized six categories of fill ranging from clear "Category 1: Residential Construction and Residential Landscape Yard Sites" to fuzzy "Category 6: Other."[23] Despite these rapid developments, DDP struggled to optimize a program capable of serving the backfill appetite of scheduled demolitions. Before the end of the year, a columnist for the *Detroit Free Press* described the logistical challenges of managing needed material:

> Last summer, demolition crews planned to use dirt scoured off of the I-96 reconstruction project to fill up basement holes. But road salt deposited on the freeway over the years contaminated the dirt too much to meet legal standards for residential neighborhoods. Demolition crews have had to buy sand and other fill from quarries at increased cost and inconvenience.[24]

16
Bob Graves, "The Motor City's Blight Busters," *Governing*, June 12, 2017, http://www.governing.com/topics/urban/gov-detroit-street-light-replacement-housing-demolition.html.

17
Kate Abbey-Lambertz, "Detroit's Abandoned Building Problem Is an Actual 'Blight Emergency,' Says City Manager," *Huffington Post*, September 16, 2013, https://www.huffingtonpost.com/2013/09/16/detroit-abandoned-building_n_3921417.html.

18
Monica Davey, "Detroit Urged to Tear Down 40,000 Buildings," *New York Times*, May 27, 2014, https://www.nytimes.com/2014/05/28/us/detroit-task-force-says-blight-cleanup-will-cost-850-million.html.

19
Glenda D. Price, Linda Smith, and Dan Gilbert, *Every Neighborhood Has a Future and It Doesn't Include Blight* (Detroit: Detroit Blight Removal Task Force and Rock Ventures, 2014), http://s3.documentcloud.org/documents/1173946/detroit-blight-removal-task-force-plan-may-2014.pdf.

20
Alan Mallach, "Hardest Hit Funds Demolition Policy Change on Track to Become a Boon for Distressed Communities," *Center for Community Progress* (blog), July 1, 2014, http://www.communityprogress.net/blog/federal-policy-change-leads-results-ground-hardest-hit-funds-demolish-derelict-houses; Dave McKinney, "Knocking Down Detroit to Revive It Comes at a Price," *Reuters*, December 15, 2015, https://www.reuters.com/article/us-usa-detroit-demolition-feature/knocking-down-detroit-to-revive-it-comes-at-a-price-idUSKBN0TY0GR20151215.

21
Detroit Hardest Hit Funds Strategic Plan (City of Detroit, 2013), http://www.detroitmi.gov/Portals/0/docs/EM/Reports/Hardest%20Hit%20Funds%20Strategic%20Plan.pdf.

22
Request for Proposal: Backfill Material Monitoring and Testing Services (Detroit Land Bank Authority, 2014).

23
Ibid.

24
John Gallagher, "Detroit Blight Removal Campaign Ramps Up, Long Way to Go," *Detroit Free Press*, December 14, 2014, https://www.freep.com/story/money/business/michigan/2014/12/14/detroit-blight-duggan/20360959.

By mid-2015, Pulitzer Prize–winning reporter Charlie LeDuff, then working at local FOX affiliate WJBK, began investigating the demolition program. In a series of televised confrontations with city leaders, LeDuff concluded the DDP was confident neither in the costs nor the quality of backfill.[25] Mayor Mike Duggan quashed public concern by linking costs to his administration's unique commitment to sustainable demolition practices.[26]

After Duggan's intervention, media attention to backfill faded while the program rapidly expanded. Finding limited supplies of local material, contractors began sourcing approved backfill from rural sand pits and quarries up to 50 miles away. Contractors responsible for new exurban and suburban housing developments shipped the spoils of basement excavations into Detroit. A big-box retailer—the hunting and fishing outfitter Cabela's—located in the small town of Dundee, 60 miles southwest of Detroit, contributed 12,601 cubic yards of backfill from a parking lot expansion.[27] In many instances, demolition contractors drew on HHF money to subsidize suburban projects by hauling away material or paying for dirt that was little more than the waste of growth. Meanwhile, Detroit real estate impresarios made clear the reason for circulating the material: new ground enables new investment.

During a 2014 press conference, Dan Gilbert—also a co-chair of the DBRTF—predicted: "Removing all blight is going to create economic value. You are going to have significant interest from profit-making capitalist folks."[28] His opinion is not restricted to the usual profit-seeking interests. One US Environmental Protection Agency (EPA) staff member remarked, "Detroit is trying to recover its public resource—land—to get back to that place like a township with undeveloped land. These cities are trying to revitalize but there's no land ready to build."[29]

The backfill program implies Detroit's revitalization is dependent on clean dirt to facilitate capital's return and to draw wealthier residents. It is a "backfill-to-the-city" movement. But the sprawling geography of backfill calls into question the benefits of blight removal. Detroit demolitions rely on material excavated by new-build suburbia to produce developable land in the core. That construction at the periphery continues unrestricted means DDP claims revitalization even while preserving dominant investment and property regimes. Thousands of transactions in state and city records register this contradiction. To wit, the records suggest $90,000 in HHF found its way to a subdivision in Auburn Hills, 40 miles north of Detroit, to source 13,890 cubic yards of material.[30] Dirt becomes money in disguise. Metropolitan real estate interests are unwilling to confront the "housing disassembly line" that simultaneously encourages suburban speculation and eradicates Detroit's existing core.[31] Backfill logistics expand demolition beyond a single property or address, implicating new geographies and property relations of decline, challenging the concept of development-ready land.

By mid-2016, Duggan claimed responsibility for 10,000 residential demolitions. During a July 19 appearance at 14097 Marlowe in the Hubbell-Lyndon neighborhood, advisors and contractors flanked the mayor while he enumerated his administration's achievements.[32] A banner hanging from the southern exposure of the lot's vacant house prominently displayed the figure "10,000" as Duggan admitted: "It took us a while to really get the hang of this, and I won't tell you we're perfect."

By imperfection, here, he means the two federal investigations into DDP. A special inspector general with the US Department of Treasury is currently investigating unusual pricing on demolitions supported by HHF.[33] A separate FBI investigation is collecting evidence on demolition bid-rigging and collusion between the mayor's office and contractors.[34]

Despite the occasional hiatus in demolitions due to investigations, weather, or auditing, the DDP is unlike any blight removal project in recent memory. The program's achievements are considerable. As of mid-September 2018, the City of Detroit's records show DDP had allocated $240,481,907.03 to regional demolition contractors for the removal of 15,156 houses at an average cost of $15,156.00 per house.[35] But another

25
Charlie LeDuff, "Is Detroit's Demolition Math Fuzzy?," *Fox 2 Detroit*, October 7, 2015, http://www.fox2detroit.com/the-americans-with-charlie-leduff/is-detroits-demolition-math-fuzzy.

26
Matt Helms and Joe Guillen, "Duggan Explains Increase in Blight Demolition Costs," *Detroit Free Press*, October 13, 2015, https://www.freep.com/story/news/2015/10/13/duggan-explains-why-blight-demolition-costs-increasing/73865790.

27
Author's analysis of demolition backfill data provided by City of Detroit following FOIA request.

28
John Gallagher, "You Tear Down the Blight in Detroit, But Then What?," *Detroit Free Press*, January 26, 2014.

29
EPA staff member, interview by author, October 18, 2016.

30
Author's analysis of demolition backfill data provided by City of Detroit following FOIA request.

31
See George Galster, *Driving Detroit: The Quest for Respect in the Motor City* (Philadelphia: University of Pennsylvania Press, 2014).

32
Matt Helms, "Detroit Reaches Blight Milestone: 10,000 Demolitions," *Detroit Free Press*, July 19, 2016, https://www.freep.com/story/news/local/michigan/detroit/2016/07/19/detroit-reaches-blight-milestone-10000-demolitions/87284392.

33
Todd Spangler, "Federal Inspector Criticizes Michigan's Demolition Spending," *Detroit Free Press*, April 26, 2017, https://www.freep.com/story/news/local/michigan/detroit/2017/04/26/tarp-michigan-demolition-programs/100892918.

34
Christine Ferretti, "FBI Investigating Detroit's Demolition Program," *Detroit News*, May 11, 2016, https://www.detroitnews.com/story/news/local/detroit-city/2016/05/11/detroit-demolition-fbi-investigate/84253412.

35
Author's calculation based on demolition data publicly available at https://data.detroitmi.gov/Government/Demolitions-Data-Lens/xhif-khyv.

feat is still more notable. Combined with systemic reluctance to confront or halt speculative development, the demolition program has enabled a massive transfer of public wealth to contractors and suburban land interests through a process that aids and abets the structural determinants of Detroit's decline.

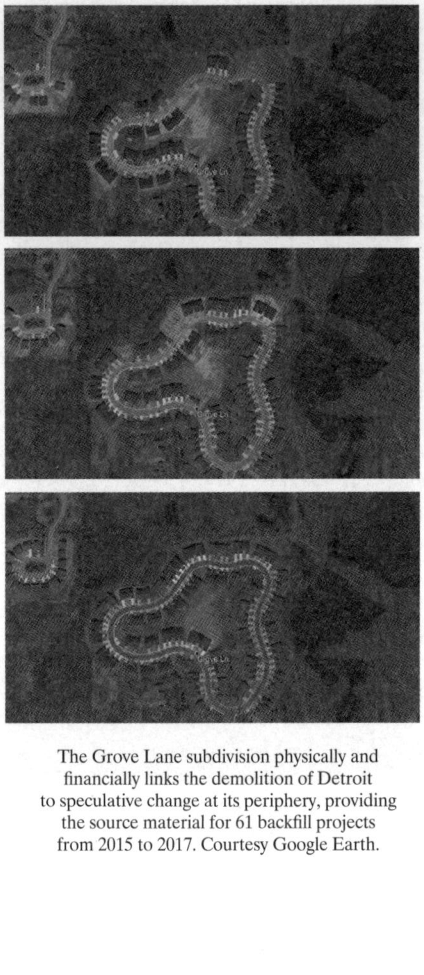

The Grove Lane subdivision physically and financially links the demolition of Detroit to speculative change at its periphery, providing the source material for 61 backfill projects from 2015 to 2017. Courtesy Google Earth.

Justifying Demolition and Governing through Blight

Countless media reports feature jubilant Detroit residents celebrating as an excavator devours a structure.[36] But exuberance differs from institutional evidence. In 2015, Dynamo Metrics, a Detroit-based spatial econometrics firm supported by Dan Gilbert, conducted research on HHF demolition and home values. Researchers observed a 4.2 percent increase in value within 500 feet of a demolition.[37] Although leaders and developers met the findings with enthusiasm, closer analysis suggests a slightly different conclusion.

The study period examines the returns on early stage HHF demolitions that were designated for Detroit's more stable neighborhoods. Critically, HHF did not choose neighborhoods at random, but rather funded targeted demolitions in strong neighborhoods that would predictably benefit from the outcome. In other words, Dynamo Metrics concluded that recovering neighborhoods in Detroit recover faster with additional resources. The demolitions thus also produced a smaller-scale redistribution of public wealth, channeling resources to protect private property and homeowner interests in "desirable" areas. These critiques have not discouraged leaders and developers from treating the study's limited findings as proof of blight removal's virtues.[38] Demolition officials continue to wield the Dynamo Metrics report and supporting anecdotal evidence as justification for intervention, even in neighborhoods outside the early HHF zones.

Detroit's future remains subject to excavators and extraction. Regionally, blight removal is an immense real estate capital-adjacent industry employing precarious low-wage labor and funneling hundreds of millions of public dollars to haulers and contractors. In many cases, the contractors that would profit from new building construction are the chief beneficiaries of blight removal expenditures. Capital stands to gain from these neighborhoods whether construction or annihilation takes place.

As planner and geographer Jason Hackworth has argued, the history of residential blight removal in Rust Belt cities does not confirm a tidy link between demolition and redevelopment. Hackworth's 2016 analysis found that since 1970, public and private actors have demolished over

36
Ronnie Dahl, "Neighbors Celebrate as Three Blighted Homes in Their Neighborhood Are Torn Down," *WXYZ Detroit*, March 2, 2016, https://www.wxyz.com/news/ronnie-dahl/neighbors-celebrate-as-three-blighted-homes-in-their-neighborhood-are-torn-down.

37
Dynamo Metrics, LLC, *Estimating Home Equity Impacts from Rapid, Targeted Residential Demolition in Detroit, MI: Application of a Spatially-Dynamic Data System for Decision Support* (Detroit: Skillman Foundation and Rock Ventures, 2015), https://static1.squarespace.com/static/55e8c061e4b018cc4b5864bc/t/55f78eeee4b07bf949e5de03/1442287342508/Detroit_DemoStudy_FinalEditedVersion.pdf.

38
Todd Spangler, "Detroit-Led Blight Fight May Spur Demolitions Across US," *Detroit Free Press*, December 18, 2015, https://www.freep.com/story/news/local/michigan/2015/12/18/detroit-led-blight-fight-may-spur-demolitions-across-us/77500028.

39
Jason Hackworth, "Demolition as Urban Policy in the American Rust Belt," *Environment and Planning A*, 48.11 (2016): 2216.

40
Nick Carey, "Detroit Area's Battle with Blight May Be Key to Survival," *Reuters*, July 25, 2013, https://www.reuters.com/article/us-usa-detroit-blight/detroit-areas-battle-with-blight-may-be-key-to-survival-idUSBRE96O02T20130725.

41
Rose Hackman, "Detroit Demolishes Its Ruins: 'The Capitalists Will Take Care of the Rest,'" *Guardian*, September 28, 2014, https://www.theguardian.com/money/2014/sep/28/detroit-demolish-ruins-capitalists-abandoned-buildings-plan.

117,000 units in Detroit. That so much demolition "has already occurred to little effect suggests that it is not an integral barrier to imminent investment."[39] At first, this fact may seem to support evidence of a managerial compulsion to obliterate empty neighborhoods or at least suggest a different temporal horizon for gentrification. Alternatively, it indicates that rent gap closure in not fundamental to profiting from prior decline. That is, demolitions in Detroit do not need to uniformly trigger reinvestment interest because blight removal is itself an accumulative process; destruction need not enable rebuilding. The demolition industry is a profit junkie hunting for the next dereliction fix.

DDP also furnishes a clear scheme for policy and finance leaders to govern decline through depoliticized intervention. Here blight removal is more than urban policy—it serves as a form of government. The clearance consensus in Detroit has evolved into a "blightocracy" that treats demolition as a technical solution to such political-economic problems as education, poverty, infrastructure, and sustainability. Blightocrats disregard historical struggles over property rights and racial discrimination in real estate development by asserting demolition as a foolproof spatial problem-solver. As Brian Farkas, a special projects director at DBA, remarked in 2013: "If you address Detroit's blight problem, you make the rest of the city's problems easier to solve."[40] Even without the certainty of demolition-dependent redevelopment, the ruling class in the Detroit region benefits by extracting public capital and by using blight removal to govern the city and its inhabitants.

Conclusion

Despite nonprofit leaders who assert, "Get the city safe, get the city clean. The capitalists will take care of the rest,"[41] the evidence in Detroit suggests a different political-economy of decline and dispossession that complicates typical gentrification narratives. Recently, scholarship on decline has analyzed neighborhood processes not automatically reducible to gentrification. For example, Joshua Akers and Eric Seymour demonstrate how investors and institutions produce decline by recycling residential properties in depopulated neighborhoods through tax foreclosure auctions and extractive land contracts. Their research suggests the limit of the rent gap thesis, proposing a wider range of exploitation in declining neighborhoods.[42] A 2017 analysis of property tax assessments concluded that thousands of tax foreclosures in Michigan were not only exceptional in scale, but also unconstitutional by state law.[43] Private and public leaders at different levels have publicly condemned Detroit's continued decline, while exerting scant institutional energy to abolish the systems that produce and profit from the city's destruction.[44] My own research agenda includes examining similar "decline machine" constellations that use alternative financial services, vampiric industries, and code enforcement to serve the urbanization interests of racial capitalism.

In sum, critical attention to the processes outlined above challenges how scholars and theorists today comprehend and contest decline. Geographers and planners can embark on new research trajectories by considering destruction and plunder as forms of city building. To borrow from Reif Larsen, decline-as-urbanization allows us to see the city materialize in old places with refreshed eyes.[45] The challenge remains enticing.

42
Joshua Akers and Eric Seymour, "Instrumental Exploitation: Predatory Property Relations at City's End," *Geoforum* 91 (May 2018): 127– 40.

43
Violet Ikonomova, "Study Finds Detroit's Foreclosure Crisis Fueled by Illegal Tax Assessments," *Detroit Metro Times*, July 12, 2017, https://www.metrotimes.com/detroit/could-detroits-tax-foreclosures-be-unconstitutional/Content?oid=4522278.

44
Tyler Scott, "Detroit Assessor's Plan to Save Some from Tax Foreclosure Stalls at County Treasurer's Office," *Michigan Radio*, October 31, 2017, http://michiganradio.org/post/detroit-assessors-plan-save-some-tax-foreclosure-stalls-county-treasurers-office.

45
Reif Larsen, "Detroit: The Most Exciting City in America?," *New York Times*, November 20, 2017, https://www.nytimes.com/2017/11/20/travel/detroit-michigan-downtown.html.

Cyberjaya and the Reality of New City Building

WADE SHEPARD

At first I thought it was a construction site. I walked into Tamarind Square, shook hands with lead designer Peter Chan, and promptly asked when the project would be completed. Chan, who happened to be dressed in a flowery green and pink Hawaiian shirt and sandals, chuckled knowingly. It was clearly not the first time the question had been asked. But Tamarind Square was not under construction—it was in vogue.

"Our projects all look unfinished," Chan explained. "This is what the tech crowd likes. Something a bit more industrial, a bit more raw, a bit more edgy: exposed ceiling and brick walls. Not like the typical office with a false ceiling and everything—that's too sleepy and too 'whatever.'"

Tamarind Square is the latest mixed-use development—office, commercial, residential—to pop up in Cyberjaya, a purpose-built new city devoted to the high-tech sector, located 40 kilometers south of Kuala Lumpur in Malaysia. As Chan led me through bare concrete corridors that were "kitsched up" with chain-link fences as well as fledgling vines and other foliage meant to someday creep over and along the walls, he stressed the importance of projecting an ideal brand and image repeatedly, to attract the community he was trying to build. Plain old hair salons and bubble tea joints were not welcome here: this was an abode for Malaysia's young entrepreneurs and innovators aspiring to disrupt the regional tech ecosystem. Chan took me to the top of one of his "treehouses"— narrow concrete pillars of stacked studios that rise from the center of the development as if mimicking trees in a forest—where companies that fit his optimal profile can rent space for less than US$100 per month.

Tamarind Square is the new face of Cyberjaya and serves as a microcosm for the place as a whole: idealistic nearly to the point of cliché, it is a project for startups in a city that is essentially a startup.

A tour with Peter Chan in Tamarind Square.
Courtesy Wade Shepard.

Square One

At the inauguration of Cyberjaya in 1997, Malaysia's then prime minister Mahathir bin Mohamad declared proudly, "The establishment of the Multimedia Super Corridor and Cyberjaya in particular will enable Malaysians to leapfrog into the Information Age. We hope to create the ideal environment that will attract world-class companies to use it as a regional multi-cultural Information Age hub."[1]

Inspired by a 1995 study by the global management consulting firm McKinsey & Company, the dream was to build an information technology (IT) themed epicenter, from scratch, on 30 square kilometers of former oil palm plantations that could someday be big enough and bad enough to attract the most prominent tech firms. Cyberjaya was one of several megaprojects the prime minister backed to jumpstart the Malaysian economy, attract foreign investment, and rebrand the nation as a modern state. It was to become the linchpin of the Multimedia Super Corridor (MSC): a sprawling special economic zone and high-tech R&D center stretching from the Petronas Towers in the heart of Kuala Lumpur all the way to the international airport, 60 kilometers to the south.

Not Exactly What They Wanted

In the early days, Cyberjaya was described with such hopeful monikers as "The Silicon Valley of Asia," "Malaysia's First Intelligent City," and "The City of the Future." It was the secret weapon that would allow Malaysia to leapfrog its neighbors and become Southeast Asia's high-tech hub. However, this vision never came to be.

Memorialized as "Malaysia's Failed Silicon Valley" by *Wired* magazine in 2016, things in Cyberjaya had not worked out as planned.[2] Rather than a vibrant "iCity hub," what was built looked more like a run-of-the-mill IT park, of the ilk easily found in a place like Provo, Utah: white and gray clinical buildings arranged in neat rows along broad, straight streets. Instead of becoming a hotbed of creativity and attracting the brightest minds globally to devise new ideas there, Cyberjaya transformed into a city of low-level white-collar workers who commuted in for work and scurried back to Kuala Lumpur as soon as the five o'clock whistle sounded.

While Cyberjaya's marketing material boasted over 40 multinational corporations and 800 information and communication technology (ICT) companies, with big names like Dell, HP, DHL, HSBC, Ericsson, Motorola, BMW, and IBM, most were simply cashing in on the new city's favorable tax policies, subsidized rent, cheap land, backup power supply, and broadband internet. Cyberjaya was a new city of high-class companies running low-class enterprises, that is, call centers. Rather than propelling Malaysia to the frontline of the global tech race, Cyberjaya was the urban equivalent of someone trying to deceive their friends with an obviously fake Rolex.

As the years went by and the digital age transitioned from the wave of tomorrow to normal everyday existence, Cyberjaya seemed like a futuristic-themed parody of itself. Streets and places with names like Persiaran Multimedia, Jalan Cyberpoint, Cyber Square, and Multimedia University may have been hip in the nineties, but they come off as passé in 2018, if not downright corny. Approaching its 20th anniversary, Cyberjaya read like a bad 1950s science-fiction novel about the year 2000. And ironically, during a period of stagnation in the years following the 1997–1998 financial downturn in Asia, Malaysia's "city of the future" was in danger of being left in the past.

New Beginnings

In 2013, Cyberjaya came to terms with the fact that it was never going to be the next Silicon Valley. But the new city's administrators and visionaries were not yet ready to give up and let it to be reduced to a distant suburb of Kuala Lumpur. There was still time left for Cyberjaya to reinvent itself and create a more realistic model for development. It was obvious then that big multinational corporations saw Cyberjaya as little more than a giant call center. To become a true hub for high-tech R&D, with an impact on the wider world outside its city limits, the innovation catalyst would have to come from within Malaysia. So Cyberjaya stopped trying to become something that it wasn't—doubling down on its strengths instead.

While new cities can rarely compete with established metropolises in terms of economic clout and social kinetics, they can offer things that such metropolises usually cannot, including:

1
Tun Dr Mahathir Mohamad, Cyberjaya groundbreaking ceremony, May 17, 1997.

2
Kobie Nicole, "Inside Cyberjaya, Malaysia's Failed Silicon Valley," *Wired UK*, April 5, 2016, https://www.wired.co.uk/article/malaysia-cyberjaya-silicon-valley-smart-cities.

The industrial, edgy aesthetic of Tamarind Square. Courtesy Wade Shepard.

The "treehouse" offices of Tamarind Square. Courtesy Wade Shepard.

1 A platform for young companies and entrepreneurs lacking the capital to set up and compete in the competitive and often high-priced environments of the established urban core. According to various promotional literature, Cyberjaya has the second most inexpensive office space in Asia.

2 A live testing ground for new urban technologies as well as innovative social and commercial schemes.

3 Physical space for expanding institutions like universities and elite private high schools.
4 Low-cost, midrange, and high-end accommodation for individuals who have been priced out of such housing in the historic city centers, that also provides a residential foothold for the emerging market's new middle class in a potentially trendy or up-and-coming area.

5 Public services and technologies that would be too complicated and expensive to deploy in more established and larger population centers. Cyberjaya was the first city in Malaysia to offer residents 1Gbps high-speed internet and a 4G LTE mobile connection.[3]

6 A more open society for the younger internationalized generation seeking new social and personal frontiers.

Cyberjaya as a Startup Hub

Abandoning its plan to become another Silicon Valley, Cyberjaya gave Malaysia something it actually needed: a sandbox for its innovators, entrepreneurs, and startups to play in.

Founded in 1996 as a joint venture between Setia Haruman (Cyberjaya's master developer), an assortment of domestic and international companies, and the Malaysian government, an agency called Cyberview was established to guide and cultivate Cyberjaya's growth as an innovation hub. Cyberview's role has ebbed with the current of the new city's development, transitioning from high-profile developer to accelerator for promising startups.

Cyberview described their mission to me:

> The goal is for Cyberjaya to be a test bed for ideas that need validation before they are implemented across the country, ultimately benefiting the nation as a whole. . . . As a smart city and a living lab for innovation, Cyberjaya is the perfect place for startups to prove the viability of their products and services and attract the attention of potential investors.[4]

With programs that provide funding, space, guidance, and instruction, successful new companies are churning out of Cyberjaya by the dozen. As an atypical accelerator program, Cyberview often seeks out young companies developing technologies that the city itself can deploy and utilize.

High-rise development in Cyberjaya.
Courtesy Wade Shepard.

For example, the Cyberjaya parking system was designed in-house by the startup Touchless, which launched after founder Mohammad Aljlal caused a traffic jam when his swipe card malfunctioned at a Kuala Lumpur parking garage. He set to work developing a better payment method and came up with an image recognition system that identifies license plates and automatically withdraws parking fees from a driver's account without having to stop at a gate or awkwardly pay on-site at a kiosk. Cyberview liked Aljlal's system and provided him funding and workshop space as he built the product. Now the goal is to spread Touchless technology beyond the gates of Cyberjaya.

Tracker Hero, another Cyberview startup, has a similar story. Reacting against Malaysia's archaic security systems, the startup sought to develop a technology to digitize, consolidate, and streamline a company's security apparatus. Upon entering buildings in Cyberjaya, I met one particular Tracker Hero product on several occasions: a touchscreen resting on a podium, designed to replace a human receptionist.

Cyberview has so far supported over 60 startups with $1.5 million of funding that has reportedly generated nearly $6 million in revenue and created 300 jobs.[5] The successes of Cyberview incubation range from the company MyCash winning the Seedstars World competition in 2016,[6] to *Forbes* naming the founders of The Lorry to its 2017 30 Under 30 Asia list.

Cyberjaya's innovative grassroots endeavors do not end with Cyberview. The new city has become an epicenter for accelerators and positioned itself as ground zero of

3
Faris Yahaya, "A Blueprint Coming True," Cyberjayamalaysia.com, August 8, 2016, http://www.cyberjayamalaysia.com.my/stories/stories/2016/08/08/a-blueprint-coming-true.

4
Cyberview representative, Cyberview, e-mail to author, October 17, 2017.

5
Cyberview representative, Cyberview, e-mail to author, October 17, 2017.

6
A Switzerland-based organization that funds competitive startups in emerging markets.

7
Hazel Abu Sama, interview by author, September 15, 2017.

Malaysia's startup scene. The Malaysian Global Innovation & Creativity Centre (MaGIC), CoInnov8, the Living Lab program, and the Futurize Center all cultivate young companies there.

As MaGIC's Hazel Abu Sama remarked, "The vision is to expand outside Cyberjaya in due time, but right now we kind of think, 'this is where it's supposed to happen.'"[7] And she explained how Cyberjaya provides the ground for new innovation by bringing together grassroots entrepreneurs, big corporations, and government-backed accelerator programs on the new city's IT-friendly infrastructure platform.

The New City as Education Hub

As can often be seen in new cities and large-scale urban developments around the world, Cyberjaya has turned to the education sector to help spur social and commercial growth. These education centers not only help solidify the image of a place as sophisticated, young, and international, but more pragmatically, they also put boots on the ground. An instant population of students who spend money on food, amenities, housing, and entertainment can overcome inertia and get the commercial ball rolling.[8] For educational institutions, the allure of a new city lies in the vastly underutilized construction land that can often be had at cheap or subsidized rates.

In China, a large education district is often a core part of a new city masterplan. For example, Nanhui's university area, College City, boasts eight schools that attract 100,000 students. Zhengdong New Area has 15 universities that account for 240,000 people on the ground. In Chenggong, a completely new area of Kunming, the educational district is the most lively part of town. And currently there is a 533-hectare university city in the works for Shanghai's Songjiang.

In Cyberjaya, Multimedia University alone brings in over 20,000 students. Three other universities and an array of elite private schools draw thousands more. The effect of this newly minted education hub can be seen in the streets: students are everywhere.

Tempered Expectations

Cyberjaya has now been in development for a little over 20 years. While that may seem like a long time, for a project of its scale and complexity two decades are hardly long enough for the first phase of development to be completed. New cities are rarely ever built in smooth, linear trajectories of development. Rather, the path to vitalization tends to look more like the jagged, menacing grin of a jack-o-lantern. They rise, they fall, they boom, they bust: at once seeming like the next global hub of tech or finance or commerce; soon after seeming like the next ghost city.

When new cities are conceived there are often few limits to planning ambitions. Marketing campaigns work in overdrive as developments are sold as the next great [fill in the blank]. People get excited, government agencies and big businesses jump in, then five or 10 years pass and reality sets in. Projections are stunted, plans downgraded, and the big dream reworked into something more manageable. In terms of tempered expectations, Cyberjaya is very similar to other new cities around the world.

New housing development, Cyberjaya.
Courtesy Wade Shepard.

Ordos Kangbashi in China's Inner Mongolia was formed during a coal boom in the early 2000s. Newly flush with cash, city officials and businesses began building a US$161 billion, 355-square-kilometer city for one million people in the Ordos desert, 25 kilometers outside the established urban core of Dongsheng. It was initially assumed that residents of the drought-prone old city would buy property and migrate to the newer modern city, designed as a man-made oasis within a series of reservoirs. But all did not go as planned.[9]

A crash in coal prices, a pair of housing market downturns, a severe local debt bubble, a wave of high-profile bankruptcies, and a global economic crisis later, Kangbashi downscaled its ambitions and decided that a 35-square-kilometer new city for 300,000 people would have to be good enough.

8
Wade Shepard, 2015. "The Truth About China's Ghost Cities." The Diplomat. Accessed October 29, 2015. https://thediplomat.com/2015/10/the-truth-about-chinas-ghost-cities.

9
Shepard, "Ghost Cities."

10
"Infamous 'Ghost City' Hopes Housing Coupon System May Solve Real Estate Glut," *Global Times*, November 14, 2016, http://www.globaltimes.cn/content/1017826.shtml.

11
Mu Xuequan, ed. "Across China: From Ghost Town to Boomtown—The New Look of Kangbashi," *Xinhuanet*, June 29, 2017, http://www.xinhuanet.com/english/2017-06/29/c_136402110.htm.

12
Sarah Moser, "Putrajaya: Malaysia's New Federal Administrative Capital," *Cities* 27.4 (2009): 285–97.

Beyond limiting the project scale and scope, Kangbashi changed course in numerous other ways. It was no longer a given that the area's newly rich would snap up its luxury homes and move in happily—more clever and proactive policies were needed to turn the place into an actual city. New construction projects were called off, developers reduced the number of new homes put on the market, and attractive incentives were offered to companies and individuals to settle there. At one point, to compensate residents who were relocated from their homes, the local government even distributed coupons that could be redeemed for unsold housing.[10]

Mixed-use development, Cyberjaya.
Courtesy Wade Shepard.

Derided as a ghost town throughout its 15 years in existence, Kangbashi now has 153,000 full-time residents according to official figures. Nearly all of the housing that has gone on the market has been sold, and real estate prices have steadily climbed over the past few years.[11] While not the luxurious boomtown originally envisioned, Kangbashi can no longer be called a ghost city.

Another new city that had to adjust planning expectations lies across the street from Cyberjaya: Putrajaya, Malaysia's purpose-built new capital city. Built in tandem and side by side, only separated by expressway route 29, both were intended to masterplan a new national identity via new city development.

Putrajaya was slated to become Malaysia's new capital—the symbolic expression of a new post-colonial national identity in concrete and steel[12]—and is also one of the earliest examples of the new city movement building across Asia and Africa. Construction on Putrajaya began in the early 1990s on the premise that it would bring in 350,000 people. While the towers of the new capital can be seen from Cyberjaya today and the national government is seated there, a mere 80,000 people actually call it home. It is easy to draw comparisons between Putrajaya and Brazil's much-maligned man-made capital, Brasilia.[13]

Similarly, South Korea's Songdo was built with the intention to become, according to author Greg Lindsay, "a weapon to fight trade wars in Asia."[14] Built on land reclaimed from the sea on the other side of a bridge from Incheon airport in the mid-nineties, Songdo was designed to accommodate Western multinationals seeking a base of operations in East Asia. According to Lindsay, at the time China was considered too risky due to the threat of intellectual property theft. South Korea wanted to elevate its economic position by providing facilities for big multinational firms. A few years and $40 billion later, a gleaming new business district appeared in Songdo. But by this time China had joined the WTO, and Songdo was quickly surpassed by cities like Shanghai, Shenzhen, and Hong Kong in competing for the attention of Western multinationals. So it "continued to grope around for new reasons."[15]

Instead of becoming a base for Fortune-500 companies, Songdo humbled its ambitions and expanded its forays into smart city technologies. As a "city of the future," or live testing ground for companies like Cisco Systems to deploy beta versions of their urban maintenance technologies. While not exactly a financial hub of Northeast Asia, Songdo is still a successful new city, attracting 130,000 full-time residents and a vibrant commercial landscape, its streets lined with restaurants, cafes, bars, boutiques, and shopping malls. The roads have a healthy amount of traffic and the central park is full of people.

Cyberjaya, Ordos Kangbashi, Putrajaya, and Songdo represent what new cities all too often become: middling new developments that are neither glorious successes nor derelict ghost towns; husks of their original visions but nevertheless viable, populated, and sustainable urban entities in their own right. New cities generally take between 20 and 30 years to develop, and are susceptible to a dizzying array of economic, climatic, and social upheavals that can derail even the most well-funded and well-considered projects, sending them on unexpected trajectories.

As global and regional economies ebb and flow, so do the fates of new cities. In the current economic upswing, Cyberjaya is again being rapidly developed: on every horizon a wall of new residential buildings is under construction, new shopping malls crop up, more businesses and more residents are moving in. New luxury developments named Garden Residence, Summer Glades, and Mirage by the Lake are in progress and thousands of new homes are scheduled to hit the market in Cyberjaya over the next few years. As real estate prices in Kuala Lumpur soar, more people today see Cyberjaya as a viable alternative where a high quality of life can be had at a more affordable price.

A commuter town for decades—a place where people worked rather than lived—Cyberjaya is now evolving its own community. Over 100,000 people call the new city home, and the first generation of Cyberjayan locals fill the schools, as shops and restaurants slowly build their

13 Joseli Macedo and Levu V. Tran, "Brasília and Putrajaya: Using Urban Morphology to Represent Identity and Power in National Capitals," *Journal of Urbanism: International Research on Placemaking and Urban Sustainability* 6.2 (2013): 139–59.

14 Greg Lindsay, interview by author, June 8, 2017.

15 Ibid.

16 Iza Sofia Kasbi, interview by author, September 15, 2017.

clientele. The population is expected to reach 200,000 by 2022, the much-heralded year when the Mass Rapid Transit (MRT) line from Kuala Lumpur will be completed, giving Cyberjaya its first real ribbon cutting. As Cyberview's Iza Sofia Kasbi explained, "We . . . look at the rest of the world as a model. . . . We pick up the best practices from around the globe . . . cities like Songdo, San Francisco, Barcelona. Of course, we are in Malaysia, so we look at what is workable here. It's a trial-and-error kind of situation."[16]

Afterword

As I rode back across town from Peter Chan's stylistically post-industrial new development, Wendy Li from Setia Haruman pointed with excitement to a long row of red brake lights ahead of us.

> "Look!" she exclaimed. "There is traffic in Cyberjaya!"

That was the first time I saw someone happy about that.

Fallow or Failure? Urbanization in the Age of Speculation

CHRISTOPHER MARCINKOSKI

The fallowing of land implies that a process of resource extraction has previously occurred. It suggests a period of intentional recovery and rest for a territory that has recently served an anthropogenically productive purpose. And it also intimates that said productive purpose—or a similar one—will soon be reinitiated on the territory in question as part of an ongoing process of land cultivation and management. In this way, to lie fallow suggests both an active, productive past and—more importantly in the context of design and planning praxis—an equally active and productive future.

Despite the potential parallels between agricultural and urbanization regimes, this familiar sequence of operations (extract, recover, extract) does not so easily apply to land that has been subjected to contemporary speculative urbanization practices.[1] In these cases, once value has been extracted from a piece of land—either economic value through a series of transactions, or environmental value as a result of stripping and denuding landcover—there is neither the guarantee of recovery or regeneration during the "fallow" period, nor the assurance of future productivity through occupation.

Regardless of the recent academic rhetoric on process and emergence, this reality manifests itself in contemporary urban planning and design practice that is still characterized by the emphasis on outcome—or the image of outcome—above all else. As others have argued, this suggests urbanization is increasingly understood as the manufacture of a saleable product, whether physical or financial, rather than the structuring of an ongoing process capable of accommodating settlement, culture, and commerce.

As I have written elsewhere, examples of speculative urbanization activities can be found throughout recorded history but have notably escalated in physical scale and intensified in frequency over the last 20 years.[2] Familiar Western examples of the failures of these activities from the early 21st century include

Ireland's so-called Ghost Estates; the substantial production and abandonmentof suburban housing throughout the US Sunbelt during this same period; and most dramatically, the massive building boom and corresponding economic bust that took place in Spain between 1998 and 2012.[3]

While most recent examples represent cautionary tales, some speculative urbanization endeavors from this same period are seen to have achieved varying degrees of success. In the Middle East, for example, both Dubai and Abu Dhabi are seen to offer replicable models of urbanization-driven economic success tied to the production of spectacular (thus highly desirable to foreign investment) urban form. And then there is of course China, which arguably has pinned much of its desire to realize a mature consumer economy squarely on the back of a real estate and construction-driven transfer of capital.[4]

Despite the range of sociocultural, economic, and political contexts in each of these and other examples of speculative urbanization, there is a consistent set of underlying conditions central to its production. These include the projection of a rapidly expanding population; belief in the need for upgraded and expanded urban facilities, in particular housing and mobility infrastructure; and the prediction of a corresponding economic boom as a direct result of projected population growth. That is, while speculative urbanization occurs in all politico-economic geographies—from state-controlled communist governments to privatized neoliberal markets—the phenomenon is most likely to occur within those polities with economies characterized as emerging.

Given the perception of success regarding speculative urbanization activities in places like China and the Emirates, their particular urban growth models and protocols are viewed by many actors in developing contexts, both state and private, as worth emulating. And it should be no surprise that these entities actively peddle their expertise in executing these models of urbanization-driven economic growth in contexts with which they have very little in common. However, despite outward impressions of accomplishment, the actual degree of economic, urbanistic, and other successes remains a serious question.[5] For example, significant state intervention is often required in these cases to subsidize or catalyze the all-important initial occupation of the settlement or to encourage occupants to remain years after so-called completion.[6]

History has shown there is an enormous economic and environmental risk associated with most large-scale speculative urbanization activities, via incompletion, low-occupancy, abandonment, and so on. Thus the potential consequences of exporting these models should not be discounted. And in fact, the urban design disciplines in particular must question their role in such activities, and the implications of promoting these urbanization-driven economic growth models in regions that lack both the political control and sufficient economic resources of their source contexts.

A New Epicenter

Here, it is worth noting a new epicenter of speculative urbanization activity that has emerged in the decade since the most recent global financial crisis. Tracing back to 2005—the peak of the most recent real estate–driven economic recession—one finds the rapid proliferation of new town schemes proposed for geographies across the African continent.[7] My ongoing research has identified no fewer than 120 such projects at a scale of at least 300 hectares or more (with most coming in between 1,000 and 4,000 hectares) each oriented towards one of nine familiar urban typologies.[8]
The projects identified in this work are located almost exclusively in exurban or peri-urban greenfield sites, well outside the frenetic complexity of existing urban centers.[9] The rhetoric and propaganda accompanying these proposals unsurprisingly suggests they are motivated both by the urgent need for upgraded housing and infrastructure due to considerable population projections, and the deficient physical state of extant urban centers and their infrastructures.

Yet despite the unquestionable need to enhance both formats of settlement and infrastructure throughout the African continent, the incongruity of the exogenous models employed by these proposals relative to their destination contexts threatens the ecological value of the land they are planned for, as well as the political and economic

1
I define speculative urbanization as any endeavor that actively instrumentalizes a proposal for (or the production of) new urban settlement and infrastructure expressly in pursuit of economic and political returns. This phenomenon includes the political redesignation and redivision of land for the specific purpose of raising its market value, and the speculative construction of housing, infrastructure, and urban amenities by both public and private entities. Projects are significant in physical size—usually hundreds of hectares or more—and are primarily situated in peri-urban or greenfield contexts.

2
See Christopher Marcinkoski, "A Brief History of Speculative Urbanization," *MONU* 19 (October 2013): 64–69.

3
The events in Spain are the subject of my recent book. See Christopher Marcinkoski, *The City That Never Was* (New York: Princeton Architectural Press, 2016).

4
For a fuller discussion, see "Recent Speculative Urbanization Events" in Marcinkoski, *The City That Never Was*, 25–33.

5
A number of economists, urbanists, and policy-makers have questioned the efficacy and translatability of these initiatives because of their conspicuous reliance on state subsidies and forced migration to generate needed populations and investment.

6
See *The Land of Many Palaces*, directed by Ting Song and Adam James Smith (2014; Cambridge, UK: Journeyman Pictures).

7
I use the continental definition of Africa as an entity rather than the UN definition that separates North Africa (the Maghreb) from Sub-Saharan Africa.

Tamensourt, Morocco: the first new town constructed for the state's ambitious Ville Nouvelle program, 2004. Courtesy C. Marcinkoski.

Overview (looking southwest) of El Cañaveral housing development at the eastern periphery of Madrid, 2014. Courtesy C. Marcinkoski.

stability of the governments often advocating for them.[10] Given the potential scale of these speculative urbanization activities—and in turn, the commensurate consequence of their potential failure—new contingent-based approaches to the physical planning, design, and initiation of urban settlement and infrastructure in developing contexts is urgently needed.

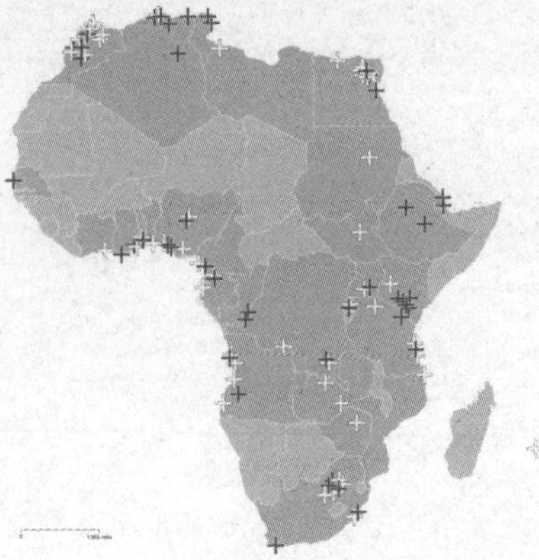

Map of African continent showing the locations of 100 new town projects proposed or initiated since 2005. Courtesy AP Photo/Kamran Jebreili.

But before delving into a specific discussion of speculative urbanization in Africa and the priorities of alternative approaches to the planning of speculative settlement, it is worthwhile to frame these activities in terms of this journal's theme of "fallow," and by extension, the bigger question of managed recovery from extractive anthropogenic activities.

Urbanistic Extraction

Speculative urbanization often takes one of two forms, both of which result in a landscape whose *value* has been extracted. One version, which I will refer to as *Plans and Proposals*, operates in the realm of legal and financial urbanistic activities, in other words, in the nonphysical. The other, *Preparation and Plots*, is perhaps the more familiar, encompassing the physical activities associated with urbanization.

Plans and Proposals can be characterized as transactional, and often begin with the planning of a piece of mobility infrastructure. Regardless of whether any part of the plan is executed, this activity has the immediate effect of raising the market value of proximate lands. Here, in theory, landowners benefit from the proposal either through increased property values or from returns received through a process of expropriation. Once infrastructure planning is initiated, adjacent property value is further influenced through changes in land-use designation or other zoning modifications. These relatively simple procedural activities have a direct impact on the market value of a territory, often leading to its eventual sale and resale.

These land-use modifications often follow the execution of a development proposal for a piece of property. This most basic of urban design activities—the plan—is thus enormously powerful. Even the most improbable or irrational proposal will serve to escalate the market's perception of a parcel's worth. The plan implies possibility. It suggests imminent transformation, although it matters little whether there is any intention of it ever being executed. Rather, the plan's "utility" is that it attracts capital by demonstrating potential.

What is extracted under this form of speculative urbanization is value; some might even say, artificial value. While the losses associated with this extraction are not physical, they are no less consequential. The tenure of the land has been fundamentally modified, and in some cases, forcefully taken from the original landowners. In turn, the potential to use the land in question for specific "low-intensity" purposes is invalidated because of its market value escalation. Land that was once productive is no longer so, at least in terms other than financial.

The second form that speculative urbanization takes is conspicuously more physical. Here land is cleared of flora and fauna; topography reshaped; watercourses diverted or channeled and covered; and ribbons of impermeable surfaces laid over formerly absorbent soils. Beneath these asphalt and concrete roadways lie miles of wire, conduit, and piping. In the parcels created by these corridors, myriad excavations are undertaken that often lead to the off-site disposal of considerable volumes of formerly fertile earth.

At the conclusion of these activities, the site is considered "prepped"— awaiting the deployment of massive amounts of concrete, steel, and brick. All of this energy and material is deployed in anticipation of a population that may not ever arrive. This is the most common state of speculative urbanization—a denuded, incomplete urban territory whose value is no longer measured in ecosystemic terms, but rather in terms that are simultaneously political and economic. Here, no amount of remediation, greenwashing or fallowing can serve to undo a potentially permanent condition oriented towards an aspirational if dubious urban future.

There has been a great deal written recently, particularly from environmental planning and critical

8
I define nine distinct typologies of speculative projects drawing from 120 or so new towns identified by my research, including 1) new national capitals; 2) dormitory or middle-class housing; 3) luxury housing enclaves; 4) touristic / resort enclaves; 5) social housing; 6) new central business district / financial center; 7) new techno-industrial cities; 8) greenfield mega-cities; and the occasional 9) radical redevelopment of existing fabric. See Marcinkoski, "Le futur urbain et spéculatif de l'Afrique," *Tracés* 4 (2016): 16–21.

9
The stated rationale for locating outside existing urban centers relates to the complexity of operating in these contexts, as well as availability and access to large pieces of contiguous land.

geography perspectives, on the implications of extractive anthropogenic activities. This discussion has principally focused on the removal of physical materials from the ground—mineral resources, fresh water, commodity-related biomass—and the severe environmental and social consequences of this activity.

Extraction in the context of speculative urbanization, however, is different. As noted above, there are significant environmental implications. But what is extracted in these cases—what is permanently lost—is as much fiscal as physiological; both economic and ecologic. The potential implications for those polities and populations involved in such pursuits are, in turn, no less catastrophic.

Speculative urbanization activities inherently reject academic notions of the urbanization process, or development in time. At the very least, they actively attempt to bypass the idea. Such activities are oriented for the near-term, motivated by immediate returns rather than long-term resolutions. More often than not, they are announced and executed (to varying degrees) on the schedule of local elections or in response to financial markets. Land is held for the minimum period possible to achieve a desired return before the acreage is disposed. Long-term management is of little interest, which shapes how these settlement proposals are conceived and planned. Speculative urbanization activities are motivated by a game of financial hot-potato dependent on interest rates and debt repayment schedules, rather than the equitable occupation and activation of urban form.

As a result, the role of urban design in these activities is often pointed towards the production of glossy, implausible, contextually incongruous renderings produced for political propaganda and to attract exogenous investment. Press releases and marketing materials are filled with aspirational references to the needs and desires of a so-called "growing middle class"—really, the consumer class—and present speculative settlements in the ethical terms of socioeconomic opportunity and access. Yet the reality of who can afford to occupy the proposed developments, particularly in emerging economies, is very different. Contradictions between promotional rhetoric and conditions on the ground are almost satirical: Luxury housing in the context of rolling blackouts; global retail opportunities in lieu of educational opportunities; high-rises before healthcare facilities. In this context physical urbanization, or at least its planning, functions as a kind of prop; an image of aspiration whose terms and currency are set by global capital and its affinity for the perceived economic successes found in the polities of China and the Middle East.

Extraction in the context of speculative urbanization is very much about the creation and mining of artificial capital value, and the creation and off-loading of debt. And in many cases, creating access to markets and other natural resources (i.e., conventional extraction) in exchange for the production of (images of) urban form. It has nothing to do with the aspirational platitudes or socioeconomic valorization of urban form. Rather, speculative urbanization in the 21st century is about attracting capital and expressing geopolitical significance.

As a result, urban designers today have become the Mad (wo)Men of the Global South—the Don Drapers of urbanization—selling an image and ideal of the 21st-century city that is more or less impossible to achieve. The optimism and good intentions of the modernist project of urban design have, in this context, metastasized into a "hand measuring contest"— to use the words of the US real-estate-developer-in-chief. This has led the familiar acronym-named design practices of the world, among many others, to proliferate grandiose plans and images of an idealized urban future with limited attention paid to the processes of getting from the realities of now to the ambitions of such fictions.

Whether these urbanization projects are executed fully does not really matter. Physical urbanization—both proposed and executed—has become a prop, a signifier of opportunity for impatient capital. As such, the thinking often goes, the more ambitious the project, the more appealing it must be to potential investment.

Volatility + Risk

Economic geographer Bent Flyvbjerg has written extensively on the volatility of what he terms "megaprojects": large-scale initiatives including transport infrastructures, telecommunications networks, cross-border pipelines, transnational power grids, and the like that have a "strikingly poor performance record in terms of economy, environment, and public support."[11] In Flyvbjerg's research "poor performance" implies the increasing correlation between environmental degradation, social disenfranchisement, severe capital loss, political instability, and the pursuit of increasingly ambitious construction projects that have become de rigueur for demonstrating global competitiveness and political power.

Despite significant differences in type and promoter (both public and private), Flyvbjerg and his colleagues have identified a set of deficiencies or negative characteristics that are consistent across projects of this scale. These include 1) substantial cost overruns; 2) "strategic misrepresentation" by project promoters (exaggeration or spin); 3) lower than estimated usage relative to demand

10
This incongruity relates primarily to financial accessibility; whom these developments are supposedly planned and built for, versus who ultimately occupies them.

Oyala, Administrative City of Djibloho, Equatorial Guinea: new capital city initiated after the discovery of oil and a coup attempt on the president in 2004. Courtesy C. Marcinkoski.

A new road under construction as part of a large "middle-class" housing estate being privately developed northwest of Nairobi, Kenya. Courtesy C. Marcinkoski.

forecasts (exacerbating cost overruns); and 4) greater than anticipated environmental impacts, both during implementation and occupation. To put it another way: mega-urban projects always cost much more than estimated, and always serve far fewer than projected.

The relevance of Flyvbjerg's research to speculative urbanization should be obvious. While much of the scholarship on "megaprojects" focuses on infrastructure, its characteristic deficiencies are translatable to the large-scale urbanization projects discussed here, precisely because of the infrastructural interventions at the basis of their undertaking.[12]

Central to Flyvbjerg's analysis is a phenomenon known as "optimism bias"; or "appraisal optimism," as he terms it.[13] This is the cognitive tendency for some actor or agency—government, institution, corporation, planner, and so on—to believe they are less susceptible to experiencing a negative event relative to an ambitious pursuit compared to others in similar circumstances, despite clear proof to the contrary in the form of past events. The presence of this "optimism" in the planning of large-scale urbanization endeavors manifests itself most frequently in the exaggerated potential of a project. Yet this exaggeration is not difficult to identify. Expressive phrases like "this time will be different," or "that circumstance is not applicable here," or "our market projections are sound," and "this project is not like the others" are strongly indicative of impending disruption and potential failure.

Arable Land

Returning to the theme of fallow and the implications of unchecked speculative urbanization across the African continent, there remains the question of arable land.

Between 60 and 65 percent of the world's uncultivated arable land—approximately 600 million hectares—is located in Africa.[14] Among a great number of natural resources, this is perhaps the continent's most valuable. Despite what seems like an enormous quantity of arable land (roughly twice the size of Argentina), in the next three decades the continent's population is projected to double to approximately 2.4 billion people. By 2100, there will likely be close to 4.4 billion people living in Africa, accounting for roughly 40 percent of the total population of the earth.[15] If ever there was an excuse to build, these population projections are it.

The phenomenon of speculative urbanization has shown that the time to worry is precisely the moment one is advised not to worry. Courtesy C. Marcinkoski.

To put the risk of speculative urbanization in some context, consider relatively recent events in Spain. In a 10-year period between 1998 and 2008, during that country's settlement- and infrastructure-driven economic boom and bust, roughly one-third of all urbanized land was created. This urbanization produced 7 million new homes, roughly 1.5–2 million of which remain empty more than a decade later. At the beginning of this period there was a need, and even demand, for housing in Spain, but never enough for the settlement that was actually produced. Contemporaneous speculative urbanization events in Ireland were similar: clear demand, extreme surplus production.[16] Even China, with its vast state-controlled expansion of settlement and infrastructure over the last three decades, established a so-called red line of reserved arable land in 2007 to ensure the country's food security and prevent urbanization from rapidly eroding agricultural land.[17]

Now extrapolate these failures to the real housing demand on the African continent at present, and the speculation that will inevitably accompany this production. The potential economic and political disruption to governments and economies that are far less mature than the preceding examples, that also lack bailout mechanisms like the European Union and the Central People's Government, cannot be overstated. And the potential environmental consequences are even more daunting.

11
Bent Flyvbjerg, *Megaprojects and Risk* (Cambridge: Cambridge University Press, 2010), 3.

12
Flyvbjerg, *Megaprojects*, 2.

13
Implying "optimism bias," Flyvberg instead uses the term "appraisal optimism," adapted from the World Bank's definition for biased cost-benefit analyses. Flyvbjerg, *Megaprojects*, 73.

14
Charles Roxburgh, Norbert Dörr, Acha Leke, Amine Tazi-Riffi, Arend van Wamelen, Susan Lund, Mutsa Chironga, et al., *Lions on the Move: The Progress and Potential of African Economies* (Seoul: McKinsey Global Institute, 2010).

15
United Nations Department of Economic and Social Affairs, Population Division, *World Population Prospects: The 2015 Revision, Key Findings and Advance Tables* (New York: United Nations, 2015), http://esa.un.org/unpd/wpp/publications/files/key_findings_wpp_2015.pdf.

16
Morgan Kelly, "The Irish Property Bubble: Causes and Consequences," *The Irish Economy*, January 15, 2009, http://www.irisheconomy.ie/Crisis/KellyCrisis.pdf.

17
Ben Blanchard, "China Draws Line in the Sand to Defend Arable Land," *Reuters*, July 12, 2007, https://www.reuters.com/article/environment-china-land-dc/china-draws-line-in-the-sand-to-defend-arable-land-idUSPEK27287720070712.

Chefie housing estate at the eastern periphery of Addis Ababa, Ethiopia. Part of one the largest ongoing social housing initiatives on the African continent. Courtesy C. Marcinkoski.

Significant loss of arable land is already occurring in rapidly urbanizing contexts like Kenya. As a recent *New York Times* feature notes: "Population swells, climate change, soil degradation, erosion, poaching, global food prices, and even the benefits of affluence are exerting incredible pressure on African land."[18] Given that the continent is the new epicenter of global speculative urbanization practices, we can only assume that this remaining arable land—and its corresponding ecosystem service capacity—is under extreme duress.

Landscape architect Richard Weller has illustrated the emerging conflict between rapidly expanding urban form in the Global South and the remnants of the earth's most important pockets of biodiversity in his *Atlas for the End of the World* (2017). Weller identifies no fewer than 70 cities whose projected growth will consume and permanently destroy significant portions of the African continent's nine biodiversity hotspots.[19] Yet these "hotspots" represent only a tiny fraction of the continent's overall ecosystem service capacity that is under threat due to, among others, intensifying speculative urbanization practices.

Conclusion

All this brings us to the essential question at the root of this ongoing research into the phenomenon of speculative urbanization: how do we, the urban design disciplines, plan and design for future urban conditions fundamentally characterized by the risk of failure or incompletion, that are moreover profoundly at odds with the ecosystem service capacity of the sites in question? The answer is not a matter of better, or smarter, or more bottom-up; but rather an essential reorientation of disciplinary priorities.

Without a doubt, design and planning rely on the notion of optimism bias discussed above. Disciplinary work is rooted in expressing the ambitions and aspirations of a potential future. But to disregard the inherent volatility and risk associated with design and planning at the global scale discussed herein is both irresponsible and unethical. As such, acknowledging the reality of this volatility indicates the need to retool contemporary urban design and planning praxis so as not to adversely contribute to, or further exacerbate, the consequences of more and more common 21st-century speculative urbanization practices.

Incidentally, one of Flyvbjerg's conclusions regarding the proliferation of megaprojects should be a fundamental conceit of contemporary urban design praxis: risk cannot be designed out of speculative urbanization, or urbanization in general.[20] Actively planning and designing for uncertainty and failure instead creates systemic frameworks that allow an urbanization project to be reliably recalibrated and readjusted over the extended timescale of its implementation and—hopefully—occupation.

Rather than focus on the preferred outcome of a proposal for new settlement—as most of such contemporary planning tends to do—a retooled urban design praxis would elaborate strategies to exploit the transactional motivation behind these speculative proposals in support of alternative urbanization logics. Near-term protocols could be redirected to examine the efficacy and value creation of planning and design strategies that manage and cultivate speculative urbanization practices over time. This would require approaches to the planning of settlement rooted in contingency, disposability, and synthesis—not outcome.

In many ways, the interim state of the urbanization process—after initiation, before occupation—can be understood as a kind of fallow state. Treating it as such, however, necessitates fundamentally reconsidering both how a project begins, and the unpredictability of its future. Until urban design praxis engages this uncertainty, it maintains complicity in the potentially catastrophic consequences of 21st-century speculative urbanization.

18
Jeffrey Gettleman, "Loss of Fertile Land Fuels 'Looming Crisis' Across Africa," *New York Times*, July 30, 2017, https://www.nytimes.com/2017/07/29/world/africa/africa-climate-change-kenya-land-disputes.html.

19
Richard Weller, Claire Hoch, and Chieh Huang, "Hotspots," *Atlas for the End of the World* (2017), http://atlas-for-the-end-of-the-world.com/hotspots_main.html.

20
Flyvbjerg, *Megaprojects*, 6.

Concrete Abstractness

A Conversation with PETER GALISON

New Geographies — One main aspect of "fallow," as conceived in this volume, concerns the periodicity of the de- and revalorization of the built (and unbuilt) environment. Often these cycles follow easily graspable timeframes; from years in terms of agriculture to perhaps decades in land speculation and the built environment. Your work on nuclear waste storage and disaster sites renders a much more difficult proposition. Rather than a single human lifespan, in this case the period of dormancy or inactivity is on the order of tens to hundreds to thousands of years. To begin: how might we critically examine the sites, strategies, scales, and imaginaries of the unused, the devalued, and the dormant across such vast temporal distances?

Peter Galison — For thousands of years, farmers rotated their crops—Leviticus commands a "Sabbath of the land" during which soil should be left alone. We know that over-intensive farming with a single crop can be disastrous—rotation is crucial for nutrients in the soil, and for stability to prevent erosion. But there are other reasons why people might want to leave land fallow, in a more metaphorical sense. For instance, think about the real estate investors who bought up land near the port in Boston. They might put up a temporary structure or parking lot and say, "we are leaving it fallow," while waiting for property prices to rise: speculative fallowness. There are also particular timescales for land infused with toxic substances. If you have a bacteria that survives only a certain number of hours or days, or a chemical that decays in the sunlight over 1, 5, or 10–15 years, regulators want that property left alone for that span, until it can be recovered for use.

For nuclear waste the scale of decay is highly variable, measured by the time during which radioactivity is cut in half (half-life). Typically, one looks at a period of 10 half-lives, or the time during which a substance becomes about 1/1000th as radioactive as it was initially. Some nuclear half-lives are short: days, hours, or even seconds. One isotope of iodine that carried a large fraction of the radioactive load at Chernobyl (iodine-131) has a half-life of eight days, so 10 half-lives is less than three months. Cesium-137 and strontium-90 carry half-lives of 30 years. For plutonium and some other isotopes above uranium on the periodic chart, it can be very long: plutonium-139 has a half-life of 24,000 years, so 10 half-lives means 240,000 years. Adding insult to injury, as plutonium-239 decays, it forms uranium-235 which has an even longer half-life.

Depending on your classification system, Homo sapiens is only 250,000 or 500,000 years old, so plutonium waste drives us to imagine a timescale about as long as the age of our species. Indeed, when the US Congress, through the Environmental Protection Agency (EPA), attempted to calculate how long to keep such nuclear waste isolated from the human biosphere, they warned people away for a period of no fewer than 10,000 years, or twice that of recorded human history! They thought 10,000 years would at least get things started at the waste burial site in New Mexico. Then our great- (x 400) grandchildren could carry the nuclear baton further into their future.

In the case of Yucca Mountain, nuclear physicists predict that the peak radiation dose absorbed by someone living near the disposal site has not yet reached its maximum. The maximum danger there will occur some 250,000 or more years in the future. Because that nuclear waste high-water mark is so much longer than 10,000 years, the National Academy of Sciences (NAS) recommended—and the courts approved—a regulatory period of one million years. By just about any count, that period is in excess of any likely historical existence of Homo sapiens. When seeking to warn those a million years in the future, we may not be talking to "our" descendants at all.

NG Your newest film, *Containment* (with Robb Moss, 2015), grapples with the problem of communicating deep into the future, raising important questions for design in relation to managing the legacy of industrial landscapes.[1] How can designers engage with what seems an "impossible challenge" to advise 400 or more generations ahead?

PG I like problems that resemble those posed by Immanuel Kant, the great 18th-century philosopher. At the beginning of his masterpiece, *Critique of Pure Reason*, he suggested that some questions are so urgent and difficult that we can neither solve nor avoid them. Such queries are riveting, even when they are far less abstract than those the philosopher posed. Now we can avoid answering "when should we go to Mars?"—nothing mandates us to respond.

Yet nuclear waste exists. We do not have a choice about that and there is no way to make it go away. You cannot destroy the waste. You cannot launch it into space (because rockets do blow up on the way out of the atmosphere and you do not want to scatter radioactive debris over half the globe). You cannot dump it in the ocean—that would violate international law. You can only try to figure out how best to contain it.

In that sense, what happens to nuclear waste is a question that we must ask. There are many debates you can have about the optimal disposal of nuclear waste, but it is pretty clear that what we are doing now—putting it in big pools of water for the long term—is the worst solution. There are plenty of weird science-fiction questions that we could, in principle, ask about almost anything in the possible future. But we must ask this question about nuclear waste. So what did the people tasked with trying to warn the future do back in 1989? First, they hired a team of futurists to imagine possible futures, scenarios that would draw attention to ways that people in the far future might inadvertently enter the waste. Then architects, including Michael Brill, used those disaster scenarios to design warning mechanisms to help avoid those cataclysmic futures. For instance, Brill designed the stunning spike fields that show up in *Containment*. Robb Moss and I introduced them with black and white 3-D animations.

There were competing ideas—people did not like monuments like Brill's. They said it was too simplistic, that we should make something ruder and cruder: bury tablets in the thousands with cautionary messages; construct large, Rosetta Stone–like guides with a variety of languages. Or enlist designers to make the Waste Isolation Pilate Plant (WIPP) site a totally uninteresting place to go. Some people worried about using valuable materials—because they might be scavenged. For example, the pyramids used to have a marble surface, which is not there anymore because marble was valuable at the time and so people carted it away pretty quickly. The pyramids themselves remain because limestone is much less precious, each stone is 2.5 tons, and the Cheops Pyramid alone weighs some six million tons. It is hard to move.

They thought about these things in 1989. They were smart people—and they were right to address this problem. Leaving the land unmarked would have been a moral hazard, because otherwise people

Yucca Mountain Nuclear Waste Repository, Nevada. Courtesy US Department of Energy.

Landscape of Thorns, a design by architect Michael Brill for the US Department of Energy.
The permanent marker is intended to communicate the danger of radioactivity 10,000 years into the future. Courtesy Peter Galison and Robb Moss.

would dig there. How do we know? Because the Permian Basin may well contain the most promising oil reserves in the world. Big oil companies are bidding billions of dollars to dig around there, in the Permian layer. In the trade they call it "permania" because they are so excited! They are prospecting all around the WIPP Site. There is no doubt at all that if the site were unmarked and unprotected, someone would dig straight into it.

NG Another issue of core importance to this volume is value. For example, while in agriculture fallowing is understood as a process of restoring latent ecological value through inactivity, in urban discourse a lack of productivity is often described negatively as abandoned or marginal, an effect produced through industrial exploitation—in other words, a valueless "wasteland." We are most interested here in two dimensions that we would like you to comment on:

a. How can we understand the historical construction of wilderness and wasteland as "zones of exclusion" that position humans and nature across an ontological abyss?

b. As environmental historian William Cronon does in his essay *The Trouble with Wilderness; or, Getting Back to the Wrong Nature,* you too advocate for something of a constructed rather than primeval or unspoiled nature, where humans are enmeshed in, rather than separate from, the world around them.[3] How can a more complex understanding of our relationship to nature provide a source for alternative ecological, social, or cultural value creation?

PG Traditionally we have seen the wasteland and the wilderness as opposite ends of a one-parameter family, as from ultraviolet to infrared, or from smaller scale to larger scale. But I think a different topology is emerging where instead of a single linear scale, with two ends maximally apart, there are actually ways in which the wasteland and the wilderness have begun to touch one another, forming what I refer to as "waste-wilderness."

These arenas function in some ways like a traditional wasteland and in some ways like a traditional wilderness. For example, one might naively picture the lands surrounding the destroyed power plants at Chernobyl and Fukushima as ruined territories, like the burnt out husks of bombed cities. But in fact the land does not look that way at all. What people are often struck by when they visit Chernobyl or Fukushima, or the nuclear weapons plant in South Carolina (the 315-sqm Savannah River Site), is that they are stunningly verdant. Some species have returned to these areas that have been missing for a long time. There are famously large-scale fauna, like the wolves of Chernobyl, or the boars of Fukushima, as well as the myriad water insects that make the Savannah River Site one of the most biodiverse of the 48 continental US states.

So, what are these places and how do we understand them? The Savannah River Site is so green you can see its boundaries from outer space, from Google Earth. That territory looks very different from the adjacent land that is either under continuous agricultural cultivation or exploited for suburban development. So by virtue of biodiversity, lack of through-traffic, and large fauna, they qualify as wilderness. On the other hand, to call them wilderness in a 19th-century sense would neglect the fact that each site contains a vast deposit of radioactive detritus.

So we need to question these categories. Nuclear contamination keeps people out and therefore allows biodiversity and the species recovery of American alligators, wolves, water insects, and all sorts of plants and snakes. That is the overall frame of my interest in your question. And it connects with some of your broader questions about value, disuse, non-use, and set-asides. What most clearly aligns these various themes is the changing relationship that we humans have to this technical land. What are we with respect to the earth, to nature, to the world around us?

William Cronon's *The Trouble with Wilderness*, which I very much admire, addresses the very real dangers of treating wilderness as primeval-pure. Cronon has always been attentive to the fact that the land is always already affected by us. It's not entirely true that the colonists lived in harmony—they fenced off their holdings to mark property and contain domestic animals, and by doing so changed the migratory pattern of many species. And if we go still further back in time, to the primeval wilderness of the Native Americans? No, Cronon says. The Native Americans living in New England were burning the shrublands so they could hunt better.

For Cronon, the land has never been primevally pure. That is important. But I disagree when he and several colleagues write about the irony of sites that are both industrial/toxic and nature preservers. I see such areas as increasingly common, as waste-wilderness. Now we have many millions of acres in the world with this status. It is not a bizarre twist of fate. It is legally, theologically, and practically structured that way. Contaminated areas can be controlled through a nature park designation—a means to remove them from certain uses (tourism, agriculture, development) that borrows from the isolation of both wilderness and wasteland.

In the US we have "withdrawn lands," which have been removed from the administration of one agency and put under special rules and regulations that dictate who can go there and for how long. They also restrict the construction of long-term habitation, laying down roads, and installing industrial infrastructure. Withdrawals are used for both wasteland and wilderness areas—there are all sorts of ways in which these lands become connected. That is what I have been writing about.

NG How can we think about the nuclear tourism emerging at some of these disaster sites, and does this lack of inhibition suggest a transformed relationship to the land?

PG Since modern tourism emerged in the late 18th to early 19th century, there has always been an element of danger; whether in seeing a half-sunk ship off the coast, a train wreck, or some other disaster. There is a long history of dark tourism.

Another feature that seems to be important about places like Chernobyl, Fukushima, and the former Nevada Test Site is that although people go there, they can only do so in a very temporary way. The reasons for this are health related. Nobody wants the tourists—no matter the potential financial gain for the local economy—to get such a big dose of radiation.

A similar position on human visitors who do not remain is written into the Wilderness Act of 1964.[4] In both cases we have a touristic relationship that allows us to visit, although we do not own the territory. So we are not permanent servants, in a romantic sense.

By talking about nuclear tourism in the context of waste-wilderness, I want to emphasize that neither alternative, "wasteland" or "wilderness" as they are traditionally understood, are alone sufficient for our day. We are not biblical masters who transform the primordial wilderness into cultivated land, despite the apocalyptic visions of those like US Secretary of the Interior James Watt. Back in the 1980s he used to say: "It is our theological obligation to use up the land"—as if anticipating some state of rapture or end of days. Nor can we quite see ourselves these days as romantic servants of a pure, untrammeled, primeval nature. In the waste-wilderness of these nuclear zones, we are visitors to nature in an existential sense. We want, or are allowed, to go to these radiological territories but they do not belong to us and we do not belong to them—lands that host both biodiversity and radioactivity.

NG The ability to own land or appropriate it for private use is the bedrock of US mythology; it is radically challenged by the idea that the land doesn't belong to us and that we do not belong to it.

PG The history of land acquisition in the US is incredibly important and we see its manifestations even now. The Louisiana Purchase of 1803—the largest territorial gain through conquest or purchase—brought a staggering amount of land under US government control that was then given away to the railroads, to homesteading, to the creation of national parks and public universities, and later to wilderness areas administered by the Bureau of Land Management. We can still see the instability in some of those relationships in the protests by cattle farmers in the Pacific Northwest, for instance, who think that environmentally set-aside land is a violation of their God-given right to use it for grazing.

NG Considering your long-standing interest in Foucault, particularly in relation to the material conditions under which scientific knowledge is produced, can his thinking also be applied to the spatialization of fallow scenarios?

PG There are two points to make here; one that is general and the other more specific. Generally, Foucault often spoke of the positivism in his approach. That is to say, he wanted to talk about things that we could observe. People—historians in particular—would accuse him of being too philosophical or metaphysical because he discussed sudden jumps and breaks in history when "everyone" knows that history is continuous and causal. Foucault argued that, on the contrary, we have never seen continuous, causally complete processes in history. He insisted that he was focusing above all on that which actually survives in the archives, what we can see. A historical narrative is after all constructed from those archives; you find a series of statements and try your best to piece them together into a series of events. But these archival bits are finite, discontinuous, and fragmentary; they do not ever amount to a complete, philosophically sound, continuous set of historical unfoldings. By ignoring the lacunae that actually correspond to gaps in the archive, Foucault contends that it is the historians who impose their own metaphysics of history on what we are supposed to see and know. For Foucault, it is not the philosopher but the historian who sees the world through an unjustified assumption of continuity and causal plenitude.

Through considerations like these, Foucault draws out the specificity in me. When people discuss abstraction, I want to ask, "Upon what concrete circumstance is that abstraction built?" If someone talks to me about nuclear waste, I want to know: where is the nuclear waste? What consistency does it have? How much of it is there? How is it handled? How does it move? What does it look like? Where does it go? That concreteness appeals to me aesthetically—I think it is interesting to see abstractions cashed out in very specific circumstances.

Pedagogically, if you want to convey what nuclear waste is, you need to remove it from the realm of a frightening, cloudy picture. People need to know where it is, what it is like, what it consists of, how much of it there is.

Politically, we want people to be able to act and make decisions in their lives. You cannot just say, oh well, that is computer privacy, or bio privacy, or that is nuclear waste. When one can see things concretely, one can act. A solution does not come without first understanding the problem.

Aesthetically, I am drawn to the sudden confrontation of ethereal ideas and their all-too-terrestrial bases. That science fiction could tie in so closely to the regulatory planning of the nuclear state, as it does in nuclear containment, is astonishing.

NG This conversation about the concrete allows us to address the complexity we are dealing with through the concept of fallowness. When you get to concrete circumstances it is very difficult to avoid thinking through the social, ecological, and political entanglements that really constitute life. Being abstract allows you to disentangle complex relationships, leaving you with a two-dimensional understanding.

PG That is absolutely right. If someone says, "I am a land speculator" or "I am making an investment in the land," then you think that is just like buying 23 shares of AT&T. It is just an investment, but to actually see what that does—what does it mean when someone invests in urban land and does not want to develop it? To allow its value to increase in time, perhaps. What are the regulations? What laws govern it? How does it affect the use of that area? What effect does it have on adjacent parts of the city and on movement in the city? These are important questions, the kind I like to ask.

Very often our abstractions hide something specific that lies at the seat of the abstraction. And to understand and intervene in our world, we need to get to that concreteness behind the abstraction. You can call it abstract concreteness or concrete abstractness, but that combination of things interests me.

NG Does this notion relate to your motivation for making film? How does the medium of film help you explore this terrain differently?

PG For me, film complements many of the questions I tackle in print, where I try to use concrete circumstances to get at things that otherwise remain fully abstract. For example, what are secrets? How are secrets created and how do they circulate, how are they guarded, how are they de-classified, what do they do to us? These concerns underlie my writing and film work in "Secrecy in Three Acts" (2010), "Removing Knowledge" (2004), and *Secrecy* (2008).[5] Similarly, surrounding our set-aside nuclear lands of waste-wilderness, there are many questions about our responsibility for vast swaths of territory on the planet today and into the far future. Those concerns take concrete form in *Containment*. Elsewhere I have tried to use railroad and cartographic technologies to examine the physics and philosophy of time. In *Objectivity* (2007), a book I did with historian Lorraine Daston, we examined those images considered to be "objective" that helped create and substantiate the notion of scientific objectivity from the 18th through the 21st centuries. How did objective depiction work? What were its procedures?

NG Inhabiting the tension in Kant's impossible-to-answer yet unavoidable questions, your films seem to hold a mirror up to humanity that reveals something more profound than what may have been your initial focus.

PG It is the reciprocal part of seeking concrete circumstances below our abstract understanding of the world. There are concrete circumstances generating this metaphorical surround that are tremendously important in what we value.

1
Containment, directed by Peter Galison and Robb Moss (Boston, MA: Redacted Pictures, 2015).

2
Immanuel Kant, *Critique of Pure Reason*, trans. Norman Kemp Smith, rev. 2nd ed. (Houndmills, Basingstoke; New York: Palgrave Macmillan, 2003).

3
William Cronon, "The Trouble with Wilderness; or, Getting Back to the Wrong Nature," *Environmental History* 1.1 (1996): 7–28.

4
US Congress, House, Wilderness Act of 1964, Pub.L. 88–577, 88th Cong., 2nd sess., introduced in House June 22, 1956, https://www.gpo.gov/fdsys/pkg/STATUTE-78/pdf/STATUTE-78-Pg890.pdf.

5
Secrecy, directed by Peter Galison and Robb Moss (New York: Docurama, 2009), DVD.

FALL
A

OW, V
ND BO

VILDN

ORDEF

ESS,
RS

Distancing the Anthropocene: Co-Creating Wildness in an Increasingly Human World

ERLE C. ELLIS

As Earth moves ever deeper into the Anthropocene epoch, most of its landscapes have been transformed into crop fields, pastures, managed forests, settlements, and other engineered ecosystems and infrastructures that sustain humans.[1] Habitats left unused persist mainly where steep slopes, poor soils, less productive climates, remoteness, and endemic disease still make land use uneconomical.[2]

Over millennia, human societies have become very good at reshaping Earth's ecology to sustain themselves. The sociocultural niche of our species now extends across this planet.[3] In the process, we have diminished, divided, and dispersed the nonhuman world across archipelagoes of remnant and recovering habitats, and immersed them in rising seas of our working landscapes, polluting industries, and warming climates. Even where extensive untransformed spaces still remain, ever more rapid changes in climate are forcing species to move. It should come as no surprise that wild species and wild spaces are disappearing at alarming rates.

Wild spaces unaltered by humans—where they still exist at all—are extremely rare and getting rarer, just as societal demands for wildlife and wildness are strengthening around the world. Without a change in Earth's contemporary anthropogenic trajectory, these living treasures of evolution could largely disappear.

Sustaining nonhuman natures in an increasingly human world is one of the greatest challenges of the Anthropocene. Yet for millennia, and even more so today, human societies have become increasingly capable of maintaining more and more people on less and less land. By broadening and accelerating long-term trends in agricultural intensification, urbanization, the demographic transition, poverty reduction, and shifting energy systems, there is every possibility to shrink societal transformation of the biosphere, even as human welfare increases through the anticipated population peak later in this century.[4]

Whether human transformation of the biosphere can be reversed remains an open question. Certainly, such a return will be possible only with unprecedented levels of local, regional, and global social ambition, creativity, and effort. It might seem paradoxical, but sustaining wild species in wild spaces free of the relentless pressures of the human world will require every tool in the human sociocultural toolkit. Existing efforts to conserve and restore wild habitats must not only be expanded dramatically—successful restoration of landscapes free of human influence will require a radical redesign of the sociocultural systems and engineered landscapes that sustain us.

Conserving nonhuman nature today demands no less than a global reshaping of the human world. The unprecedented challenge of such an effort is exemplified by two seemingly unrelated proposals. The Half-Earth Project aims to create a globally interconnected conservation reserve covering half of Earth's surface[5]; while designed autonomy seeks to enable nonhumans to live unpressured by humans even deep within the human world, by using artificial intelligence to support nonhuman needs.[6] In thinking through these wildly ambitious visions for reversing the human social construction of nature, new landscapes designed by humans, for nonhumans, come into view.

Sharing Half a Planet

The proposal to conserve half of this planet for all nonhuman life—as envisioned by conservationist Harvey Locke and others in 2013, and prominently promoted by E. O. Wilson in 2016—is likely the most aspirational conservation goal ever.[7] If implemented, it would also represent the broadest and most challenging social and geopolitical project of land reallocation and management in history, with profound implications for food production, land tenure regimes, and land ownership around the world.[8] Implemented poorly, Half-Earth could become the greatest green grab in human history, with the potential to disenfranchise the world's most impoverished and vulnerable people, establish a top-down global regime of land management, impede rural development, and invoke a destabilizing social backlash against conservation from the bottom up.[9]

Yet from a conservation point of view, a global-scale system of interconnected reserves covering half of the surface of this planet is more likely to sustain nonhuman nature into the deep future than any other project yet proposed.[10] With 15 percent of the Earth's land already protected and another 2 percent on the way, the 50 percent target is at least imaginable. To date, lands set aside have typically been deemed undesirable for other uses, an approach that must change as conserved surface area gets beyond about 25 percent, depending on the region.[11] And most importantly, the Half-Earth vision is radically simple, crisp, and clear: a shared biosphere for nonhuman nature can be a better biosphere for us all. Ideally realized simultaneously from bottom up and top down, a Half-Earth movement could rally the broadest segment of humanity ever to invest in the future of nonhuman nature—precisely what is required to achieve such a global mission.

1
Erle C. Ellis, Jed O. Kaplan, Dorian Q. Fuller, Steve Vavrus, Kees Klein Goldewijk, and Peter H. Verburg, "Used Planet: A Global History," *Proceedings of the National Academy of Sciences of the United States of America* 110.20 (2013): 7978–85.

2
Erle C. Ellis, Kees Klein Goldewijk, Stefan Siebert, Deborah Lightman, and Navin Ramankutty, "Anthropogenic Transformation of the Biomes, 1700 to 2000," *Global Ecology and Biogeography* 19.5 (September 2010): 589–606.

3
Erle C. Ellis, "Ecology in an Anthropogenic Biosphere," *Ecological Monographs* 85.3 (August 2015): 287–331.

4
Ellis, "Ecology in an Anthropogenic Biosphere"; Andrew Balmford, Rhys Green, and Jörn P. W. Scharlemann, "Sparing Land for Nature: Exploring the Potential Impact of Changes in Agricultural Yield on the Area Needed for Crop Production," *Global Change Biology* 11.1 (October 2005): 1594–1605; Jesse H. Ausubel, "The Great Reversal: Nature's Chance to Restore Land and Sea," *Technology in Society* 22.3 (August 2000): 289–301; Marina Fischer-Kowalski and Mark Swilling, *Decoupling Natural Resource Use and Environmental Impacts from Economic Growth* (Nairobi: United Nations Environment Program, 2011); David Tilman, Christian Balzer, Jason Hill, and Belinda L. Befort, "Global Food Demand and the Sustainable Intensification of Agriculture," *Proceedings of the National Academy of Sciences* 108.50 (December 2011): 20260–64.

5
Andrew Balmford and Rhys Green, "How to Spare Half a Planet," *Nature*, 552 (December 2017): 175; Eric Dinerstein, David Olson, Anup Joshi, Carly Vynne, Neil D. Burgess, Eric Wikramanayake, Nathan Hahn et al., "An Ecoregion-Based Approach to Protecting Half the Terrestrial Realm," *Bioscience* 67.6 (June 2017): 534–45; Edward O. Wilson, *Half-Earth: Our Planet's Fight for Life* (New York: Liveright, 2016).

6
Bradley Cantrell, Laura J. Martin, and Erle C. Ellis, "Designing Autonomy: Opportunities for New Wildness in the Anthropocene," *Trends in Ecology & Evolution* 32.3 (2017): 156–66.

7
Dinerstein et al., "A Protecting Half the Terrestrial Realm"; Wilson, *Half-Earth*; Harvey Locke, "Nature Needs Half: A Necessary and Hopeful New Agenda for Protected Areas," *IUCN Parks* 19.2 (2013): 13–22; Erle C. Ellis, "Nature for the People: Toward A Democratic Vision for the Biosphere," *Breakthrough Journal* 17 (2017): 15–25.

8
Zia Mehrabi, Erle C. Ellis, and Navin Ramankutty, "The Challenge of Feeding the World While Conserving Half the Planet," *Nature Sustainability* 1 (2018): 409–12.

9
Bram Büscher, Robert Fletcher, Dan Brockington, Chris Sandbrook, William M. Adams, Lisa Campbell, Catherine Corson et al., "Half-Earth or Whole Earth? Radical Ideas for Conservation, and Their Implications," *Oryx* (2016): 1–4.

10
Dinerstein et al., "A Protecting Half the Terrestrial Realm"; James E. M. Watson and Oscar Venter, "Ecology: A Global Plan for Nature Conservation," *Nature* 550 (2017): 48.

11
Ellis, "Nature for the People"; Mehrabi, "Feeding the World."

If Half-Earth were to succeed, what might the terrestrial biosphere of 2100 look like? At this early stage, many important questions remain unanswered. Still, as a shared social project operating across generations of people to reshape, reconnect, and manage dynamic environments worldwide at local, regional, and global scales, the landscapes formed by Half-Earth will most certainly differ from one place to another. In some regions, landscapes may evolve into a binary world of half urbanity and intensive agriculture, half protected reserves. Elsewhere, the old dichotomy between used lands and protected areas may continue to transition into a continuum of strategies for sharing the biosphere, by connecting regional national parks, indigenous reserves, urban green spaces, prairie strips, hedgerows, wildlife bridges, dam removals, and other new experiments in conservation and restoration.[12] In this linked and multivalent assemblage of controlled and wild spaces, Half-Earth would in fact make the Earth whole, through the project of planet sharing—not dividing.

Previews of future Half-Earth landscapes have emerged through social collaborations between private and public stakeholders at the local, national, and regional levels in transnational initiatives like the Yellowstone to Yukon Conservation Initiative,[13] the Convention on Biological Diversity, the World Business Council for Sustainable Development's report on landscape connectivity,[14] Natura 2000,[15] and many others. The scientific, technical, and social capacities needed to establish and sustain high-quality, transcontinental habitats are challenging in themselves, requiring diverse creative solutions. Yet the ultimate key to sharing the biosphere with nonhuman nature is to make such efforts valuable enough to people that they will support wild nature into the unforeseeable future.

Designing Wildness: Reversing the Social Construction of Nature

The pressures of human societies are an inevitable obstacle to creating and sustaining wild spaces for nonhuman nature. Even in designated nature conservation areas, human influence is pervasive and ever present, from species invasions to nutrient enrichment, altered fire regimes, and pollution, including anthropogenic light and noise. Infrastructures—from roads and dams to cities, croplands, canals, and ditches—divide and isolate nonhuman populations and challenge both migration patterns and daily movement, limiting habitat, breeding possibilities, and posing other problems potentially leading to extinction. Even just the intermittent presence of humans and domesticated animals (pets and commensals like rats) can affect food and water availability (influenced by bird feeders, boreholes, cornfields, garbage dumps, among others), profoundly shaping the conditions under which wild species live and evolve. Without intending to, we have greatly enhanced populations of anthropophilic species like raccoons, sparrows, and *Ailanthus* while making life nearly impossible for anthropophobes like cougars, gorillas and the California condor. Human alteration of the nonhuman world extends far beyond our intentions and even our awareness.

In the face of such insidious pressures, wildlife conservation efforts increasingly require intensive human management, from culling, spraying, and exterminating invasive species to reintroducing others, as well as continuous monitoring, controlled breeding, soil remediation, translocation, and fencing. These interventions obviously constitute human alteration of ecological patterns and processes, and much has been learned the hard way about the negative consequences of such control. For example, large-scale wildfires and harm to fire-dependent species were long produced through well-intended efforts at fire suppression.

The urge to control the nonhuman world is potent and enduring. Indeed, must one simply stand by when fire, common weeds, or rats threaten to burn up, overrun, feast on, or otherwise endanger the rarest of species? What should be done about the dangerous carnivore that has just consumed a treasured pet? And who gets to decide? The social-ecological tradeoffs and inadvertent consequences inherent in managing wild species in wild spaces create some of the most complex and wicked problems imaginable.[16]

Engaging human sociocultural connections with nature will always be fundamental to successful efforts to care for the nonhuman world.[17] On the other hand, these connections incorporate the equally deep human need to control and shape nature to fit expectations and desires, even among the most well-informed scientific managers. Despite best intentions, efforts to manage ecological complexity regularly yield negative or unintended outcomes, no

12
Kathy MacKinnon, Harry Jonas, Nigel Dudley, Marc Hockings, Dan Laffoley, David MacKinnon, and Stephen Woodley, eds., *Guidelines for Recognizing and Reporting Other Effective Area-Based Conservation Measures*, version 1 (draft), (Gland: International Union for Conservation of Nature World Commission on Protected Areas, 2018), 26.

13
Charles C. Chester, "Responding to the Idea of Transboundary Conservation," *Journal of Sustainable Forestry* 17.1–2 (2003): 103–25.

14
Sasha Alexander, Anais Blasco, Ettore Capri, Ehsan Dullo, Douglas Jeroen, Natalia Estrada-Carmona, Roberta Iley et al., *Landscape Connectivity: A Call to Action* (Geneva: World Business Council for Sustainable Development, 2017).

15
Vanya Simeonova, Irene Bouwma, Edgar van der Grift, Carlos Sunyer, Lola Manteiga, Mart Külvik, Monika Suškevičs et al., *Natura 2000 and Spatial Planning* (Brussels: European Commission, 2017), http://ec.europa.eu/environment/nature/knowledge/pdf/Natura_2000_and_spatial_planning_final_for_publication.pdf.

16
Ruth DeFries and Harini Nagendra, "Ecosystem Management as a Wicked Problem," *Science* 356 (2017): 265–70.

17
Ellis, "Ecology in an Anthropogenic Biosphere"; Edward O. Wilson, *Biophilia*, (Cambridge, MA: Harvard University Press, 1984).

matter the scope of human individual and social intelligence brought to bear on the process.

But what if another form of nonhuman intelligence could be engaged in the curation of nonhuman natures? With the concept of designed autonomy, landscape architect Bradley Cantrell, environmental scientist Laura Williams, and I have proposed to go beyond human intelligence to better sustain wild spaces within an increasingly human world.[18] With deep reinforcement learning technologies, computational systems are gaining capacities to solve ever more complex problems. By engaging this unprecedented capability, it may yet be possible to surpass human curatorial limitations to design a more distanced authorship in the creation and care of wild spaces for nonhuman life.[19] To accomplish this, a conceptual design for a "wildness creator" replaces human curatorial interactions with responsive technologies (sensing, monitoring, robotics) guided by an artificial intelligence that has learned to assist the nonhuman species and spaces in its care through its own observations and experiences, rather than through human programming. Thus removed from (limiting) management priorities defined by humans, the wildness creator derives its specific priorities from an evolving computational intelligence emergent from direct interaction with nonhuman species and environmental processes. While the construction of such autonomous systems may exceed societal technological capacities for at least another decade, the potential for coupling deep reinforcement learning with constant real-time observation, feedback, and experimentation could offer novel solutions outside conventional conservation strategies.

Acoustic monitoring has already been combined with machine learning to sense the activities of rats preying on endangered island birds, and bird population recovery subsequent to rat removal. Coral reef invasion by the corallivorous crown-of-thorns starfish (COTS) is currently being controlled by submarine drones that use imaging and machine learning. After identifying COTS for eradication, the drones inject them with toxins.

Considering the potential for designed autonomy in creating wild spaces, the story of the "Lions of Los Angeles"—cougars that even now successfully navigate the human world of Southern California—is an important example.[20] Hiding in the shadows, traveling at night, and narrowly avoiding death by vehicle collision, a small population of cougars is learning how to survive and reproduce among humans. Designed autonomy engaged in improving cougar habitat and conservation would amplify existing efforts to assist cougar movement through landscapes using bridges and other corridors. Through continual monitoring of cougar activity (movement, feeding, reproduction), new means of reducing conflict between cougars and humans (their livestock and pets) may be found, such as encouraging cougar movement through less conflictive spaces, or by discouraging people and livestock from nearing cougar spaces—in real time. These examples only scratch the surface of what could become routine if advanced artificial intelligence is empowered to sustain nonhumans embedded within the human world.

Distancing the Anthropocene

Reshaping nature has always been a human social project; most of the biosphere already bears the fingerprints of ancient and ongoing social change. Yet even as the human species today is increasingly globally interconnected and interdependent, with a stabilizing population and rising welfare, new levels of social cooperation are needed to serve the interests of all species, not only humans.

It is time to redesign the human world to empower the natural world once again. To do so we must first discard outdated sociocultural conceptions of nature as being somewhere else by welcoming the nonhuman world into ours.[21] Efforts to create enough space for nonhuman nature to continue its evolution beyond ours must become part of everything we do. And the challenges have never been greater, demanding shared social projects of unprecedented scale and the most powerful design tools ever developed. Ultimately, in distancing our authorship of the nonhuman world, we might redefine this human epoch for the better.

18
Cantrell, B., L. J. Martin, and E. C. Ellis. 2017. Designing Autonomy: Opportunities for New Wildness in the Anthropocene. Trends in *Ecology & Evolution* 32:156-166.

19
Charles Waldheim, "Strategies of Indeterminacy in Recent Landscape Practice," *Public* 33 (Spring 2006): 80–86.

20
Dana Goodyear, "Lions of Los Angeles," *New Yorker*, February 13 & 20, 2017, https://www.newyorker.com/magazine/2017/02/13/lions-of-los-angeles.

21
Ellis, "Ecology in an Anthropogenic Biosphere"; Ian Jared Miller, *The Nature of the Beasts: Empire and Exhibition at the Tokyo Imperial Zoo* (Berkeley: University of California Press, 2013).

From Fallow to Wild

JILL DESIMINI

Fallow, in many ways, is a fallacy. That is, defined as a period of inactivity. On any piece of land, there is always activity—and while resting might breed uncertainty in some contexts, the agricultural definition of fallow implies that dormancy is a requirement of sustained growth. Within this period of dormancy, there is action: plowing, tilling, and even the planting of cover crops. Fallow is a necessary pause, akin to the necessity for ruination, described by landscape writer and cultural geographer J. B. Jackson.[1] He argues that periods of ruin are required for cultural evolution. The economist Joseph Schumpeter made a similar claim about capitalism, that destruction is an integral part of the process.[2] Downturn demands creativity.

Urban abandonment has been described both in terms of ruins: its buildings, economies, infrastructures; and fallowness: its landscape. In fact, describing abandoned property as fallow acknowledges its liminal state. A ruin is irreversible but potentially of value. A vacancy—the common term for discarded urban plots—is undesirable, associated with seemingly perpetual demise rather than temporary inoccupation. Vacant seems to be without value.

Fallow is both reversible and valuable, if indirectly so. By suspending immediate cultivation, future yield is greater. A time of fallowness increases fertility and is arguably necessary for longevity. With waiting comes reward. The condition of agricultural fallowness, however, is different from that of urban fallowness, because it is planned with a relatively predictable outcome.

By contrast, urban fallowness is unplanned and has an unknown future. This irregular and uncertain condition has vexed architects, landscape architects, urban designers, and planners for decades. Numerous design studies and competitions have highlighted the anxious energy surrounding abandoned urban space, most notably, the Vacant Lots project (1987), a collaboration between the Architectural League and the New York City Department of Housing Preservation; the Shrinking Cities international ideas competition (2004), initiated by the Kulturstiftung des Bundes (German Federal Cultural Foundation) and the magazine *Archplus*; and the competitions Urban Voids (2005–06) and Future Ground (2014–15), administered by the Van Alen Institute. There is an urge to do something. This fallow is rarely seen as a healthy pause.

In fact, it is difficult, naive, even dangerous, to embrace a fallow condition, to forget the years of exploitation, or to give up on the dream of rebuilding. It is human nature to want to replace building with building, store with store, office with office. It is distressing to see the built environment dissolving, pulling economic resources and social support systems down in its wake. And it is tragic to live in its midst.

At the same time, it is rejuvenating to see the expansive sky open up above vacant fields, to watch volunteer plants take root and grow tall, to allow water to infiltrate through soil once sealed in concrete, to generate energy through new climatic conditions, to see animals and people at play, work, and rest in these fallow urban landscapes. The people and the land have embodied resources—and pauses in activity, oddly, allow these resources to flourish. By letting go temporarily, diversity takes hold. With time, even, the fallow turns wild.

Fallow and wild both contrast with cultivation—and it could be argued that fallow spaces either return to active use or become wild. In fact, their classification as fallow is really an indication of reduced human engagement rather than of one of inactivity. Fallow means less human control, and less human control means increased spontaneity—both by other humans and by other species of flora and fauna. A fallow landscape of a year returns to crop production. A fallow landscape of a few years becomes a wild meadow. A fallow landscape of 40 years becomes a wild woodland.

Fallow and wild, at first glance, appear at odds. One is the result of a deliberate management practice. The other is deliberately unmanaged. One is cleared. The other is dense and tangled. One plow-ready, the other unruly. But understood differently, fallow is a beneficial first step towards wildness. Wildness, in fact, is one of the untapped potentials of land left fallow.

It is this wild potential that I will focus on more deeply here, particularly in relation to the cultural, ecological, and urban contributions of a 100-acre (40-hectare) woodland in Boston, the Allandale Woods, and its 400-year journey from wild to cultivated to fallow and back to wild.

To the untrained eye, there are landscapes that look as if they have existed, in their present form, forever. The effortless existence of these spaces masks their past struggles. Their size, depth, and weight belie their youthfulness. I remember my first realization about such a landscape—in the Pennsylvania Coal Country—the setting of my first landscape architecture studio. I was driving with a scientist from the United States Environmental Protection Agency, who was pointing left and right to sizable tree-covered hills that had formed from mine excavations decades earlier. I was stunned, my nascent landscape brain struggling to reconcile these hills as the positive forms of the mine pits I had been tracing and traversing all semester. From that moment, my eyes sharpened to look carefully at woodlands for their strange juxtapositions, for the relics that reveal the surprises of the past and clues for the future. The many layers, some subtle and others all-encompassing, are what make hybrid landscapes rich and compelling social and ecological spaces. Allandale Woods is one hybrid landscape that seems to have existed as extensive and continuous woodland for a long time. The rich canopy seeps out of its built confines. The trees reach out to beckon visitors even though the designated entrances are hard to find. Circumnavigation is required to spot the small breaks in walls, with paths leading down into the woods, or the narrow stairs hidden behind buildings and parking lots that form the true entrances to the space. As you descend or ascend into the woodland, the perception of it as an ordinary New England forest of oaks and maples quickly fades. Interruptions—ponds, vernal pools, walls, foundations, rusting tools, apple orchards—dot the undulating forest carpet. The oddities are both slight and rampant. The singularity of the woodland is quickly discarded. This is a space constructed over time, at the hands of many—human and nonhuman—agents.

Outcroppings of Roxbury puddingstone—a conglomerate dating back more than 500 million years—indicate the deep time associated with Allandale Woods, while twisted black cherry trees signal more recent transformations. Old and crumbling stone walls indicate centuries-old human appropriation of the land. An unrelenting concrete-and-stone-clad boundary wall suggests more recent human attempts at conquest. Online debates and protests over a new housing development planned to abut and capture some of the woodland speaks to future annexation. The Allandale Woods is dynamic in its formation, from the species level to the extent of the territory. And contestation makes it even more alluring and unnerving.

For example, the concrete boundary wall is remarkable. It follows straight lines despite topographic variation, a flat inscription on the plan enacted without reference to undulating ground. It breaks with trees, begging the question of provenance. What gives way to what? What existed first, and what came after? Why is this here? Does it matter? A walk through the woods invites contemplation, awe, imagination. The wall is phenomenal to walk along or on top of, to come across, to see from a distance. The misalignment of logics—of boundary making and forest dynamics—plays out materially, to great delight.

It is easy to grasp the remnants: in view of abandoned building foundations, one can imagine a small barn

1 J. B. Jackson, *The Necessity for Ruins* (Amherst: University of Massachusetts Press, 1980).

2 Joseph A. Schumpeter, *Capitalism, Socialism, and Democracy* (1942; Taylor & Francis e-Library, 2003).

Three panoramic images showing: light filtering through the successional woodland (top); farming and building relics hidden among the trees (middle); and the pond, with Paul Sutton, the Urban Wilds program manager for the Boston Parks and Recreation Department and Elliot Rhodeside, whose initial work aided in the future conservation of the woods, enjoying the view (bottom). Courtesy Jill Desimini.

The boundary wall built to delineate public and private claims, weaves in and out of the trees.
Time and weathering are evident in the polychromatic foliage and differential material conditions. Courtesy Nathalie Mitchell.

occupying a morsel of the woods. But it is more difficult to put all the pieces together to envision the wholesale transformation of the entire tract of land. A few apple trees do not immediately call up an orchard. A dry stone wall does not transcend its present material condition to evoke the agricultural fields it once enclosed. A 100-year-old sugar maple may look out of place but it is a stretch to identify individual species and see curving estate roads, manor houses, and fields. To take in the woodland as a rolling agricultural landscape is hard enough. And to think that the landscape transformed from forest to cropland and back again in just under 400 years forces a reconsideration of our current predilection to resist dramatic adaptations.

Allandale Woods is a strange landscape to conjure as fallow—because its past fallowness has elapsed and its future fallowness is yet to come. However, the wood's most recent fallow period was not that long ago, and still within memory for some. Most likely, it occurred in the mid-20th century as estates fell into disrepair and grazing lands were left overgrown. Aging fields pervaded the landscape, suspended in a liminal state before new growth emerged. That fallowness was of a different era, when Boston underwent a moment of economic transition. Prosperity was less certain, populations were drifting outward, and old districts of the city were razed or abandoned.

This was the same moment that landscape architect Elliot Rhodeside and his colleagues at the Boston Redevelopment Authority became intrigued by the rugged exposure of many of the city's landscapes[3]; an innate quality they found to be a kind of urban wildness. They surveyed the city—on foot and by air—searching for uncultivated landscapes that evoked the natural history of the region. They were drawn to marshes, woodlands, and outcroppings, and ultimately identified 176 sites as urban wilds that should eventually be conserved as significant markers of the bio-geophysical characteristics of the city. As Rhodeside explained, "For Bostonians, the city has an even more precious side: the unprotected natural areas of remarkable beauty—Boston's Urban Wilds—remaining hidden among the development areas which represent a historical picture of Boston much older than the [American] Revolution."[4]

The area around and including Allandale Woods is a nexus of these wild spaces. And while they play an important ecological role in the city fabric, their social significance, both historical and contemporary, is underplayed. Rhodeside and his fellow advocates thought of them as natural rather than hybrid, as long-standing rather than constantly evolving. As a result, their wildness has been contained, their fallowness misunderstood, and their future rendered lackluster.

As woodland, Allandale offers a pleasant but unremarkable respite in the city. Ask people what they remember from a visit and they will invariably mention the wall or the springhouse or another structural intrusion. These historical appurtenances give value. But the woodland itself remains vulnerable. Development has eaten away at its edges and continues to hem in the site. There is a current battle underway over a housing project that sees the wooded backdrop as an amenity to capitalize rather than a landscape to steward. Arguments for the importance of the Allandale Woods point to its ecological capacity to address changing environmental conditions and only rarely mention its key presence in the social, economic, and political formation of the city of Boston. Yet as an "approximate archaeology" of the site indicates, the pillaging of the woodland is not a new practice.[5]

The woodland is, rather, an example of the cyclical nature of the city—analogous to the cyclical rotation of crop fields—where spaces fall fallow only to grow again, quietly, after regaining focus in the pause produced by inactivity. Allandale Woods, with its puddingstone outcroppings, springs, and vernal pools, does contain markers of a history older than the American Revolution. This timeworn history is juxtaposed with another long history of continued and varied human use and misuse, from the colonial period through to the present day. The site itself is liminal, occupying both sides of a physical and temporal boundary.

Within this complex history, there are traces of a bright future. Our tendency to conserve ecological landscapes is to tame them. Our other tendency is to supplant them (especially the novel ones) to create naive substitutions. Ecologies need moments of fallowness to take root. They need moments of disruption in order to evolve. They need maturation to invoke the excitement and imagination required for social resonance. Hybrid conditions, developed over long time spans with periods of fallowness and of wildness, create the strange juxtapositions necessary for such intrigue. Allandale Woods would not be the same without its rocks, walls, rusty tools, agricultural specimens, dogs, forts, and fungi.[6] If you visit once, would you be curious enough about its landscape to return and fight for its potential futures? Ideally as many to equal those of its uncanny pasts.

3
The Boston Redevelopment Authority, now called the Boston Planning and Development Agency, is the urban planning and economic development agency of Boston, Massachusetts. It was established in 1957 to pursue development opportunities for the city.

4
Elliot Rhodeside, "Boston Urban Wilds: A Natural Conservation Program for City Neighborhoods," *Environmental Comment*, 1977: 10.

5
This approximate archaeology is based on conversations with Elliot Rhodeside, Paul Sutton, and Peter Del Tredici, and on the following article by Richard Heath and Richard B. Primack, "Allandale Woods: A Fragment of the First Families of Boston," *Arnoldia*, 51.2 (Summer 1991): 32–39. It has further been supported by a Harvard University Graduate School of Design Dean's Junior Faculty Research Grant and the work of research assistants Timothy Wei and Michelle Franco.

6
My ongoing discovery of Allandale Woods has benefited greatly from the work of the students in my Fall 2017 seminar at the Harvard University Graduate School of Design, "It's a Wild World: Future Scenarios for Feral Landscapes." Especially Madeleine Aronson, Je Sung Lee, Nathalie Mitchell, L. Stacy Passmore, and Moritz Schudel, who took on the woods themselves; and Ana Garcia, Keith Hartwig, Grace McEniry, Avery Normandin, Greta Ruedisueli, Zephaniah Ruggles, AJ Sus, and Seok Min Yeo, who indirectly touched upon them.

Unbuilding: Process and Preservation

CAITLIN DeSILVEY

The below extract from my book *Curated Decay: Heritage Beyond Saving* (University of Minnesota Press, 2017) describes a site in the far southwest of the United Kingdom, in the county of Cornwall.[1] I've lived in Cornwall for a decade now, but its landscape still perplexes me. Having grown up in New England, I was accustomed to encountering traces of lost landscapes in the moss-topped fieldstone walls scattered through dense woodland, sunken cellar holes, oxidized farm implements, feral orchards. In Cornwall the remnants of prior occupation are of another order altogether. In the most remote locations—atop an upland moor or along a thickly wooded riverbank—one frequently comes across the ruins of massive masonry structures: wheel pits and processing works, engine houses and auxiliary buildings, and other relics of intensive mining, quarrying, milling, and manufacture. Cornwall's industrialization was precocious and, ultimately, precarious. Kennall Vale is just one of many sites that have been abandoned for a century or more. Here the "interval of neglect"—to borrow a turn of phrase from J. B. Jackson—has persisted long enough that remnant structures have since been colonized by other ecologies, and thus have begun to shed their value as purely cultural artifacts.[2]

The most common response to this kind of incipient hybridity—in both nature conservation and historic preservation contexts—is to consolidate the meaning of the object of concern, be it rare species or significant structure, by reestablishing the boundary between natural and cultural substance. Various practices are involved in the labor of boundary maintenance: repair, restoration, rehabilitation, conservation. Yet all are directed towards the achievement of a specific desired state (i.e., measured by the presence of target species, or the integrity of the original building fabric). The ultimate aim is framed as "averting loss," and the greater the evidence of cross-contamination—through incursions of undesirable culture into natural habitats, or through the degradation of cultural artifacts by environmental processes—the greater the assumed risk. Through discussion of the boundary work that has taken place in Kennall Vale to maintain the distinction between natural and cultural heritage, the potential for an expanded heritage practice comes into view, in which the distinction between making and growing, built and unbuilt, begins to break down. Such an expanded practice allows that structures and artifacts have biological as well as social lives, and that ecosystems have deeply cultural properties as well as natural ones.

This way of thinking resonates, perhaps, with ideas in architecture and design about the unfinished quality of buildings, and the ways in which their lives are continually extended through acts of alteration, amendment, destruction, and wear.[3] Moshen Mostafavi and David Leatherbarrow write of building weathering as a "form of completion" and ask whether "it is possible that weathering is not only a problem to be solved, or a fact to be neglected, but is an inevitable occurrence to be recognized and made use of in the uncertainties of its manifestation."[4] In the sites examined in *Curated Decay*, the unfinished extends to the point of unbuilding. Ruination, however, does not signal the collapse of order and structure, but opens instead onto radically different forms of organization.[5]

Images from Kennall Vale.
Courtesy of Caitlin DeSilvey.

Extract from *Curated Decay: Heritage Beyond Saving*

The gunpowder works at Kennall Vale were established in 1812 to produce explosives, primarily for industrial use. Here, in a steep-sided, thickly wooded valley, manufacture harnessed the hydropower of the Kennall River to process saltpeter, sulfur, charcoal, and graphite into a (relatively) stable product. Mines used the gunpowder to extract ore from below-ground shafts, and quarries used it to loosen massive blocks of stone. Mistakes were sometimes made (one accident was caused by a hot roasted potato in the press house), and several workers lost their lives in accidental explosions. Production declined in the early part of the 20th century with the development of new nitroglycerin-based explosive technologies, demand accelerated by the onset of World War I. Back in Kennall Vale, at the edge of the disused gunpowder works, a granite quarry was established, specializing in fine-grained granite for use in memorials to fallen soldiers.

Now, over a century since the closure of the works, the landscape holds little to alert the casual visitor to the intensity and the volatility of its past life. When my family first moved to Cornwall, we lived only a couple of miles away from Kennall Vale, and we used to visit often. We walked the paths cut along the side of the valley, following an elaborate system of leats that once directed waterpower to a series of incorporating mills. The mills and other industrial structures were now overgrown with ivy and ferns, picturesque relics that attracted local photographers to document their dereliction. Bluebells carpeted the forest floor in the spring, up to the base of the massive blast wall at the top of the valley, which had been built to protect adjacent properties. On the side of the valley across from the mills, the granite quarry void had filled to a still, shaded pool. Mosses encased blocks of waste granite, forming soft green cubes.

Everywhere there were trees. Mature beech, sycamore, ash, and oak grew densely through the valley and rooted in the halfling structures. My favorite specimen was a young sycamore that had grown up next to a blocky concrete foundation. Nudged by the wind against a sharp corner in the structure as it grew, it had crafted an ingenious solution by molding its trunk with a matching right angle, which now rested on the concrete ledge like an elbow propped on a wall. Many of the older trees were

1
Excerpt from "Boundary Work" from *Curated Decay: Heritage Beyond Saving* by Caitlin DeSilvey (University of Minnesota Press, 2017), 138–44. Copyright 2017 by the Regents of the University of Minnesota. Used by permission of the University of Minnesota Press.

2
J. B. Jackson, *The Necessity for Ruins* (Amherst: University of Massachusetts Press, 1980).

3
Jeremy Till, *Architecture Depends* (Cambridge, MA: MIT Press, 2009); Douglas Murphy, *The Architecture of Failure* (Winchester: Zero Books, 2012); Fred Scott, *On Altering Architecture* (London: Routledge, 2008); Roger Harbison, *The Built, The Unbuilt, and the Unbuildable* (Cambridge, MA: MIT Press, 1991); Ed Hollis, *The Secret Lives of Buildings* (London: Portobello Books, 2010); Stewart Brand, *How Buildings Learn* (New York: Penguin, 1994); Stephen Cairns and Jane Jacobs, *Buildings Must Die: A Perverse View of Architecture* (Cambridge, MA: MIT Press, 2014).

4
Moshen Mostafavi and David Leatherbarrow, *On Weathering: The Life of Buildings in Time* (Cambridge, MA: MIT Press, 1999), 16.

5
Karen Dale and Gibson Burrell, "Disturbing Structure: Reading the Ruins," *Culture and Organization* 17.2 (2011): 108.

deliberately planted by the gunpowder works employees to keep humidity levels high in the valley. The hope was that their presence would reduce the likelihood of accidental detonations and contain them if they did occur—a sort of green blast chamber.[6] With the withdrawal of active industry, the trees accelerated their occupation of the landscape. By 1985, the valley was sufficiently renaturalized to merit its designation as a nature reserve, managed by the Cornwall Wildlife Trust. The derelict walls and structures provided habitat for pioneer plant species, and greater horseshoe bats roosted in nearby mine shafts. Kingfishers and song thrushes were spotted in the valley, trout and eels in the river and leats.

The first historic and archaeological survey of the site was completed in 1986, a year after the designation of the reserve.[7] The historic value of the site was deemed to be significant enough for the remains of the gunpowder works to be designated as a Scheduled Monument in 1999. Management of the structures up to this point had been minimal, but an archaeological assessment prepared in the same year as the listing identified some potential issues:

> The effects of mature trees falling onto structures or damaging them as roots are lifted is a serious concern. Some leats have already been affected by falling trees. Saplings have also begun to establish themselves on and in the walls of some buildings. Dealing with the latter should cause no problems to the CWT [Cornwall Wildlife Trust] but the extensive and awkward tree surgery needed to ensure that important remains are not damaged by falling trees will not only be expensive but may also lead to clashes with nature conservation aims, not least the retention of the large mature trees and their communities of invertebrates, bryophytes, lichens, fungi, etc. It should also be expected that the opening up of numerous small glades around buildings will probably lead to the development of scrub woodland whose root systems may also have a negative impact on the archaeological remains and will certainly render them less easily visible. The historic character of the reserve, in which the trees were themselves used as devices to minimise the impact of any explosions in the gunpowder works, would also be altered by the fragmentation of the woodland.[8]

In the passage above, the trees are cast in at least three distinct roles: they are ecological entities, offering essential habitat for specific species and providing structure within the broader ecosystem; they are unintentional agents of destruction, threatening to undermine buildings and obscure archaeological remains; and they are cultural artifacts in their own right, their presence contributing to the historic character of the reserve by signaling their past enrollment in the industrial process. This passage was written a quarter of a century ago, and, as my recent exploration of the site suggests, the trees are still there, and their identity remains unfixed. If anything, they have accrued another part in the performance, as the nonnative beech and sycamore (planted during the period of active industry) are occasionally demoted to second-class citizenship in favor of indigenous oak and ash.[9] At Kennall Vale, nature conservation value and cultural heritage value seem to be treated with a rough equivalence. The boundary work that does take place is, for the most part, selective, and focused on specific interventions rather than wholesale restoration. The 1999 report recommended removing ivy and saplings from the structures, and over the years there has been a fair amount of this kind of remedial maintenance, but much of the vegetation has grown back over time.

In 2009, a spike of anxiety about the gradual deterioration of the structures led a group of volunteers and historic environment professionals to carry out a photographic survey of all buildings and structures within the reserve. Scrub and saplings were removed from around the structures to make them visible for

6 Shaun Lewin, "Field Trip 3: Hydroplutonic Kernow," The Falmouth Convention, Cornwall, UK, May 21, 2009, https://www.urbanomic.com/event/hydroplutonic-kernow/.

7 J. R. Smith, *Kennall Vale Archaeological Report* (Truro, UK: Cornwall Trust for Nature Conservation, 1986).

8 Peter Herring, *Kennall Vale Reserve Archaeological Assessment: A Report to the Cornwall Wildlife Trust* (Truro, UK: Cornwall Archaeological Unit, Cornwall County Council, 1999).

9 S. Adams, "Management and Monitoring Plan: Kennall Vale Nature Reserve, 2001–2006: A Report to Cornwall Wildlife Trust," May 2000.

the photographs. The survey identified vandalism (local youths were fond of taking loose stones from the buildings and tossing them into the river) and "tree-throw and tree-root damage" (a variation on vandalism, but with arboreal rather than human agents of destruction) as the key factors undermining the condition of structures. Trees were considered to pose "major threats" to public safety and to the historic buildings.[10] A flurry of activity followed over the next several years. Across the site, ostensibly overmature trees were felled, and selected buildings were reclaimed and repointed.

Those who carried out the work were aware that structures without a protective covering of ivy and moss were more likely to be the target of vandals. In removing the vegetation, they were stabilizing the structures but simultaneously increasing their vulnerability. On some buildings, new mortar was covered with earth to encourage moss and lichen to recolonize—an ecological and aesthetic strategy of camouflage. In other areas, vine and root had come to provide structural support, taking the place of decayed mortar, and reconstruction involved difficult decisions. A set of steps next to one of the mill buildings had been assembled using recycled millstones, but because "the roots of a large tree [were] intimately wound around the steps, with one root even forming one of the steps," the work they could do was limited.[11] The willingness to negotiate, or even collaborate, with vegetative agents has its parallels in the practice of "soft capping" ruined structures with layers of protective, living matter.[12]

The language in recent reports and the management plans for Kennall Vale retains an element of ambiguity. A 2011 report prepared by English Heritage's senior field officer in Cornwall stresses the need to hold back the "ongoing tide of natural decay and vandalism," without acknowledging that decay is an essential process in any woodland ecosystem.[13] On the ground, however, managers attempt to find synergies between seemingly disparate goals. Recent repairs of the leat system, which involved the removal of several mature trees, also apparently provided a more consistent flow in the watercourses for plants, bryophytes, and wildlife. "Removing inappropriate species and improving the woodlands structure by selective felling, ride creation, restoring glades and rotational coppicing" has been found to create new pockets of habitat while simultaneously protecting the structures from the effects of unpredictable "tree-throw."[14] Although there is an air of convenient coincidence about the rationale put forward for these management actions, there is also a sense that the managers on this site are attuned to the way their labor must continually negotiate the nature–culture boundary. They accept that there will be compromises and that sometimes different aims will clash, but for the most part Kennall Vale seems held in a precarious balance. A visit to the valley can still offer an illusion of nonintervention, the structures surrendered to a state of pleasing decay, surrounded by semi-wild nature.

10
Ann Preston-Jones, *Kennall Vale, Ponsanooth, Cornwall: Archaeological Management and Interpretation* (Truro, UK: Cornwall Council Historic Environment Projects, 2011).

11
Ibid., 17.

12
Robin Kent, "Thirlwall Castle: The Use of Soft Capping in Conserving Ruined Ancient Monuments," *Journal of Architectural Conservation* 19.1 (2013): 35–48; Chris Wood, "Soft Capping: Justifying a Return to the Picturesque," *Context* 90 (2005): 22–24. Other sites where this approach has been applied in the United Kingdom include Wigmore Castle, Jervaulx Abbey, Fountain's Abbey, and Tintagel.

13
Preston-Jones, *Kennall Vale*, 20.

14
Nick Marriott, personal communication to author, October 6, 2014.

Fence and Fallow

BENJAMIN R. COHEN

There is a meandering wall at Storm King Art Center, an outdoor sculpture park in the Hudson River Valley of New York. The wall was built without mortar—a "dry" wall—and stands through the integrity of carefully assembled stones, small boulders, and right-size pebbles. It follows a nonlinear path snaking down a slope and weaving in and out of trees, until eventually slipping into a lake. When it emerges on the other side, it runs up a hill and defines a straight line to the edge of the park. Officially, it is the *Storm King Wall* (1997–1998) by British artist Andy Goldsworthy. But some call it the "wall that went for a walk," and others the "running wall." Both epithets are nice; the action in each having two senses. In that of running a wire under a carpet, the wall walks or runs along a slope. But it also runs down the hill, as in actually moving, sliding, or rolling forward freely.[1]

The wall plays with common concepts of fencing off, enclosing, dividing, containing, or controlling space. Fallow fields operate under similar principles, and function under assumptions of controlled space and time. Both fence and fallow field require care and maintenance. Although appearing static and docile, they are in fact active and in motion; they walk and run across time and space. Goldsworthy has worked to make this point about fences. Reading fallow in the same way can help designers consider agricultural lands and nonagricultural urban spaces alike. Cinching the two together, fence and fallow, is a renewed demand for maintenance and active management.

First, the wall. Artist and environmentalist Andy Goldsworthy designed it in keeping with a body of work that seeks to reveal nature: its flow, lifecycles, and ephemerality. His installations have limited life spans. Some last an hour, like the ice sculptures that melt along with the sun's rise; some only a few days;

Andy Goldsworthy, *Storm King Wall* (1997–1998). Storm King Art Center, New York, 2011.
Courtesy bobistraveling, licensed under a Creative Commons Attribution License 2.0.

and others, like *Storm King Wall*, many decades. A documentary on his work, *Rivers and Tides* (2002), shows Goldsworthy's use of meandering paths and twisting patterns in a number of media. There are clay walls built with a snaking pattern, strings of leaves floating down streams, and lines on paper drawing looped forms.

The serpentine wall is a larger, physically emboldened version of the same theme. And it is sneaky. It pushes against ideas of physical separation and linear demarcation, the notion that fences separate and define two spaces. It is also indebted to a sense of time, of how long things last. The wall is ephemeral on the generational timescale of tree growth. Eventually, those trees that flourish will grow trunks large enough to upend the base of the wall and topple its stones. Eventually.[2]

In other words, the separation between spaces matters less than the time such presumed separation can be managed. In this sense, Goldsworthy's wall is most notable for the way it asks viewers to envision spatial and temporal scales at the same time. The wall—a fence—separates one space into two. When you come upon a fence or wall, you witness one point along a timeline. How long has it been there? How long will it stand? The effect is that of encountering an old stone wall in the middle of woodlands, a common occurrence on the East Coast and other historic settlement areas of the US. In Virginia, where I lived for many years, I often walked the trails at a nature preserve, wondering about the disheveled stone walls cutting through it. They were remnants—testament to a bygone era when the area had been an active farm.

Storm King Art Center is a remarkable landscape in its own right, with a particular history. It is set on old farmland in a river valley famous for its connection to both agricultural livelihoods and westward expansion. Think of its geographical position in the 19th century: take the Hudson River north, cut west across the Erie Canal to the Great Lakes, and find the interior of the continent. The area was also famous for grand artistic representations by the Hudson River School of landscape painters, founded by Thomas Cole. These were contemporaries of Ralph Waldo Emerson and Henry David Thoreau working and living in New York, painting broad canvases with distant views of hillsides, sublime mountain peaks, and waterfalls. The Hudson River artists captured a sense of geological history in their work, depicting generations of valley life and expressing the long-term identity of the place. Goldsworthy's wall loops in and out of hundred-year-old trees planted in the generation after Cole painted its landscape in the mid-19th century.[3]

In the more near term, the remains of earlier farm lanes etch paths in the contours of the hills and meadows at the sculpture park. The farmlands are a palimpsest. This is not an auxiliary point, since even the impetus for the original wall was agricultural. The fields of Goldsworthy's native Scotland, lined with stone walls that defined enclosures, were part of his inspiration. Those walls grew up over generations as farmers and shepherds tossed newly unearthed stones aside each spring to clear grazing areas. The spring thaw is a particular moment of relaxation for the earth. After a frozen winter, the "breathing" of the crust is visible in newly upturned rocks. The land exhales stones.

Agricultural metaphors remain prominent in post-industrial language because, like biological metaphors, they are the substance of human relations to our surroundings. Cultivate, grow, tend, make fertile, flourish, nourish, blossom, and bloom are things we want for our children. They are what we do with land. And they take time. Over the years, piles of discarded stones became material for walls and borders. Over decades, farmers defined space and distinguished "in" from "out" in keeping with the scale of generational change.

The insistence on timescales is significant here because they are seldom held alongside spatial scales in conceptual schemas and design plans. Yet Goldsworthy's serpentine wall requires just this. Its shape is its most characteristic feature because it contradicts common assumptions about linearity—it does a poor job of clean divisions. But even more, it does a poor job of demarcating the land definitely. It will not last forever. So what use is it? What does it do—if not hold spaces apart?

One insight from the "wall that went for a walk" may be that utility means different things in land management. Commonly understood as a virtue of functionality, or making things happen, utility is an economic term. But Goldsworthy's wall sets value beyond economic terms, or non-market valuation, economists would say. In her essays on humanity, Marilynne Robinson writes, "Our best is so often artistic more than utilitarian, in the usual sense of both words," because art is a broader and more enduring concept. "It is a fact with which we should learn to be at peace." Goldsworthy's work is not utilitarian in the usual sense but it is useful, still, here. His stone fence escapes the economical reductions of the "utilitarian."[4] It challenges the functional assumption that fences divide neatly, instead weaving in and out of trees and explicitly avoiding linearity.

1
Andy Goldsworthy and Kenneth Baker, *Wall: At Storm King* (New York: Harry N. Abrams, 2000); Robert Chianese, "Storm King 'Running' Wall," *American Scientist* 101 (May–June 2013): 188.

2
Rivers and Tides: Andy Goldsworthy Working in Time, directed by Thomas Riedelsheimer (2001; Edinburgh: Skyline Productions). See also Kima O'Connell, "The Walking Wall: On Andy Goldsworthy's Gift to Storm-King," *Landscape Architecture* 90 (2000): 16; Robert Fulford, "Andy Goldsworthy: Nature's Collaborator, Art's Alchemist," *Queen's Quarterly* 114 (2007): 597–606; Kylie Stevenson, "The River in a Landscape of Creative Practice: Creative River Journeys," *Landscapes* 5 (2013): 1–19.

3
See Thomas Cole, "A Essay on American Scenery," *American Monthly Magazine* 1 (January 1836): 1–12; Rebecca Bedell, *The Anatomy of Nature: Geology and American Landscape Painting* (Princeton, NJ: Princeton University Press, 2001); David Schuyler, *Sanctified Landscape: Writers, Artists, and the Hudson River Valley, 1820–1909* (Ithaca, NY: Cornell University Press, 2012).

4
Marilynne Robinson, *What Are We Doing Here?* (New York: Farrar, Straus & Giroux, 2018), 92.

Walls, borders, and fences do work because they exert claims on what is protected and what excluded, distinguishing one side from the other, one use and another. In this sense, they are always social and environmental, temporal, and spatial. And they require work and maintenance to keep going, to keep working, to keep dividing.

Fallow operates in a similar way. Historically, fallow fields served an environmentally regenerative purpose. Although common definitions consider them inert and unused, they are active sites of fertility generation. Dormancy is a misnomer that connotes an absence. Fallow challenges that connotation. Allowing one plot to play a different role than its neighboring space benefits both. But it requires patience. As active sites of agricultural and biological processes, fallow fields are defined by their contribution to overall farming operations by enhancing fertile soil, helping biomass accumulation, and managing weeds. They too are simultaneously social and environmental. They organize human practices and separate environmental (agricultural) spaces.

Leaving fields fallow is part of longstanding practice. An ancient directive in a Sumerian agricultural guide, the *Farmer's Instructions*, "opens with 40 lines on the renewed cropping of fallow land . . . [making] reference to the common practice of leaving arable fields unseeded after plowing for a period of time in order to recover natural fertility on alternate years."[5] Biblical strictures also dictated a Sabbath for the soil, by leaving a field uncultivated every seventh year.[6] This credo embedded religious codes of conduct into agricultural codes of cultivation. In the ancient two-field system, where one field was cultivated and one left fallow, the restorative land rotated every two years rather than awaiting the biblical seven. Such a "biannual fallow period and pastoral animal herding [which enriched soil with organic manure] became predominant in the temperate regions beginning in antiquity."[7] The three-field system emerged at the end of the first millennium. This meant that a field was planted in fall, again in spring, and left fallow in summer, or some variation thereof. Or it could also mean a field was rotated every three years. Some time later, in the American colonial period, it was a "common practice of leaving land fallow for 20 years" for tobacco farmers in the Chesapeake region. Two, three, seven, or 20, all fallows stipulate patience and a particular timescale.[8]

Despite the mistaken view that fallow fields imply inactivity, they are in practice a flourishing and healthy part of a broader agrarian ecology. Cole's contemporary, Thoreau, objected to this misunderstanding too. Granted, as a surveyor he measured more than just fallow fields, so his were observations of public space writ large. But the concern over a misperception of emptiness and absence bothered him just the same. "Between those lines indicating roads," he wrote in his journal about a mapping job, "is a plain blank space in the form of a square or triangle or polygon or segment of a circle, and there is naught to distinguish this from another area of similar size and form." Yet, as historian Daegan Miller writes, "These blank spaces irritated Thoreau, because they weren't, in fact, blank." As opposed to maps of old that denoted where there may be monsters, Thoreau understood that an economically utilitarian view saw absence where the land was always full.[9]

Considering fallow as dormant echoes the misinterpretation in Auden's famous eulogy for Yeats that "poetry makes nothing happen." It takes a kind of invisible work to hold and manage things, Auden suggests, to seem as if "nothing" is happening. Later in the same poem he notes that poetry survives and builds meaning, that it is "a way of happening" as opposed to a tool whose actions are visible, materially present. Survival takes time. "Nothing" may look like an absence, but Auden's point is that poetry's "nothing"—its lack of immediacy—offers a means to work over time. Fallow too takes time. Fallow makes fertility happen.

The fallow field is comparable to the fence or wall on the level of temporal change. The two are comparable in another way. If the old stone wall is the long-term outcome of an annual process, of the earth heaving stones to its surface, year after year, the wall also manifests a relationship of respiration from underneath to aboveground. The upward movement of the rocks makes a wall possible. Fallow, too, is the outcome of annual processes of nitrogen exchange between the air and grasses. "During a period of fallow, soil bacteria will convert atmospheric nitrogen into soil nitrogen, leaving new reserves for the next crop."[10] In this way, fallow manifests a relationship of respiration from the sky above to the ground below. Nitrogen in the atmosphere moves downward to be grabbed by bacteria in the roots of grasses that return it to the soil.

The patience required by fallow is difficult to hold in our accelerated world. Because knowledge systems are similarly built through long-term experience, they too take

5
Christopher Isett and Stephen Miller, *The Social History of Agriculture: From the Origins to the Current Crisis* (Lanham, MD: Rowman & Littlefield, 2016), 15.

6
Lv. 25:4.

7
Marcel Mazoyer and Laurence Roudart, *A History of World Agriculture: From the Neolithic Age to the Current Crisis*, trans. James H. Membrez (New York: Monthly Review Press, 2006), 219.

8
Isett and Miller, *The Social History of Agriculture*, 160. See also H. S. A. Fox, "The Alleged Transformation from Two-Field to Three-Field Systems in Medieval England," *The Economic History Review* 39 (1986): 526–48; Joseph Gies and Francis Gies, *Cathedral, Forge, and Waterwheel: Technology and Invention in the Middle Ages* (New York: Harper Perennial, 1995).

9
Thoreau, quoted in Daegan Miller, *This Radical Land: A Natural History of American Dissent* (Chicago: University of Chicago Press, 2017), 37. Not incidentally, the economic utilitarian view stemming from a Lockean concept of use-value informed the perspective that Native lands were empty and ready for settlement. See for example Mark Spence, *Dispossessing the Wilderness: Indian Removal and the Making of the National Parks* (Oxford: Oxford University Press, 1999).

10
Mark Overton, *Agricultural Revolution in England, 1500–1850* (Cambridge: Cambridge University Press, 1996), 17.

time. Before the introduction of a science of agriculture in the 19th century, farmers and agrarian people understood the ways in which fields gained fertility through the kinds of crops they planted and how they amended the soil with animal and mineral manures. These ways of knowing soil fertility were built from the political virtues of agricultural lives and community structures. They were, that is, equally social and environmental processes. Developments in fertilization technique followed from these practices, aiding the cultivation of community and land. But soon agricultural chemistry offered a shortcut. It took less time.[11]

This was neither good nor bad, but it was consequential. The new agricultural technology cleaved the environmental from the social, where the functional demands of soil fertility were aimed very directly at the soil, and did not address the agrarian livelihoods associated with its management. It challenged the prominence of fallow fields with a more utilitarian work-around, eschewing generational patterns of cultivation, field rotation, and soil management. Of course, this was a tendency, not absolute. Organic farming, permaculture, and other methods of soil amendment remain in use today, particularly with strengthening awareness of the ecological exploitation of industrial agriculture. In any case, the perception that fallow makes nothing happen became widespread during the age of modern agricultural science. It was wasteful, underutilized. These descriptors follow from a commitment to intensive rather than extensive agriculture. With limited arable land, one must find different ways to regenerate the soil. Chemical fertilizers, pesticides, herbicides, and the like have met this challenge for the past century and a half. Because we do not have enough time for fallow. We are too busy. There is not enough space—so the argument goes.

The modern notion that fallow is defined by inactivity is thus the product of a historical process, one too long to describe fully here. And more critically, the historically produced view of fallow as absence or idleness is not one we have to perpetuate. Goldsworthy does not. Designers need not either.

What, then, holds fence and fallow together? Both are examples of technologies operating with attention to temporal and spatial scales. And they are bound together by their agricultural function, working in tandem. The fence makes the field.

There is a more actionable part, too. Fence and fallow field thrive with long-term maintenance, which parallels the temporal and spatial dimensions of agriculture. As a model for land management, they offer a means to consider the value of nonagricultural space as well: how it is conceived and organized for a purported use or imperceptible (seemingly dormant) function.

An emerging field in technology studies helps this cause. Rather than innovation and invention (making things happen in the dominant industrial sense), it demands greater attention to maintenance and management. The principle observation from that field is that a great majority of technological work throughout history, and today, is the too-often concealed labor of engineers, practitioners, users, and everyday citizens in simply keeping things going. The time needed to create and envision a new approach to a problem—whether a device, roadway, network, or city—pales in comparison to the amount of work required to build, implement, manage, and maintain it for any length of time.[12]

The notion of keeping things going is of course well known as underpinning modern narratives of sustainability. But as a principle of activity rather than a purely ecological ethos, scholars too should promote a maintenance-focused view. Sociologists, for example, speak of a theory of repair in social life, where repair is another metaphor for maintenance. Rather than the utilitarian sense of fixing something, in its theoretical deployment repair is "a process of maintaining social order," as Chris Henke writes, and "social order is a practical everyday accomplishment, negotiated over and over again."[13] We need not leave the land to think about maintenance in this way. Animal husbandry—managing livestock and farm animals—does the same work. Historian Brian Donahue describes it as "the careful balance and integration of diverse elements across a varied and difficult landscape."[14] The key terms here are active: care, balance, process, negotiation.

For an infrastructural analogy, consider the barn as it is used. That use holds repair, maintenance, husbandry, and sustainability together. Old barns that are neglected fall into disrepair after a few seasons, with rotting boards, loosening nails, and sinking roofs. An in-use barn benefits from constant traffic and necessary upkeep: modulated airflow, reinforced joinery, re-pounded nails, smoothed edges, and other minor tunings that result from sustained use. Rather than any large restoration efforts, a barn in use benefits from often unseen or unaccounted for daily tinkering, understood as a practice of everyday life. Its maintenance plan is neither onerous nor intensive, but attentive and consistent.

While there is no lack of ways to think about process-driven or ongoing activity, organizers and designers

11
Benjamin R. Cohen, *Notes from the Ground: Science, Soil & Society in the American Countryside* (New Haven, CT: Yale University Press, 2009).

12
David Edge, *The Shock of the Old: Technology and Global History since 1900* (Cambridge: Cambridge University Press, 2007); Andrew Russell and Lee Vinsel, "Hail the Maintainers," *Aeon*, April 7, 2016, https://aeon.co/essays/innovation-is-overvalued-maintenance-often-matters-more; Andrew Russell and Lee Vinsel, "Making Maintainers: Engineering Education and the Ethics of Care," in *The Innovator Imperative*, ed. Matt Wisnioski, Eric Hintz, and Marie Stettler Klein (Cambridge, MA: MIT Press, forthcoming); Patrick McCray, "It's Not All Lightbulbs," *Aeon*, October 12, 2016, https://aeon.co/essays/most-of-the-time-innovators-don-t-move-fast-and-break-things.

13
Chris Henke, *Cultivating Science, Harvesting Power: Science and Industrial Agriculture in California* (Cambridge, MA: MIT Press, 2008), 10.

14
Brian Donahue, *The Great Meadow: Farmers and the Land in Colonial Concord* (New Haven, CT: Yale University Press, 2004), xv.

struggle to enact these concepts in practice, particularly as planners, policy-makers, and reporters urge them on to the allure of the new. Yet constant, subtle attention is what matters most.

Here, scholarship on maintenance and management is helpful. In rejecting innovation's overzealous mantra, historians Andrew Russell and Lee Vinsel argue that "the most unappreciated and undervalued forms of technological labor are also the most ordinary: those who repair and maintain technologies that already exist, that were 'innovated' long ago." Looking at infrastructure or "old, existing things rather than novel ones reminds us of the absolute centrality of the work that goes into keeping the entire world going."[15]

This view is significant for both fence and fallow. What we need today is the conceptual ability to pursue designs that are temporally attentive and generative, not inactive. Like Goldsworthy's *Storm King Wall*, the fallow/non-fallow relationship reveals the flow, lifecycle, and ephemeral scale of artificial separation. Fallow fields can operate according to 2-, 3-, 7-, or 20-year cycles, but they continuously operate whether we take notice or not. Tactically, identifying spaces to set apart in the short term can help spaces to be cultivated more actively. The difference is in degree of activity, not presence or absence. And over the long term, public spaces can benefit from these principles as much as agricultural ones. Fallow makes things happen.

15
Russell and Vinsel, "Hail the Maintainers." Notably, this kind of endless and underappreciated daily work often has a gendered dimension. The unpaid labor of household management, for example, has left women out of the history of technological development for centuries. And emotional labor, volunteer labor, and community philanthropy have traditionally weighed more heavily on women than on men. For an earlier study of this subject, see Arlie Hochschild, *The Managed Heart: Commercialization of Human Feeling* (Berkeley: University of California Press, [1983] 2012).

From Fallows to Permaculture: The City as a Special Landscape

THOMAS SIEVERTS

The Ambivalence of the Term

The term *brache*, the German language equivalent of "fallow," is ambivalent: on the one hand, it indicates a leftover, characterized by idleness, emptiness, negligence, and destruction. It is regarded as an unwanted lesion in the urban fabric that needs to be mended. In many cases, this form of fallow is caused by former use, and requires constructive rehabilitation. At first, this fallow has a negative connotation.

On the other hand, fallow is a matter of care. The practice originated in the era of traditional farming, when a field was left idle for one or more years of cultivation. The field needed "sleep," because it was exhausted and needed to recover. In the soil, with time, myriad bacteria work to restore fertility. During this idle sleep, the farmer may seed certain plants that help improve fertility when ploughed into the soil. In some cases these intermediate plants and their flowers are of great beauty. This kind of fallow is not a passive matter, but an active one, even if hardly visible. Here fallow has a positive and productive connotation.

It might be useful to apply both connotations of fallow, the negative and the positive, to the city in a metaphorical way. This framing could be used to characterize the handling of a negative leftover of the Industrial Revolution, as a result of ruthless exploitation, and to reflect on the potentially constructive role of fallow in active city development.

In the German language, the terms *brache* (fallow) and *bauen* (to build) correspond to the contrasting verbs *brachfallen* (to become fallow) and *anbauen* (to cultivate), respectively. However, *brache* has a slightly different connotation than does "fallow" in American English. This nuance influences the reflections that follow, extending the metaphor to also elicit subtle romantic and poetic connotations.

The Fallow of Exploitation

To illustrate the handling of an exploited fallow, I will reflect on my experience with the *Internationale Bauausstellung Emscher Park* (IBA Emscher Park) from 1989 to 1999 in the Ruhr region of North Rhine-Westphalia, Germany. The situation of industrial decay and dereliction had left behind destroyed soils, poisoned landscapes, and dangerous surfaces. These fallows were unused for a decade or more, and needed a period of repair and active restoration before they could be developed again.

The IBA Emscher Park project handled fallows on a large scale, which had also been deeply exploited. The land had lost its productivity through injury from a heavily industrial past. This loss of productivity can perhaps be compared to the farmland's loss of fertility, and the need of treatment in the form of a "recovering sleep." But these similarities should be considered carefully, lest they transgress the limit of a productive comparability.

For example, the injuries treated at IBA Emscher Park were of different character, encompassing both "physical, material" and "spiritual, symbolic" injuries. The former included destruction, contamination, poisoning, and general instability of the site. Of equal importance, however, were the latter; evident in how the positive connotation, image, and "aura" of the place had simply been devastated. This spiritual destruction was caused by bad memories of dangerous and unjust working conditions, by the exclusion of ordinary people, and by loss of life. As a result of these various injuries, a differentiated "healing process" was required, with a program of more than technical improvement. Such complex fallows need special care and attention, for example, by way of historical analysis conducted through interviews with people once employed on site, and through keen observation of its present informal, sometimes illegal patterns of use. This form of care is also known as "deep understanding."

Westpark Bochum (1995–2010)

The development process of the Westpark in Bochum, Germany, is a useful case study of a complex fallow, with many typical features such as traces of industry, soil contamination, and a rich ruderal vegetation.[1]

This fallow was the site of one of the oldest steelworks in the Ruhr region, in operation from 1850 to 1985. When the steelwork first opened it was situated far outside the small town of Bochum, which had about 4,000 inhabitants. By the time it closed 130 years later, it was surrounded by a city with a population of 300,000.[2] The steelworks itself constituted a "forbidden city" within Bochum, fortified by a high brick wall that was inaccessible to ordinary citizens. Now located in a central position in the city, the site had been deemed unsuitable for heavy industry. To attract modern service industries to the area instead, a decision was made to redevelop the steelworks as a park.

The status quo condition of the site, however, was unsuitable for immediate use as a recreational area. When commissioned to design the park, our office found an extensive abandoned and fallowed site of nearly 20 hectares that had been forgotten by most people, because it was inaccessible for so long. The only remaining structure was an immense industrial building, the *Jahrhunderthalle*. Furthermore, the entirety of the fallow—soils, water, vegetation, structures—was contaminated. Before any kind of reuse, there would need to be a complex process to restore its ecological, cultural, and (ultimately) economic productivity.

Treating the physical injuries to the site was an intricate task. Rainwater was collected in separate basins, so as not to poison the groundwater through soil infiltration. Highly toxic pockets of land were packed and isolated in clay and "buried" at safe depths. The topography of the site had been shaped by heavy industrial use over a long period of time, resulting in dramatic artificial contours, many of which were physically unstable and in need of bracing by new constructions. Not all these changes were negative, however. In only a decade of idleness, a remarkable but vulnerable ruderal birch tree woodland had grown up, which required careful cultivation. So before beginning work on the park, the fallow was partly converted into a covered and contained toxic site with rainwater storage and a cultivated forest. All of these actions were later integrated as unique features of the park, eventually contributing to its special character.

But these rehabilitation activities concerned only the site's physical qualities. The treatment of its spiritual and symbolic injuries was of a different nature altogether.

1
Karl Ganser, Tom Sieverts, and Jens Trautmann, *Westpark Bochum: Geschichte und Geschichten* (Essen: Klartext Verlag, 2007).

2
Helga Grebing, "Die Geschichte des Bochumer Vereins," in *Industrielandschaft: Das Bochum Projekt* (Darmstadt: Kunsthalle Darmstadt/Kunstverein Darmstadt, 1992), 11–22.

Through conversations with former employees of the steelworks and their families, we soon understood the difficult history of dangerous working conditions and the tragic accidents that also weighed heavily on the fallow. And we grasped the sense of alienation felt towards the area, where limited access was granted to only those facilities where the former employees had worked, if they were allowed to see anything at all.

After these experiences it seemed necessary to find a deeper understanding of the fallow as described above.[3] Through actively engaging the history of the site we became involved with the fallow intellectually, as well as sensorially, to better acquaint ourselves with the atmosphere, smell, sound, and other immaterial qualities. We tried to track what was happening, socially, through the (excluded) external community (i. e., children, teens, tramps, young couples) already creeping through cracks in the walls by mapping their trails and secret gathering places as indicators of certain site qualities.

In the final phase of exploring the fallow, a group of art students under the guidance of Werner Durth came to work on site. They organized an exhibition of their installations, drawings, and paintings in the *Jahrhunderthalle* and invited the neighborhood to the opening.[4] For most, it was the first ever visit to the forbidden city. This artistic event was followed by classical music and dance performances in the *Jahrhunderthalle*.

These cultural events began the process of converting the bad image associated with the site into a more positive one, by meaningfully connecting the deserted fallow to forms of beauty, culture, and social celebration. As the park's designers, we exaggerated this change into a mythological transformation: The god of the blacksmiths and iron founders, Vulcanus, had departed, and elves began to inhabit the new woods until the goddess of the arts, theater, dance, and music, Thalia, arrived. Hermes, the god of commerce, was already waiting outside. Finally, the fallow was ripe to begin a new life.

The Fallow of Productive Transition

If humankind is to survive, the time of ruthless exploitation, of looting and destroying nature, must come to an end. Consequently, urban design must be directed towards a cultural–economic transition, integrated with nature. To work in this context, the designer must conceive of the built environment as neither static nor fixed, but in a continuous process of transformation.

When considering city development as a sequence of different stages, the notion of the fallow and its positive connotations plays a strategic central role.

In each sequence of transformation, the fallow forms both the end and the beginning of a stage. It is the "degree zero" of this sequential transition. Thus, the fallow is a critical phase, during which the content and direction of development may change. It is a soft, sensitive, and vulnerable phase which needs special attention and care.

Traditionally, urban fallows served certain intermediate uses: the circus constructed its tent there for several weeks, a special market might occupy the empty space for a few days, or a festival might be staged there for a weekend. Today, instead of regarding fallows as idle time and space which is easily abandoned, they should be a matter of careful design and consideration as intermediate spaces of freedom, play, and experimentation.

This conception of fallow could be intensified and developed further. Both after the end of a stage of commercial use and before the start of a new one, a "planned fallow" could systematically serve as an opportunity for intermediate uses that are too weak economically to pay profitable rents, but nevertheless contribute to the agility of the city, its vitality and variety. Such a fallow could contribute to the city's short-term adaptability, offering space for revisable experiments and becoming a test field for the future. In certain aspects, the capacity of such site-improving intermediate uses could perhaps be compared to the green fertilizing of the fallow on the farm.

In this context, the fallow could become more than the degree zero between two development stages of the built environment. For example, it might provide a certain amount of time for the built environment to reconnect with the realm of nature through a piece of rich ruderal vegetation. Consequently, the fallow has the potential to play a significant role in the age-old battle between the city and nature.

Ultimately, it will be necessary to find ways to organize and realize such intermediate activities of experimentation and natural restoration, which neither fit the scheme of conventionally capitalist real estate markets nor the neat bureaucracy of administrative technocrats.

3
Thomas Sieverts, "The Notion of Deep Understanding" in *Planning, Theory, and Practice*, 11.4 (December 2010): 597–619.

4
Dorit Marhenke, ed., *Industrielandschaft: Das Bochum Projekt* (Darmstadt: Kunsthalle Darmstadt/Kunstverein Darmstadt, 1992).

The City as Special Landscape

There is a fundamental question behind the term "fallow" when used in relation to urban development as described above. Will fallow continue to be an adequate metaphor, characterizing an important strategic phase in the process of development? Or will it be necessary to build the city without producing fallows?

Perhaps the growth of humankind and the doubling population will force us to minimize energy consumption and further exploitation of the earth, so as not to destroy human life utterly.[5] In other words, it may soon be necessary to work within a built city structure that will never disappear completely, but will remain in a state of permanent transition. Under these conditions, a permanent city would consist of elements of varied lifetimes; for example, preexisting infrastructure could be used to support lighter and softer elements that can be exchanged and recycled in different cycles. This kind of permanence allows periodic and gradual adaption to new demands, without risking disappearance.[6]

Furthermore, in the Anthropocene era, the categorical differences between culture and nature, between building and landscape, will become more and more blurred, as there will be no more nature that has not been deeply transformed by humankind. Here I am tempted to interpret the future permanent city as a new kind of urban landscape, bridging the old hostile conflict between city and nature.

At present, the conflict between city and landscape in Germany is managed by the legal planning tool known as *Ausgleichsfläche*, a space purposely left to nature to compensate for destructive building activities. To some extent it recalls the *Ablasshandel*, or the selling of indulgences during the Middle Ages, when the Catholic Church accepted monetary compensation in exchange for the relief of sins, and a clear conscience.

While the *Ausgleichsfläche* may be necessary for the time being, it cannot be the final solution to the city-nature conflict. Seen from a global dimension—considering how many cities will double in the next decades, thus chiefly producing and chiefly suffering from climate change—cities must transform to actively mitigate global warming and minimize ecological exploitation. They must become an integral part of a new conception of "nature," that is, of landscape.[7]

Perhaps future cities will be seen as the most important new man-made mineral-geological formations,[8] contributing to the character of the Anthropocene by providing habitats for human and nonhuman life.[9] Already today the number and variety of species in the city—both flora and fauna—is much more distinctive than in the surrounding industrialized agricultural landscape.[10] For certain species the contemporary city provides better living conditions than an exploited natural environment.[11]

The merging of city and nature may also be a sign of the weakening categorical differences between nature and the man-made in the Anthropocene era: even *Homo sapiens* with big brains are nevertheless poor creatures, very much dependent on nature, who can only manipulate it favorably to a certain limit.

In the city, today, one can typically find: fugitive flora and fauna from industrialized agricultural landscapes; many well-structured urban biotopes; natural, if poor, soils nevertheless dense with flowers, insects, and beehives; and finally, a warm urban microclimate that serves as a laboratory for a future of climate change. It may not be absurd to view the city as a special type of landscape, even a kind of oasis or Noah's Ark in a desert of industrialized landscapes. Furthermore, the city reflects the most basic feature of the Anthropocene era: the anthropogenic character of significant parts of the earth's surface.

The densely packed global city could thus perhaps be conceived as a "porous rocky landscape" containing both habitats for man, plants, and animals—with building roofs supporting both gardens and wilderness, and walls housing plants, insects, and birds. In various attempts to establish new branches of, for example, "Animal-Aided Design" (AAD) and others, complementary approaches to urban design are already emerging that take the needs of nonhuman nature into consideration.[12]

Conceived as a special landscape, such a city would develop no longer through linear sequences of gradual aging, falling into and out of a fallow state, but rather through countless different interrelated lifecycles that would amount to a continuous transformation. This kind of city would share some characteristics of a permaculture—its buildings would be kept in use beyond the one or two generations common today, but for 100 years or more,

5
Dimitri Zenghelis and Nicholas Stern, "This Is Humankind's 'Great Urbanization': We Must Do It Right, or the Planet Will Pay," *Guardian*, November 8, 2016, https://www.theguardian.com/cities/2016/nov/08/mankind-great-urbanisation-era-act-now-planet-pay.

6
N. John Habraken, *Supports: An Alternative to Mass Housing*, trans. B. Valkenburg (London: Architectural Press, 1972).

7
Thomas Sieverts, *Zwischenstadt: Zwischen Ort und Welt, Raum und Zeit, Stadt und Land* (Basel: Birkhäuser, 1997), 51, 68.

8
Undine Giseke, *Gottfried Semper Architekturpreis: Undine Giseke* (Dresden: Sächsische Akademie der Künste, 2016), 12–17.

9
P. J. Crutzen, Mike Davis, Michael D. Mastrandrea, Stephan H. Schneider, Peter Sloterdijk, *Das Raumschiff Erde hat keinen Notausgang* (Berlin: Suhrkamp, 2011); Jens Kersten, "Das Anthropozän-Konzept," *Rechtswissenschaft* 5.3 (2014): 378–414.

10
Herbert Sukopp, ed., *Stadtökologie: Am Beispiel Berlin* (Berlin: Dietrich Reimer, 1990).

11
Josef H. Reicholf, *Stadtnatur: Eine neue Heimat für Tiere und Pflanzen* (Munich: Oekom Verlag, 2007).

as was typical historically, to reduce gray energy and the exploitation of natural resources.[13]

In this context new buildings must no longer be designed for a specific function, but must be made fit for continuous adaptation to ever changing demands. Buildings should thus be composed of elements with different lifetimes. To make another daring comparison, such a building should behave like an organism that renews certain organ systems, like skin, according to short intervals, while others like the bones of the skeleton have to last a lifetime.

In the course of different city life cycles, the traditional fallow will not disappear altogether, though it will likely change its character. Perhaps the common fallow will dissolve into those elements of the built environment programmed to transition to another element, with another use and another function, without necessarily becoming a fallow in the traditional sense.

Reflecting on the city as a permaculture maintains a metaphorical connection to the realm of agricultural production. Could the term "permaculture" thus possibly be supplementary to "fallow" as a means of stimulating new imaginaries of the urban environment? We must think of the city as a special landscape—as a habitat for both human and nonhuman life in non-exploitative form—that will not destroy our planet, but enhance it materially and spiritually.

12
Thomas E. Hauck and Wolfgang W. Weisser, *AAD: Animal Aided Design* (Freising: TU München/Universität Kassel, 2016).

13
"Gray energy" refers to the energy invested in a building's production, in terms of both materials and construction.

Dormant Dumps vs. Leaky Landfills: An Examination of Visual Representations of the Great Pacific Garbage Patch

NICOLE BENNETT

The National Oceanic and Atmospheric Administration (NOAA) held their first Marine Debris calendar art contest during the 2012–13 scholastic year, when over 600 elementary and middle school students from 21 states submitted artwork to be published in NOAA's 2014 calendar. Of the 13 winners chosen, many illustrated sea animals threatened by marine debris, and featured calls for action foregrounding contaminated scenery. The submission of Aleena Fayaz stood apart from these winners. While it depicts a sea animal (a turtle) and a directive ("Keep the sea free of debris!"), Aleena's artwork displays an apprehension of marine pollution that differed from the imagination of her contest peers. Against a simple white background, she drew two turtles separated by a wiggly blue line. On the right is a turtle seen from the outside, which, unlike the other submissions, swims unobstructed in a light blue ocean. On the left, the debris that seemed to be missing from Aleena's ocean appears. Inside the body of the turtle, she illustrates the plastic pollution that other students depicted external to the animals, floating in the ocean itself: plastic bags, aluminum cans, fishing nets, and other unidentifiable shapes clearly meant to convey a profusion of trash within an otherwise normal-looking sea creature.

Surprisingly, Aleena's drawing bears a striking resemblance to the cover artwork for the first edition of Captain Charles Moore's *Plastic Ocean* (2011). Moore, a chemistry-trained oceanographer and founder of the marine research and education organization Algalita, is popularly known as the discoverer of the Great Pacific Garbage Patch.[1] Moore's 2011 book features the outline of a fish against a plain white background. Filling in the outline is a colorful textural layer that is in fact a detail from an overhead view of plastic waste littering what appears to be a shoreline. Dozens of beverage bottles and

Aleena Fayaz's winning submission to the 2014 NOAA "Keep the Sea Free of Debris" calendar art contest.

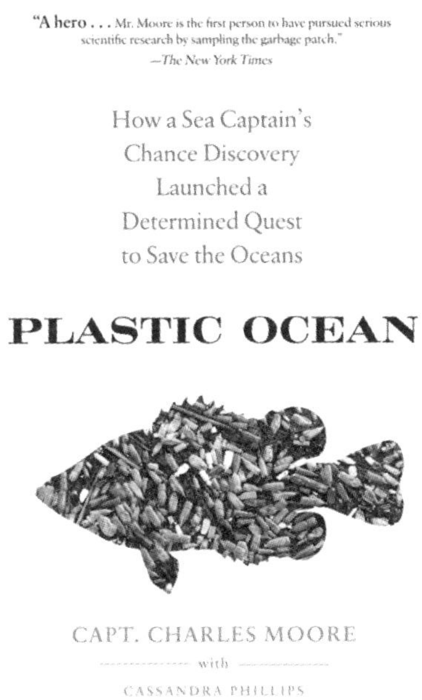

Plastic Ocean. Jacket design by Andrea Ho.

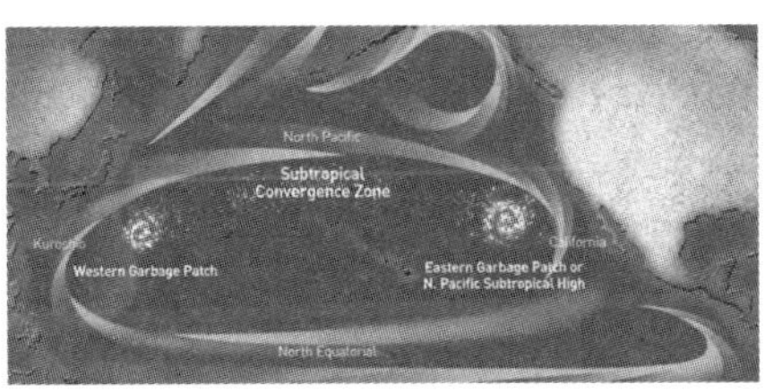

Illustration of the Great Pacific Garbage Patch by the NOAA Marine Debris Program.

other unidentifiable pieces of plastic intermingle with slim fragments of driftwood. The "plastic ocean" that Moore describes in his book is here depicted as a plastic-packed marine animal.

The submissions to the NOAA Marine Debris calendar contest and the cover of Moore's book succinctly outline two distinct yet parallel trends in the visual representation of ocean pollution. In the first, waste remains on the outside; it is easily visible drifting in ocean waters or blanketing coastlines. And in the other, waste is harder to see. Instead of lingering among marine creatures, the pollution is *inside* them. Taking these trends as a starting point, this paper critically examines popular visual representations of the Great Pacific Garbage Patch. In particular, through an illustration of the Great Pacific Garbage Patch produced by NOAA's Marine Debris Program and through a series of photographs of decaying albatross corpses in the northwestern Hawaiian Islands. However disparate, by bringing these widely circulated works together this paper will analyze the techniques through which artists and institutions attempt to visualize the Great Pacific Garbage Patch. Focusing on the spatial and temporal scales in these representations shows how they either illuminate or misinterpret the Great Pacific Garbage Patch. Finally, consideration is given to the ethical imperative at work in these pictures, and how effectively (or not) it generates an ecological consciousness in the viewer.

Failure to Notice: An Abbreviated History of the Great Pacific Garbage Patch

Though the Great Pacific Garbage Patch has been hyped recently, oceanic plastic pollution was first discovered in the northern Atlantic in 1972. In an article published in *Science*, Edward J. Carpenter and K. L. Smith describe and quantify the presence of plastic debris across a distance of 1300 km in an ocean gyre east of the continental United States. Toward the conclusion, they write: "The incorporation of PCB's [polychlorinated biphenyls] by marine organisms is possible."[2] Carpenter and Smith not only noted plastic pollution, but also correctly predicted it would become a pervasive problem both in the ocean and inside the bodies of marine animals.

At the time, Carpenter and Smith's essay did not generate any discernable interest. Sustained attention was not focused on oceanic plastic pollution until 1997, when Captain Charles Moore unexpectedly encountered plastic

1
An accumulation of widely dispersed, mostly plastic debris that has been captured in giant, oceanic gyres, the Great Pacific Garbage Patch is actually the name for two garbage patches found in the northern Pacific Ocean. Designated as the East and West Garbage Patches, these two zones and the area between them, known as the Subtropical Convergence Zone, together make up what is more commonly referred to as the Great Pacific Garbage Patch. Although some have credited Moore with naming the garbage patch, he attributes the name to Curtis Ebbesmeyer. See: Captain Charles Moore and Cassandra Phillips, *Plastic Ocean: How a Sea Captain's Chance Discovery Launched a Determined Quest to Save the Oceans* (New York: Avery, 2011), 53.

debris in the northern Pacific Ocean while sailing from Hawaii to Santa Barbara, California. Though scientifically trained, Moore had no idea that plastic could be found so far out at sea. Shortly after returning to California, he petitioned the board of directors of his nonprofit foundation, Algalita, to support a research mission with the aim of "verifying and quantifying the presence of plastics" in the northern Pacific,[3] resuming Carpenter and Smith's survey 25 years later.

Algalita's first research mission departed in August 1999. Since 2000, the foundation has sponsored biennial gyre research expeditions through the present day.[4] Despite growing scientific attention on plastic pollution in the Pacific Ocean, mainstream media outlets were slow to address the issue. Only when Kenneth Weiss and Usha Lee McFarling published the five-part series "Altered Oceans" in the *Los Angeles Times* in 2006 did the existence of the Great Pacific Garbage Patch seem to strike a chord with the general public[5]—after which the number of newspaper articles and television features on the subject of oceanic debris in general and the Great Pacific Garbage Patch specifically increased significantly.

The Dormant Dump: Imaging the Great Pacific Garbage Patch

As the public became increasingly interested in marine pollution, the US government created an entity to study it. In 2006, Congress authorized NOAA's Marine Debris Program (MDP). In addition to sponsoring elementary and middle school art contests, the MDP published on its website its own visualization of the Great Pacific Garbage Patch. Zoomed out to a hemispheric scale, the image illustrates the ocean currents that surround the Western and Eastern Garbage Patches as well as the Subtropical Convergence Zone. Oceanic debris is depicted as tiny, colored pigment that accumulates in specific areas on the map. The patches are seen as bright spirals containing many colorful pigments, while the convergence zone appears more like loose confetti strewn across the mid-Pacific. The image does well to give the viewer a sense of the approximate geographic location of the Western and Eastern Garbage Patches and the Subtropical Convergence Zone. Beyond providing an awareness of the broadly affected area, however, the MDP illustration is incredibly misleading.

By producing an image in which the Great Pacific Garbage Patch is distinctly located, static, and effortlessly visible (even from a great distance), the MDP depiction reinforces entrenched and troublesome misunderstandings about how an oceanic garbage patch in fact behaves.[6] One could easily presume a garbage patch to be a dormant dump rather than a dynamic entity. And representing debris as tiny, colored dots scattered over a deep blue background gives the impression that marine pollution simply hovers on the surface of the Pacific Ocean.[7] In reality, much of the plastic pollution has either sunk to the ocean floor or floats just below the surface.[8] Although the colorful swirls of debris and the sweeping lines indicating ocean currents imply motion, the MDP image remains static. Without proper context, a viewer might assume the Great Pacific Garbage Patch to be fixed in remote areas of the ocean, thus posing little danger to humans and wildlife. Yet in reality, ocean debris is constantly on the move and can even wash up on coastal shores.[9] Finally, because the MDP image shows the entire northern Pacific, it appears as if taken from outer space, although the Great Pacific Garbage Patch cannot actually be seen from the stratosphere. For reasons outlined above (constant circulation and subsurface position), satellite imaging is currently impossible. Finally, while it is possible to find larger plastic items, most debris consists of microplastics which, if seen at all, appear more like a filmy ocean soup than an isolated patch of garbage.[10]

Rather than highlighting the pernicious environmental problem of oceanic pollution, the MDP image instead exposes the spatiotemporal challenges to any visual representation of the Great Pacific Garbage Patch. Spatiality plays an important role, as the patch is not only immense, but also widely dispersed and composed of microplastics. For this reason, the question of scale is crucial; zooming too far out essentially makes the patch invisible, while zooming too far in fails to give an adequate sense of its size. Temporality is also a problem with visual representation, especially through static images. Both eastern and western portions of the Great Pacific Garbage Patch constantly swirl with ocean currents, and the entire

2
Edward J. Carpenter and K. L. Smith, "Plastics on the Sargasso Sea Surface," *Science* 175 (1972): 1240–41.

3
Moore, *Plastic Ocean*, 19.

4
Except the years 2004 and 2013.

5
Weiss, McFarling, and Rick Loomis earned the 2007 Pulitzer Prize for Explanatory Reporting for the "Altered Oceans" series.

6
Moore also suggests that the name itself leads to misconceptions: "Let it be said straight up that what we came upon was *not* a mountain of trash, an island of trash, a raft of trash, or a swirling vortex of trash—all media concocted embellishments of the truth." Moore, *Plastic Ocean*, 4.

7
Perpetuating one of the most common misunderstandings about the Great Pacific Garbage Patch, many popular photographs show boats floating through blankets of aquatically suspended trash. These images actually depict waters that are located much closer to land. Most famous, perhaps, is the photo of a man canoeing through the trash-strewn waters of Manila Bay.

8
Merel Kooi et al. "The Effect of Particle Properties on the Depth Profile of Buoyant Plastics in the Ocean," *Scientific Reports*, 6 (October 2016): www.nature.com/articles/srep33882.

garbage patch can move longitudinally depending on climate phenomena such as El Niño.[11] Varying with time and according to weather patterns, currents, and volume of debris, plastic pollution does not stay in the same place even as it accumulates. Imaging the Great Pacific Garbage Patch is like trying to photograph a moving target that assembles and dissipates in different places at different times. It is therefore inaccurate, and perhaps even harmful, to imagine the Great Pacific Garbage Patch as a static, inactive area where our waste remains in its place.

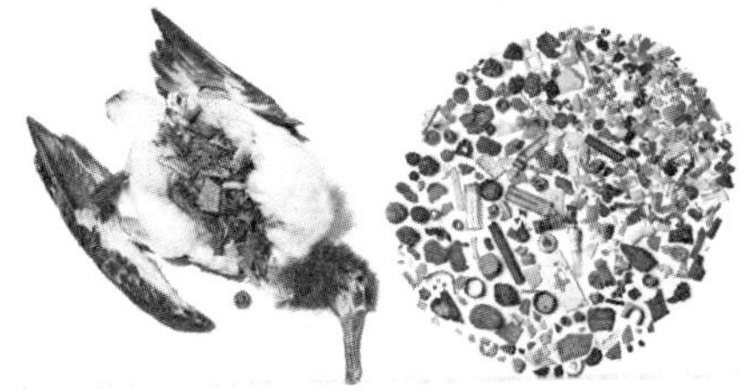

Susan Middleton's photographs of the Shed Bird autopsy.

Leaky Landfills: The Albatross Corpse as Environmental Allegory

In contrast to the MDP image, photographic representations of the Great Pacific Garbage Patch opt for a much closer view. Among these, the albatross has frequently served as a focal point for illustrating plastics pollution. In the same way that polar bears have come to serve as symbols of climate change, now albatrosses, too, figure as harbingers of troubling environmental degradation. The albatross occupies this central role principally because the birds have begun to feed on plastics from the Great Pacific Garbage Patch.[12] As essentially marathon runners of the avian family, albatrosses fly impressively long distances out to sea to procure food for themselves and their children. Besides plastics, the northern Pacific Ocean gyres and convergence zone accumulate marine life such as krill, octopus, sardines, and fish eggs, all of which are central to the albatross diet. The birds mistake brightly colored items—bottle caps, disposable lighters, shotgun shells—for their typical seafood staples, and bring the plastic debris back to breeding grounds such as the northwestern Hawaiian Islands, to feed to their offspring.[13]

Photographers have exposed the plastic-filled stomachs of albatrosses for at least 15 years. *Plastic Ocean* contains two images (c. 2002), credited to Cynthia Vanderlip, of albatross corpses in advanced stages of decay with a profusion of plastic scraps, mostly bottle caps, trapped within their rib cages. In October 2005, *National Geographic* published photographs taken by Susan Middleton and David Liittschwager in the northwestern Hawaiian Islands. One depicts a recently deceased adolescent Laysan albatross ("Shed Bird") whose stomach has been cut open to reveal an abundance of plastic debris. A second shows each piece of plastic that Middleton meticulously removed from the bird's stomach and arranged into an egg shape. The same year, the National Geographic Society published *Archipelago: Portraits of Life in the World's Most Remote Island Sanctuary* (2005). The coffee-table book contains essays by Middleton and Liittschwager about their journey and more photographs from the northwestern Hawaiian Islands, including several images of albatross corpses found near the Kure Atoll in various stages of decay, all with plastic debris in their abdomens.

Like Aleena's turtle drawing and Moore's book cover, Middleton and Liitschwager's albatross autopsy photographs get beneath the surface. The images clearly expose ocean pollution as a contaminant lurking within the bodies of marine animals. And like the plastic bags, bottles, and aluminum cans that fill up the animal outlines in Aleena's and Moore's illustrations, it is also easy to recognize the quotidian items released from Shed Bird's stomach. As the image caption makes clear, Middleton found "cigarette lighters, [a] pump-top sprayer, nut shells, [a] shotgun shell, [and] broken clothespins." The viewer is not only struck by the extreme incongruence of these items but also disturbed to learn that the distinction between food and garbage is no longer so well defined.

The allegory of the albatross, symbol of oceanic plastic pollution, is also taken up by Chris Jordan in his series *Midway: Messages from the Gyre* (2009),[14] published in *Ecotone* magazine. Before encountering any photos, however, the reader is confronted by a blank white page printed with the title of the series, the name of the artist, and the following text:

9
Jeannie Evers, ed., "Great Pacific Garbage Patch," *National Geographic Society Online Encyclopedia*, September 2014, http://www.nationalgeographic.org/encyclopedia/great-pacific-garbage-patch/.

10
Moore describes the Great Pacific Garbage Patch as "a thin plastic soup, a soup lightly seasoned with plastic flakes, bulked out here and there with 'dumplings': buoys, net clumps, floats, crates, and other 'macro debris.'" Moore, *Plastic Ocean*, 4.

For an account of commodity spills from shipping containers, see Curtis Ebbesmeyer and Eric Scigliano, *Flotsametrics and the Floating World: How One Man's Obsession with Runaway Sneakers and Rubber Ducks Revolutionized Ocean Science* (New York: Harper, 2009).

11
Moore first encountered the Eastern Garbage Patch during an El Niño year, because it had moved much farther south than usual. Moore, *Plastic Ocean*, 54.

12
Moore calls the albatross "the poster child for plastics ingestion." Moore, *Plastic Ocean*, 215.

13
As early as 1963, scientists were studying the presence of plastic in the stomach of the albatross. But as in the case of the Sargasso Sea study, at the time, the impact of the findings was minimal. Moore describes the early albatross study as "a fine example of science unhinged from public awareness." Moore, *Plastic Ocean*, 219.

Two photographs from Chris Jordan's series *Midway: Messages from the Gyre.*

These photographs of albatross chicks were made on Midway Atoll, a tiny stretch of sand and coral near the middle of the north Pacific. The nesting babies are fed bellies-full of plastic by their parents, who soar out over the vast polluted ocean and collect what looks to them like food to bring back to their young. On this diet of human trash, every year tens of thousands of albatross chicks die on Midway from starvation, toxicity, and choking.

To document this phenomenon as faithfully as possible, none of the plastic in any of these photographs was moved, placed, manipulated, arranged, or altered in any way. These images depict the untouched stomach contents of baby birds in one of the world's most remote marine sanctuaries, more than two thousand miles from the nearest continent.[15]

The introductory text is significant on a number of levels. First, it offers the audience contextual information about the photographs, describing what the viewer will see, why it looks the way it does, and where the images were taken. Second, it attempts to engender an affective response with negative connotations like "vast polluted ocean" and "diet of human trash" as well as the quantification of tragedy—the death of "tens of thousands of albatross chicks" every year. Drawing the reader's attention to the extent of the pollution and the harm it produces, the text prompts the emotional responses of disgust, sadness, and pity. And because the photos are exclusively trained on the albatross corpse, the text provides a supplemental, broader scope through which to think about them. The concluding line describes an extreme distance, remote areas "more than two thousand miles" from any continent, implying that the photos operate on two scales: the unfathomably far and the intimately close. The text ends by foreclosing viewer suspicion, through the legitimating assertion that no item was moved or placed. Neither staged nor composed, the images thus represent things as they are. Yet the very need to affirm their veracity emphasizes how unrealistic they seem.

The 16 photographs following Jordan's introduction depict variously decayed albatross corpses. Positioned two per page, one image atop another, the carcasses seem to ceaselessly repeat. Even despite the photographer's cautionary text, the cumulative effect of viewing so many dead birds and the disturbing pervasiveness of plastic—in every albatross abdomen—is nevertheless striking.

In *Camera Lucida* (1980), Roland Barthes theorizes a particular feature of photography, the "punctum," as a searing aspect that stands out from the rest of the image: "this wound, this prick, this mark made by a pointed instrument . . . that accident which pricks me (but also bruises me, is poignant to me)."[16] In *Midway*, plastic operates as the punctum. It seems to leap from the images, its bright colors contrasting with the neutral browns, grays, and whites of the earth, bones, and feathers. The sharp edges of many shards and pieces are unsettling when considering the fragile, penetrable stomach of each bird. Even more jarring, however, is the disturbing out-of-placeness of the plastic. In recognizing a bottle cap or disposable lighter, it becomes impossible to ignore the troubling connections between one's own habits of consumption and the bird's distressing diet.

The presence of decay in Jordan's photos sets them apart from Middleton's Shed Bird autopsy photo. By removing debris from the bird's stomach, Middleton made the confounding abundance of waste present inside the albatross evident, exposing how the Great Pacific Garbage Patch disturbs distinctions between plastic waste and nutritional sustenance. In an image caption from *Archipelago*, Middleton and Liitschwager write: "Long after the flesh, bones, and feathers disintegrate and return to the earth, the plastic will remain."[17] By contrast, Jordan's photographs reveal that when there is little left of the albatross itself, the shape of a cigarette lighter, a bottle cap, a pen barrel, or the cap of a spray bottle remain clearly visible. Ostensibly presenting albatross remains, the actual subject of the *Midway* series is the persistence of plastic. Here, death and decay are revelations; as much as we would like to believe our trash disappears when we dispose of it, in fact it stubbornly and harmfully remains.

Unlike the artwork of Aleena and her peers, Jordan's, Vanderlip's, Middleton's, and Liitschwager's photographic representations of the Great Pacific Garbage Patch—via the albatross—do not impose an explicit ethical claim on their audience. Even the text contextualizing *Midway*, though guiding an affective response, refrains from making an explicit appeal to the viewer. Despite lacking any call to action, the tragic surprise evoked by these images opens up the possibility for environmental concern. The subtitle of Jordan's series also encourages a deeper reading of his repeated images of death; "Messages from the Gyre" suggests that both the plastic debris and the dead birds have something to tell us, a desire to communicate.

What distinguishes these photographic representations from the MDP scientific illustration is that they abandon any attempt to comprehensively represent their subject, instead relying on suggestion, allegory, and affect to engage the viewer's attention and stimulate concern. Jordan, Middleton, and Liitschwager are able to overcome

14
The *Midway* series is concerned entirely with the plastic-polluted albatross. See Chris Jordan, "Midway: Message from the Gyre," *Ecotone* 5.2 (Spring 2010): 110–18. Because *Archipelago* includes images of a variety of animals in the northwestern Hawaiian Islands, my analysis here focuses on the *Midway* photographs, although much equally applies to Middleton and Liitschwager's striking early images of the albatross. See David Liittschwager and Susan Middleton, *Archipelago: Portraits of Life in the World's Most Remote Island Sanctuary* (Washington, DC: National Geographic Society, 2005), 212.

15
Jordan, "Midway," 110.

16
Roland Barthes, *Camera Lucida: Reflections on Photography*, trans. Richard Howard (New York: Hill and Wang, 1980), 26–27.

17
Liittschwager and Middleton, *Archipelago*, 212.

the spatiotemporal imprecision of the MDP image. By focusing on the albatross, the photographs account for the remoteness of the Great Pacific Garbage Patch in both the location of the bird's habitat—what Middleton and Liitschwager refer to as "the world's most remote island sanctuary"—and the distance the albatross must travel, hundreds or even thousands of miles, to procure plastic from the gyres. The images also avoid the misleading suggestion that plastic debris is visible on the surface of the ocean. Instead, they rely on themes of death and decay to expose the reality that oceanic plastic pollution is often very difficult to see. Finally, they illuminate the temporal aspects of the Great Pacific Garbage Patch in their revelations of accumulation (it takes time for plastic to accrue inside the albatross) and persistence (plastics—not bone, feather, or flesh—are the real remains).

Concentrating on oceanic pollution's effect on the bodies of marine wildlife pushes back against attempts to visualize the Great Pacific Garbage Patch as if it were a static and contained waste site. This is a problem for the conceptualization of not only oceanic pollution, but of land-based waste disposal sites in general. As Joshua Reno has argued in *Waste Away: Working and Living with a North American Landfill* (2016), large-scale waste disposal sites are better imagined as leaky bodies than sealed containers. While Reno focuses his analysis on a landfill site in Michigan, the concept equally applies to unregulated and uncontrolled sites of waste accumulation like the Great Pacific Garbage Patch. By exposing the accumulation of plastic waste within the belly of the albatross, photographers like Middleton, Liitschwager, and Jordan demonstrate the ways in which our waste exceeds our efforts to contain it—leaking out of our trash bins and landfills and catastrophically into bodies of water and birds.

FALL

O

OW AI

RGAN

ND SO
ZATIO

CIAL

ON

Fallow Appalachia

AUSTIN ZWICK

After working three decades for the US Navy, my mother retired to the Florida Panhandle. Referred to as the Emerald Coast in state tourism pamphlets, it is affectionately known to locals as the Redneck Riviera. Every summer humble Appalachian folk come down from the mountains to vacation on Florida's pristine, and exceptionally affordable, white sand beaches. Nearly every Southern accent imaginable can be heard as they "gone fishing"—often with more beer than bait—or lie in the sun until turning to leather. At the end of summer the mountaineers head home, leaving locals behind for the mild if desolate winters. Stores board up, partly for the coming hurricane season, but mostly due to the annual economic cycle: spring blooms, summer booms, winter winds bring rest, only to renew. Back in Appalachia, the mountaineers can only dream of such predictability. Communities lie fallow; restless hands wait indefinitely for spring to come once again.

Appalachia—the rocky terrain speckled with small towns that stretches from northern Alabama to the southern tier of New York—is a beautiful disaster. A contrast of verdant land and human tragedy. Rural poverty hides beneath the deciduous canopy, following the rivers as they bend along the mountainsides. The underlying strength of the region in the 19th century—natural endowments coupled with the grit of its people—is an enduring liability, as such assets have become extraneous to the modern economy. As technology continues its unrelenting march forward, so too has the traditional regional livelihood of subsistence agriculture and resource extraction (mainly coal) been slipping away for decades. A global transformative wave shipped once-steady jobs to foreign shores, or battered aging bodies to insentience, leaving a latent skilled workforce in its wake.

The myth of Appalachia as a place where "time stood still" was first introduced in the closing decades of the 19th century, but it did not take root in the public imagination until the 1960s.[1] An article by Roul Tunley published in the *Saturday Evening Post (*1960) first contrasted the natural beauty of the landscape with its "chronic, grinding poverty."[2] And Jack Willis's documentary, *Appalachia: Rich Land, Poor People* (1968), broadcast the plight of coal miners into the nation's living rooms, revealing lands rich in coal and other natural resources, and residents without adequate food, housing, and medical care. At the time, approximately two-thirds of Appalachian counties fell into the lowest 20 percent of median household income in the country.[3] Historian Henry D. Shapiro suggested that because the peculiarity of the mountaineers could not easily be explained either by residence in a foreign land or being of an "inferior" people, their contemporaries rhetorically assigned Appalachians un-American status. Appalachia is "a discrete region defined by a particular pattern of culture as well as by its location, and inhabited by a legitimately distinct population."[4] The mountaineers became the nation's "contemporary ancestors"—living relics of another age.[5]

When I traveled through Appalachia for dissertation fieldwork in the summer of 2016, that stereotype is not exactly what I found. The rural poverty of this region feels a world, or an era, away; not a short drive from some of largest, densest metropolitan areas in the country. "Centuries of isolation and economic privation . . . made [Appalachia] as distant from the rest of the country in culture and politics as it was in miles."[6]

Stereotypes exist for a reason. There was no shortage of dilapidated barns still in use, empty fields that had decades ago ceased cultivation, or abandoned factories in the former "arsenal of democracy." Most striking were the still-occupied derelict homes in former coal company towns. Though the industry is long gone, its people remain. Even in the face of innumerable economic and environmental challenges—a legacy born from an extractive process that left rivers toxic and land sterile, not to mention the current opioid epidemic[7]—the people of Appalachia continue to adhere to their small, cohesive communities and maintain a strong connection to the land.[8]

Despite this, the people in Appalachia were not the caricatures seen on television. Some were upbeat, others distressed, all trying to get by in a world full of uncertainty. Many could have easily been confused with urban hipsters in T-shirts and blue jeans, speckled with tattoos, and expressing concerns about healthcare, family, and most importantly, lack of employment. Some were optimistic that the future held a brighter tomorrow, and some filled with despair. In other words, people were not much different from those in New York City. But the past few decades had not been as kind to this region. Nostalgia for what used to be, and resentment for what is, has become engrained in the cultural fabric here.

Sociologist Jack Weller's *Yesterday's People* (1965), a seminal study that controversially idealized (homely, hardworking) and derided (fatalistic, backward) the Appalachian way of life, still echoes true today.[9] Some desperation yields resourcefulness. In his recent *New York Times* bestseller, writer J. D. Vance recounts how some entrepreneurs literally scrape by with a pickax and a pickup truck, hand-digging surface coal from the side of the highway to sell to unscrupulous buyers.[10] But even those lucky enough to still have jobs in the coal industry do not want the same for their children, though there is not much else for the local economy to offer. After all, coal-mining is more than a job, it is an identity: "Coal created its own geographical area and culture."[11] Though a few jobs have popped up at Walmart stores and for local state parks, retail and tourism do not play powerfully in the imagination of the region, in stories, music, or forging identity.
As a presidential candidate, Barack Obama once caused a mini scandal by (correctly) observing that Appalachians cling to what remains: their guns, their religion, their antipathy to those unlike them, and their way of life.[12]

1
Ronald L. Lewis, "Industrialization," in *High Mountains Rising: Appalachia in Time and Place*, eds. Richard A. Straw and H. Tyler Blethen (Urbana: University of Illinois Press, 2004), 63.

2
Roul Tunley, "The Strange Case of West Virginia," *Saturday Evening Post*, February 6, 1960, 19–21, 64–66.

3
Jerry Bruce Thomas, *An Appalachian Awakening: West Virginia and the Perils of the New Machine Age, 1945–1972* (Morgantown: West Virginia University Press, 2010).

4
Henry D. Shapiro, *Appalachia on Our Mind: The Southern Mountains and the Mountaineers in the American Consciousness, 1870–1920* (Chapel Hill: University of North Carolina Press, 1978), 119.

5
William G. Frost, "Our Contemporary Ancestors in the Southern Mountains," *Atlantic Monthly* 83 (March 1899): 311–19.

6
Brit Hume, *Death and the Mines: Rebellion and Murder in the United Mine Workers* (New York: Grossman, 1971), 94.

7
Lara Moody, Emily Satterwhite, and Warren Bickel, "Substance Use in Rural Central Appalachia: Current Status and Treatment Considerations," *Rural Mental Health* 41.2 (2017): 123–35.

8
Christopher Cooper, Gibbs Knotts, and Don Livingston, "Appalachian Identity and Policy Opinions," *Journal of Appalachian Studies* 16.1–2 (Spring/Fall 2010): 26–41.

9
Jack Weller, *Yesterday's People: Life in Contemporary Appalachia* (Lexington: University of Kentucky Press, 1965).

10
J. D. Vance, *Hillbilly Elegy: A Memoir of a Family and Culture in Crisis* (New York: Harper Collins, 2016).

11
Barbara Freese, quoted in Karen Heller, "Coal No Longer Fuels America. But the Legacy—and the Myth—Remain," *Washington Post*, July 9, 2017, https://www.washingtonpost.com/lifestyle/style/coal-no-longer-fuels-america-but-the-legacy--and-the-myth--remain/2017/07/07/d8a8bcb4-582b-11e7-b38e-35fd8e0c288f_story.html.

12
Potus08blog, "Barack Obama's Small Town Guns and Religion Comments," YouTube video, 1:38, April 11, 2008, https://www.youtube.com/watch?v=DTxXUufI3jA.

Cliff tops on Mount Le Conte, in the Great Smoky Mountains of Sevier County, Tennessee, 2007. Courtesy Aviator31.

Under these conditions, fracking came "a-knockin." Towanda, Pennsylvania (population 2,850), is a two-stoplight town on the Susquehanna River where State Highway 6 and State Highway 220 come together. It is ground zero of fracking country in northeastern Pennsylvania; Bradford County has the highest drilling activity in the region. An old, rusted-out railroad car in front of a closed-up US Post Office greets strangers driving through on Main Street. The old Towanda Iron and Metal factory—the town's bygone linchpin—is now used as a landfill. Older painted wooden homes built at the turn of the century are boarded up, some with shattered windows. The newer houses, mostly constructed in the 1960s, are clad in vinyl siding and charcoal roof shingles; materials manufactured elsewhere but purchased cheaply from a local Ace Hardware store.

Marcellus Shale Gas Well,
Jackson Township/Butler County, PA.
Courtesy WCN 24/7.

Main Street was eerily quiet in the middle of a sunny Friday afternoon. More than a third of its storefronts lay vacant. The American Legion and Elks Lodge had seen better days, but their flags still proudly waved, reminiscent of Bruce Springsteen's 1984 hit, *Born in the USA*. The County Peddler and other antique shops were selling off the town's history at bargain bin prices. Law offices lined the street up and down from the County Courthouse, in position to negotiate mineral rights leases, or prepare plea bargains in opioid-related criminal cases—all for a hefty fee of course. The only brand-new brick and glass storefront was the Social Security Administration, for processing government pension checks so that Towanda retirees can survive another day. One of the largest employers in the region is the State Correctional Institute at Muncy, a prison built in 1913 that employs over 500 people to secure 1,300 inmates. It was government money—money made elsewhere—that kept the little town alive.

Red Rose Diner, Towanda, Pennsylvania.
Courtesy Doug Kerr.

Appalachia was once a land that made things. But at some point, production stopped. As I stood outside the Red Rose Diner eating a meal mountaineers take great pride in—hot dog stuffed with sauerkraut and pickles, a Coca-Cola—I realized all the ingredients had been made somewhere else, too. Food writer Ronni Lundy suggests that in the context of Appalachia, the way people eat "is not simply about availability, convenience, inexpensive price, or taste preference, but is also largely fueled … [by who] they aspire to be … like those they've seen selling food on billboards and on TV."[13] Ironically, the modern Appalachian diet, heavy in processed foods like soda, Wonder Bread, and potato chips, aims to reflect an image of the rest of America, whereas city folk—customers at Appalachian farmers markets and roadside stands—want to buy traditional jars of homemade preserves and pickled vegetables for an "authentic experience."

For all its faults, fracking briefly brought hope to the area. Hands were no longer restless, trucking construction materials and building drilling rigs. The land was no longer fallow, gushing black gold and sour gas. However, fracking is no long-term solution—only the latest iteration of the resource-extraction industry's boom-bust cycle. Jobs may arrive today, but the transient nature of the business means the work may be gone tomorrow. Worse still, the environmental degradation wrought is irreparable. So if not fracking, then what?

As city planner Daniel Burnham instructed: "Make no little plans; they have no magic to stir men's blood and probably themselves will not be realized. Make big plans; aim high in hope and work . . . asserting itself with ever-growing insistency."[14] Yet every big plan for Appalachia to date has been proposed by outsiders unfamiliar with the mountaineers, who may not have their best interests at heart. Thus such plans have continuously met with local resistance; and planners are seen as trying to impose the state government or Washington's will. Most initiatives—such as

13
Ronni Lundy, *Victuals* (New York: Clarkson Potter, 2016), 211.

14
Daniel Burnham [1907], quoted in Charles Moore, *Daniel H. Burnham: Architect, Planner of Cities*, vol. 2 (Boston: Houghton Mifflin, 1921), 147.

15
Particularly contentious conservation efforts in the region include those that successfully created the Allegheny, Daniel Boone, and Monongahela National Forests, among others.

16
Katie Colaneri, "Pennsylvania Towns with No Zoning Rules Unlikely to Limit Gas Drilling," *State Impact Pennsylvania*, February 11, 2014, https://stateimpact.npr.org/pennsylvania/2014/02/11/pa-towns-with-no-zoning-rules-unlikely-to-limit-gas-drilling-2.

worker retraining programs with the Appalachian Regional Commission in the 1960s, and environmental conservation efforts in the early 20th century—were either violently opposed at the ballot box or scuttled by politicians representing the region.[15] The people of Appalachia "are not rich . . . but what they do own is their land and they are very proud of that."[16] To rebuild, the first thing to understand is that Appalachia resists change. The key to the region lies in appreciating what it uniquely has to offer, and a future in building on old strengths and values.

Unlike the regional commissions that came before, the nonprofit Bipartisan Policy Center engaged stakeholders of every stripe to draft a plan for the future, published in *The Appalachia Initiative: A Bipartisan Approach for the 21st Century* (2017). The report was authored by a task force of Senators Joe Manchin (D-WV), David Perdue (R-GA), Thom Tillis (R-NC), and Mark Warner (D-VA), aided by an advisory committee of 40 academics and practitioners from across Appalachia, including bureaucrats (ARC), nonprofits (Golden Leaf Foundation, US Chamber of Commerce), unions (United Mine Workers), and for-profit corporations (Shell Oil Company). Unsurprisingly, the Bipartisan Policy Center concluded that there is no silver bullet; they proposed no big plan to save Appalachia. Instead, a program of small interventions was recommended to partner local people and companies, including initiatives to provide resources and regulatory flexibility to empower local leaders, public-private partnerships to facilitate and formalize workforce-training partnerships, and investments in solar panels and wind farms to transition from an energy-extraction to an energy-creation region.[17]

Wind farm turbines, West Virginia.
Courtesy The Nature Conservancy.

What is missing, however, is an effort to reshape how people feel about the region. Rebranding is needed to transform Appalachia's liabilities into assets. Here the formerly great factory cities of Cleveland and Detroit provide a model for doing so. In the cultural narrative of "Rust-Belt chic," the corroded factories of the last generation have given rise to a unique character derived from "the warmth of the faded . . . part old-world . . . like the simple pleasures associated with bagged lunch meat and beaten boots in the corner. And then there is grit."[18] That branding not only changed the way outsiders viewed those cities, but how locals understood themselves as well.

Appalachia can do even better by mythologizing rural roots. It is a land of contradictions: beautiful nature, desolate people; hopeful for the future, nostalgic for the past; proud, yet desiring to be better. The blood, sweat, and tears of Appalachians helped lay the foundation for the US; from uncles descending deep into coal mines to sons sent off to great wars. With ingenuity and grit Appalachians continue to fight for survival and a better future for their children. Not only our "contemporary ancestors," that sentiment applies to us all, despite our origins. And as Americans, it is what we have always been.

Appalachia as America Distilled

That a message can remake Appalachia without sacrificing its past demonstrates that the path forward is to honor the integrity of the region rather than demean its unenviable condition. The idea of small-town America—where neighbors greet each other across their front porches, keeping one eye on the children playing freely in open fields—can be packaged and sold, from mason jars to boutique barns to bourbon bottles. Recruit tourists to kayak down countless Appalachian streams, hike through lush forests, descend into dormant mines, and finish the day by washing down freshly fried pork rinds with moonshine. Locals will no longer look to the Redneck Riviera for escape, but cherish the fruits of their own garden paradise. As designers, geographers, and planners, our job is to turn this fallow ground fertile, to make spring come once again.

And the time is now. In the immediate aftermath of the 2016 presidential election, Americans called for a renewed embrace of their brethren on the forgotten frontier. Yet the eyes of the country are like the wind that blows through Appalachia, without wavering for the mountains and forests, and without yielding. Rebranding, restoration, and rebuilding are urgently needed lest we forget this fallow land and its people once more. In what could easily be read as a contemporary account, Malcolm Ross described the history of Appalachia thus:

> A machine age twilight has settled over the coal hills . . . a region of small farmers was made momentarily prosperous by a sudden invasion of industry; the wave passed, leaving them spoilt for the old way of life and helpless to face the new.[19]

17
Mark Warner, David Perdue, Joe Manchin, and Thom Tillis, *The Appalachia Initiative: A Bipartisan Approach for the 21st Century* (Washington, DC: Bipartisan Policy Center, 2017), https://bipartisanpolicy.org/wp-content/uploads/2017/09/BPC-Economy-The-Appalachia-Initiative.pdf. NOAA National Centers for Environmental Information, State of the Climate: Global Climate Report for Annual 2017, January 2018, https://www.ncdc.noaa.gov/sotc/global/201713.

18
Richey Piiparinen and Anne Trubek, eds. *Rust Belt Chic: The Cleveland Anthology* (Cleveland: Rust Belt Chic Press, 2012).

19
Malcolm Ross, *Machine Age in the Hills* (New York: Macmillan Company, 1933), 3–4.

Waiting in the Sky: Test Beds for a Vertical Future in Torre David

ALFREDO BRILLEMBOURG, HUBERT KLUMPNER, and KLEARJOS EDUARDO PAPANICOLAOU

At around three in the morning on July 22, 2014, as the sound of running on adjacent floors grew louder, Humberto Hidalgo began to realize what was happening. Not entirely surprised, and with few alternatives to consider, he decided to follow the most orderly course of action possible. If lucky, he, his wife, and their 10 children would be gone before the police arrived on their floor. After collecting their few belongings into plastic bags, the family descended six flights of bare concrete stairs to the ground floor, joining the other soon-to-be ex-residents of Torre David. After 14 years of informal occupation in the center of Caracas, Venezuela, the phenomenon referred to by some as "the world's tallest vertical squat" appeared to have ended.[1]

Appearances, however, can be deceiving. In a city where beginnings and endings—of prosperity, or democracy—are interchangeable depending on the person asked, the successive life cycles of this tower represent something more complex. The project began in 1989 as the crown jewel of the city's financial district before becoming a derelict giant, later transforming into a hybrid vessel for a resourceful community of squatters until the 2014 eviction. Since then the tower has been mostly empty, with the exception of intermittent low-level squatting. As the Venezuelan government meanwhile fails to deliver effective housing solutions, the tower resembles the city in microcosm, its entropic energy pairing beginnings and endings not with birth and stagnation, but rather with the transition from order to disorder and back again.

This raises the question: if the tower's current state of emptiness constitutes disorder (or order), then what form will the return of order (or disorder) take, and what stakeholders will administer it?

The Centro Financiero Confianzas, also known as Torre David. Courtesy ETH-Zurich, UTT, and Daniel Schwartz.

While this query may seem particular to Torre David, and to Caracas, it is by no means singular to them. The life cycles of dozens of other tall, empty buildings scattered across the globe can be understood similarly.[2] With skyscraper construction set to rise exponentially in the coming decades (both in prosperous western democracies and in socially and politically volatile cities like Caracas[3]), questioning their program for the long term is no longer absurd.

In navigating this vertical future, we turn briefly to the urbanization of densely populated cities during the industrial periods of the 19th and 20th centuries and the history of horizontal "sprawl." Understanding the urban life cycles of those areas—from productive districts to "waiting lands"—sheds light on the future of Torre David, and onto the thousands of (existing and imagined) towers in India, China, South Africa, Lagos, and beyond.

The Centro Financiero Confinanzas

Developed in 1992 in Caracas, Venezuela, the Centro Financiero Confinanzas— colloquially known as "Torre David" or "Torre de David"—represented the meteoric boom of Venezuela's economy: a 47-story financial tower comprising a hotel, reception hall, apartments, and other luxury amenities, crowned by a helipad. Within a few years of construction, however, a cocktail of unfortunate events befell the project, including the death of its main financier and the tower's namesake, David Brillembourg, along with an economic bust of the same dramatic proportions as the preceding boom.

The lifespan of the tower's intended program was cut remarkably short, and yet it remained standing, an immense concrete colossus looming over a city gripped by a housing crisis.[4] Within months the barriers enclosing the empty tower were breached by dozens—then hundreds—of families in search of a roof over their heads. In the years that followed, their occupation and subsequent bottom-up development transformed the tower into something unprecedented. This new iteration of the tower hosted an assortment of businesses and social programs as well as housing 3,200 residents at the height of the occupation. While the tower continued to resemble a ruin from the outside, as residents were unable to finish its facades, their collective labor completed 22 floors that the government could not afford to do. Torre David became a "city-within-a-city"; its residents' assertion of space through (informal) development embodying Henri Lefebvre and David Harvey's notion of the "right to the city."[5]

This new and unintended phase of the tower's program split opinions. The Caracas establishment could not condone an occupation that manifested what they perceived as the degeneration of their city, once hailed as a beacon of modernism and development. Despite hostility to the speculative environment that produced the tower, the Venezuelan government also opposed the squatters. For Hugo Chávez, then Nicolás Maduro, the spontaneity of the occupation—and their inability to control it—was cause for concern. The irony was perhaps lost on them: without a coherent social housing policy, and failing to recognize the ingenuity of the tower occupation, the Chávez government instead encouraged citizens to squat wealthier parts of the city.[6]

But others marveled at the resourcefulness of tower residents, whose occupation inadvertently pointed to alternative uses for the skyscraper typology, while addressing the issue of empty space in urban centers and articulating innovative solutions for low-environmental-impact living in densely populated areas.[7]

The accumulated weight of contestation eventually provoked the Venezuelan government to action, leading to the eviction of the tower residents on July 22, 2014. Once again it looms empty over an expanding city with little capacity to accommodate newcomers, let alone existing residents. Yet despite its current physical emptiness, the tower's position within the densely populated and growing urban center of Caracas means that it is ill suited for abandonment. Rather, it is a waiting land, with latent potential resting in an invisible tug-of-war between multiple stakeholders.[8] These diverse stakeholders, in turn, see such a waiting land as a metaphor for those parts of the city where degeneration presents opportunity for renewal; as in agriculture, optimal sites for future fertilization are defined by lands left fallow. City authorities, would-be squatters, and investors alike fix their gaze on the unusual situation, none (yet) making a decisive case over another.

Waiting lands do not collapse as their programs expire, but rather become raw materials for developing new forms of urbanity.[9] By raising questions about land value and use value in a context of the acutely mismatched supply and demand of urban space, the vacant Torre David is a departure point for considering the potential of the vertical built environment.

1
"Venezuela: Desalojo en Torre de David, el 'rascacielos-favela' de Caracas," *Perú21*, July 27, 2014, https://peru21.pe/mundo/venezuela-desalojo-torre-david-rascacielos-favela-caracas-174815.

2
Sufia Banu, "10 Abandoned Skyscrapers & Vast Empty Towers of the World," *Urban Ghosts*, May 28, 2015, https://www.urbanghostsmedia.com/2015/05/10-abandoned-skyscrapers-derelict-towers-of-world.

3
Sophie Warnes, "Vanity Height: How Much Space in Skyscrapers Is Unoccupiable?," *Guardian*, February 3, 2017, https://www.theguardian.com/cities/2017/feb/03/skyscrapers-vanity-height-graphics-numbers.

4
Rory Carroll, "Chávez Tackles Housing Crisis by Urging Poor to Squat Wealthy Parts of Caracas," *Guardian*, January 26, 2011, https://www.theguardian.com/world/2011/jan/26/venezuela-chavez-housing-crisis-squats-caracas.

5
David Harvey, "The Right to the City," *New Left Review* 53 (September–October 2008): 23–40.

6
"Squatters Move out of Venezuela's 'Tower of David' Super Slum in Caracas," *ABC*, July 24, 2014, http://www.abc.net.au/news/2014-07-24/venezuela-caracas-super-slum-tower-of-david/5620814.

Ground floor space serves as a gymnasium and provides room for sports fields. Courtesy ETH-Zurich, UTT, and Daniel Schwartz.

At the height of the occupation period, dozens of small business and service providers emerged within Torre David.
Courtesy ETH-Zurich, UTT, and Daniel Schwartz.

This brings the notion of waiting lands into a new framework, that of the city's verticalization, at a time when thinkers like Edward Glaeser argue that it is cheaper and also more coherent to build vertical structures in megacities rather than continue horizontal sprawl—economically, socially, and culturally.[10] The 2017 Chicago Architecture Biennial echoed this sentiment, prompting architects to reinterpret the Tribune Building through numerous alternative visions for tall buildings.[11] Yet while Torre David's dimensions may point to a vertical future, its emptiness describes an older vision of the future.

Guided by Lefebvre and Harvey's notion of the right to the city, and Glaeser's top-down reasoning on the benefits of urban verticalization, here we consider waiting lands—post-industrial peri-urban built environments completed throughout the 19th and 20th centuries—as a blueprint to better analyze this long-sighted future perspective.

Waiting Lands

Of the various signs differentiating stagnation from latent potential, a curious one can be found among the thousands of abandoned structures in Detroit, Michigan: orange paint. The ambiguous effect is the intention of the artistic collective behind the phenomenon, Object Orange. Their simple performance of coating dilapidated buildings in highly visible "triggerific orange"—the same shade as a common traffic cone—is both a protest and an attempt to redefine space.[12] By turning urban neglect into a cultural object, inadvertently rebranding Detroit as an urban "industrial ruin," their action expresses a desire to reinvent.[13]

The artists behind Object Orange join Gordon Matta-Clark (Fake Estates, 1973–1974[14]) and Robert Smithson (Hotel Palenque, 1969–1972[15]) in considering the departure of industry from urban peripheries as not only the end of a process, but a point of departure for another. Our documentation of Detroit with Camilo José Vergara in 1995 corroborated this, as we together observed the city's dilapidation as well as its latent post-industrial potential to foster creative production.[16] In Detroit, residents themselves highlight this phenomenon in orange.

When one views the urban environment as fluid or "in the making,"[17] for waiting lands, retrofitting is a matter of course in the recreation of space. Common areas identified as waiting lands, like harbors and train stations (clear nodes in global networks), become hotspots of activity, with groups ranging from squatters to artists adapting the space to fit unrequited urban needs. These areas are bottom-up test beds for new and alternative uses of urban space, in contrast to the monocultural visions often imposed by top-down planning. Adaptability and resilience here are key; and even the reclamation of space by nature plays a role, either aesthetically (overgrown greenery on walls and building facades) or functionally (urban farms and other reclaimed green spaces).[18]

For designers, politicians, real estate developers, and cultural producers, among other stakeholders, the waiting land is a site of interaction and collaboration. It requires an urban strategy to identify the programs emerging within it, from all directions. Here the resulting democratization of design—enriching bottom-up processes with top-down expertise and planning—charts a new path in the development of these areas, uncoupling them from the full brunt of market fluctuations.

Given the variety of stakeholders involved, each waiting land necessarily develops its potential in different forms. Two former industrial plants in central London illustrate the divergence of such paths: Tate Modern (formerly Bankside Power Station) and Battersea Power Station. While both are crucial to London's economy, the former is a free art museum (producing culture), and the latter a luxury residential and commercial development (producing wealth). This elasticity of waiting lands is what makes them interesting.

Elasticity, however, is often accompanied by conflict. Beyond the diverging agendas of top-down and bottom-up stakeholders, there are also related issues of gentrification, with consequent subcycles of valuation and devaluation. Waiting lands, in other words, must be understood as part of broader urban dynamics.

7
Alfredo Brillembourg and Hubert Klumpner, eds., *Torre David: Informal Vertical Communities* (Zurich: Lars Müller Publishers, 2013). Urban-Think Tank studied the occupation over several years, consolidating findings into a book, film, and exhibition. The latter, titled *Common Ground*, was presented at the Venice Architecture Biennale in 2012, where it received a Golden Lion for best project. Even then, opinion was split. Why, critics asked, should a tower considered a manifest architectural failure be awarded one of the profession's top prizes?

8
See Kees Christiaanse, Han van den Born, Gietma Ruurd, Irma van Oort, *Situation/KCAP: Architects & Planners* (Rotterdam: NAi Publishers, 2005).

9
See Reto Westermann, Roman Züst, and Tibor Joanelly, *Waiting Lands: Strategien für Industriebrachen* (Sulgen: Niggli Verlag, 2008).

10
Edward Glaeser, "How Skyscrapers Can Save the City," *The Atlantic* (March 2011), https://www.theatlantic.com/magazine/archive/2011/03/how-skyscrapers-can-save-the-city/308387.

11
See Leo Shaw, "How the Chicago Tribune Tower Competition Changed Architecture Forever—and Why It's Worth Revisiting," *Chicago Architecture Biennial* (blog), October 3, 2017, http://chicagoarchitecturebiennial.org/blog/how-the-tribune-tower-competition-changed-architecture-forever-and-why-its-worth-revisiting.

12
The group was formerly known as Detroit. Demolition. Disneyland. See the DDD Project, "Detroit. Demolition. Disneyland.," *Detroiter* (November 2005), http://www.thedetroiter.com/nov05/disneydemolition.php.

13
See Hanna Katharina Göbel, *The Re-Use of Urban Ruins: Atmospheric Inquiries of the City* (New York: Routledge, 2014).

14
Nancy Spector, "Gordon Matta-Clark, Reality Properties: Fake Estates, Little Alley Block 2497, Lot 42," *Solomon R. Guggenheim Museum Collection Online*, https://www.guggenheim.org/artwork/5210.

What remains unaddressed is how the parameters of the waiting land may shift beyond a horizontal paradigm. Features like density and geographical location not only point to new contexts and stakeholders, but also to emerging potential. While most contemporary tall buildings do not lend themselves to such study, with programs typically protected by stakeholders as wealthy as they are few, some cases do exist. Among them is Torre David.

Waiting in the Sky

How can Torre David be read not only as an empty skyscraper in a politically unstable city, but also as an entity within the broader urban fabric of Caracas? In the city's mixture of modernist structures and informal settlements, all situated under a shared layer of decay, we found a suitable analogue to the futurist retrofitting employed by director Ridley Scott in *Blade Runner* (1982).[19]

Torre David makes this metaphor intelligible, turning the vision of progress embodied by the skyscraper into one of dereliction, and suggesting that the future is already old. Seeing the tower in this light demonstrates the need to reassess how urban space is managed and developed, and underlines the omnipresent hazard of singular utopian visions, which so easily turn dystopian.

Our research envisioned ways in which existing bottom-up initiatives at Torre David—such as the complex tasks of providing water, electricity, and sanitation facilities, at the time fulfilled by small crews of volunteers—could be upgraded through collaboration and negotiation with other stakeholders. These included architects, like us; service providers like water, gas, and electricity companies; and eventually the city itself. Solar panels, wind farms, and a water retainment system were among our proposed interventions to strengthen the living framework for residents by increasing their self-sufficiency through sustainable and low-impact means.

Eager to understand how an occupied skyscraper could function without elevators, with the help of the Swiss elevator giant Schindler Group, we proposed a mostly nonelectric system based on concepts for public transport, featuring specific routes that counterweighted passengers with goods traveling up and down the tower. A timetable would inform residents when they could use the service. New programs continued to emerge in the tower until the event of its eviction. One vision developed with residents saw the "greening" of the building's exterior walls in parallel with a water distribution system. In another, we devised a system of elevated corridors connecting various parts of the building, to generate increased mobility within the tower programs and to foster sociability between residents.

Before the 2014 eviction, the activity and innovation within Torre David had gained enough momentum for potential incorporation into formal urban frameworks. New links with city officials were being made, as were draft contracts with water and electricity firms. This exuberant period of experimentation, collaboration, and negotiation between multiple stakeholders, however, was cut short.

Today, Torre David waits in a different phase, its floors now mostly vacant, its collaborative spirit muted. One finding from our research, however, remains firmly in mind: the imperative to work with diverse stakeholders. In the vertical context of Torre David this effective group was particularly heterogeneous, including service providers (of water, gas, transport, and sanitation; making human life possible far above ground), as well as planners, architects, and politicians, together with citizens (and noncitizens) of every ilk.

Stakeholders, like spaces and structures, are also in flux. Before Chávez and Maduro there was Rafael Caldera; their successors, too, will change with time. Venezuela's rate of urbanism is currently at 89.1 percent and rising 1.38 percentage points per year.[20] In a system with continuously moving parts, deploying waiting lands also means defining and redefining new beginnings and endings, too.

The Future Is Waiting

Eventually, Humberto Hidalgo and his family, along with other ex-residents of Torre David, were rehoused by the government that had evicted them. Imagine, however, that he wished to return there, to live in the city center closer to jobs and services. What lessons would the previous cycle of occupation provide? And what other kinds of people and activity might join Humberto's return?

Considering the city in three dimensions, the abandoned skyscraper is a density-friendly ecosystem in waiting. Multiple stakeholders from the bottom and the top will be required for its realization. And if current rates of urban densification continue (or increase), tall buildings must become flexible typologies.

The 19th-century adage today proves prescient: "Buy land—they're not making it anymore."[21] As if in response, Glaeser gives the issue of land value an existential spin, by suggesting that "skyscrapers can save the city." As Asian cities have already made clear, building

15
Nancy Spector, "Robert Smithson, Hotel Palenque," *Solomon R. Guggenheim Museum Collection Online*, https://www.guggenheim.org/artwork/5321.

16
Focusing on urban decay in the US, Camilo José Vergara is a pioneer in sociological photography.

17
Bruno Latour and Albena Yaneva, "'Give Me a Gun and I Will Make All Buildings Move': An Ant's View of Architecture," in *Explorations in Architecture: Teaching, Design, Research*, ed. Reto Geiser (Basel: Birkhäuser, 2008), 80–89.

18
Homo Sapiens, directed by Nikolaus Geyrhalter (Vienna: Geyrhalter Filmproduktion, 2016).

19
Hubertus Adam, "Blade Runner in the Tropics," *Neue Zürcher Zeitung*, September 18, 2018, https://www.nzz.ch/article7NJJ5-1.476858.

Imagined alternative futures for the Centro Financiero Confinanzas (Torre David). Courtesy ETH-Zurich, UTT, and Daniel Schwartz.

vertically is an efficient way to ease the pressure of high density where land is scarce. With its ubiquitous protected walkways, the example of Hong Kong shows that vertical density is not only possible, but highly productive.

Elsewhere, a new skyscraper is planned for Detroit, touted as a "vertical statement" tantamount to a city-within-a-city.[22] The lessons of urban space valuation and devaluation would imply that such an endeavor be programmed flexibly, allowing the tower to withstand economic vicissitudes, but it is not immediately apparent whether that is the case. With big money behind the initiative—a financial mogul and hedge fund manager—another Torre David may be on the horizon.

Ultimately, there is no singular solution for an urban future of either horizontal or vertical dimensions—only blueprints to refer to. Torre David currently awaits its next cycle, though not passively. In 2015, an investment proposal from a Chinese firm indicated a new direction for the tower and the city. However that path, too, was short-lived; the firm slowly withdrew as volatility in the city grew in recent years.[23] Whenever order (or disorder) does return to Torre David, we must ask: who will be stakeholders? Will its fabric be multipurpose, cosmopolitan? We pose these questions skeptically, with the shadow of the tower still looming precipitously over Caracas.

20
"South America: Venezuela," *The World Factbook 2018* (Washington, DC: Central Intelligence Agency, 2018), https://www.cia.gov/library/publications/the-world-factbook/geos/ve.html.

21
Peter M. Wolf, *Land in America: Its Value, Use, and Control* (New York: Pantheon Books, 1981), 6.

22
Daniel Howes, "Could We Be on the Edge of Detroit's New Entrepreneurial Age?," *Detroit Journalism Cooperative*, December 20, 2017, https://www.detroitjournalism.org/2017/12/20/edge-detroits-new-entrepreneurial-age.

23
Nate Berg, "Inside the Tower of Torre David: Venezuela's Vertical Slum," *Daily Beast*, April 24, 2016, https://www.thedailybeast.com/inside-the-tower-of-david-venezuelas-vertical-slum.

Fulcrum, Fallow: On Tempelhofer Feld

KEITH BROWER BROWN

I

Just south of the center of Berlin, the 750 acres of Tempelhofer Feld gape open. Two airstrips lie dormant, and chest-high grasses break through the cement. A few low trees are scattered across the expanse; from their shade, the old terminals on the northwest side lie quiet, the refugee camp in their hold largely out of sight. The city stretches for miles on every side, built high on shattered layers of the past. This field is a void in a major metropole on the continent, and it startles. What cleared this land and kept it open?

In the summer of 2017, I lived by Tempelhofer Feld. I was the first in my family to return to make a life in the city, ending eight decades of collective exile. On long June evenings under the 53rd parallel, I ran, or reclined, or spoke in halting German on the grass. Historical placards around the field pulled me in. I dove into its story, drawn deeper by neighbors' memories, *Faust's Metropolis* (1998) by Alexandra Richie, and Benjamin Deboosere and Wouter de Raeve's *On Tempelhofer Feld* (2016).[1] As I unearthed more, telling the story of Tempelhof became a way to ground the roiling past of this society, and to know myself stuck in it.

That fall I began studying towards a doctorate in geography, and my attention was caught by one long thread found throughout the Western canon: storytelling land to define a people. Herodotus defined Greece by the bounds of a way of life on the land, against its inverse in the surrounding barbarians. Paul Vidal de la Blache wrote romances for the valleys of France and how the lives of the villages suited each perfectly—diary entries for the project of nationalism.[2]

Carl Sauer wrote on the landscapes and peoples of northern Mexico, mutually culturing one another across centuries.[3]

In each of these canonical geographies, what matters most is not only principle, but prose. After all, these geographers were not principally working with maps, oratory, or figures, but in writing. Prose was their chosen medium for carrying the sense of landscape.

How does prose turn a landscape into a story of society? The writer makes freighted choices, consciously and not, in the selection of subjects and objects, the cadence of sentences, and the lyrics of evocation. Especially important in writing the land are the chosen scope and scale. Which marks of the past will be described? Which material presences will be taken as static or given, and which will be told in flux?

These are choices both aesthetic and political, at very least. Land can be given voice in words and a tempo following the writer's sensed experience of the place, in pursuit of common understanding. A utopian hope can animate the landscape, finding everywhere its destiny. Or, too often, language can meter the land in the inherited terms of a national myth.

Storytelling through land should not be done recklessly, blind to how often such prose has made a singular claim to land for a single people. The annals of Western geography and politics overflow with stories of land in service of nationalism and colonialism. And what story of land and people has conveyed more horror than one wrought here in Germany, of "blood and soil"?

In Berlin, I pledged to never carry on a nationalist story of land and descent. The country's nationalist project had nearly snuffed my family out of history; I would neither write us back into that story nor try to make it our own. Instead, I wanted to discover a lasting sense of how nations, borders, and other landed projects of race ran against the source of my being, nearly precluding it. I wanted a sense of connection to place without possession, of heritage without hierarchy.

If I found that sense anywhere, it was on Tempelhofer Feld. Learning and telling a story of its landscape became my effort to draw meaning from a nearly overwhelming tangle of self, society, and land. The forces that kept open that plain have also tied knots; this essay is a practice in working them loose.

II

The story begins in the meadow, in the Middle Ages. Two miles below this flat bluff, on a soggy riverine plain, a small town slowly grows; someday it will be Berlin.

Around the 13th century enter the Knights Templar. The mercenary Catholics will later be a mythic archetype for Prussian militarists, but for now they are flush with riches from the Crusades. They buy the land on the bluffs from a local lord, and recruit 20 families of landless farmers to join the settlement as peasant smallholders. The meadow becomes common grazing land, though little record remains of how it was tended and shared.

Wars, remembered by their length in decades, tear Europe to shreds for the next few horrible centuries. The meadow is overrun by invading armies, cleared, then overrun again. The grass grows thickly as livestock are hidden or stolen away, only for the soil to turn to mud in seasons of battle.

New lords take hold of the town downhill. By the early 18th century, Berlin is the seat of a Prussian state coalescing great power. Military discipline as imperial backbone and social order alike is the aim of the autocrats. The meadow on the bluff becomes a principal marching ground for the army, as the capital grows up around much of the clearing. It is a stage where the young men of the state make practice of might; a simulation of the battlefields to come, where they will meet the other armies of Europe. Tempelhofer Feld is a fulcrum of the force that Prussia's rulers hurl across Europe, for nine sanguine generations. It takes the desolate armistice of 1918 to oust the monarchs and quell the army's ambitions, if only briefly.

For a few years, the meadow lies fallow to state power, as economic collapse and hunger reign. Neighbors dig potatoes in the tilth. Furtive revolutions are put down in the surrounding city. The Weimar government proposes a civilian airport for the field, and eventually opens a small terminal and runway in 1927. Adjacent to the airport, municipal leaders erect a model city, named the Gartenstadt, or Garden City, for its open, verdant plan. The streets are named after drab public functionaries.

In 1933, the National Socialists win control of the government, and within a few months, tens of thousands of party members line Tempelhofer Feld, in tight formation. Military discipline has returned, and now civilians too must drill in the performance of power. The new regime swiftly renames the Gartenstadt avenues after World War I fighter pilots, lettered in old Gothic script. Over the next few years, government crews vastly expand the airport, installing two concrete runways nearly spanning the breadth of the field. Hulking new terminals are the biggest buildings, by volume, in the world. Their spare rooms soon become offices for *Schutzstafel* (SS), or secret police. Daily flights arriving from

1 Alexandra Richie, *Faust's Metropolis: A History of Berlin* (New York: Carroll & Graf, 1999); Benjamin Deboosere and Wouter de Raeve, eds., *On Tempelhofer Feld* (Leipzig: Spector Books, 2016).

2 Paul Vidal de la Blache, *Tableau de la Géographie de la France* (Paris: Librairie Hachette & Co., 1908).

3 Carl Ortwin Sauer, *The Morphology of Landscape* (Berkeley: University of California Press, 1925).

Madrid and Rome are greeted by severe brown limestone facades, the new gateway of the fascist "world capital."

At this juncture in the story, my family takes off. Two generations prior, they moved from a small city in eastern Prussia to the neighborhoods near Tempelhof. Word had spread among Jewish enclaves that economic and cultural integration was possible in Berlin like nowhere else. And for my family, that did happen for a time. By the eve of the Fascist takeover, my grandmother Kate later told me, they identified as culturally German and only dimly Jewish. The gardens and tennis courts of the neighborhood felt fully hers for play, the salons and cafés hers for reading Rilke. It could have been the rallies on the meadow—their frenzied performance echoing down adjacent streets—that made her realize the family had to get out. In the course of a year, she convinced her sister and father to leave. They packed light bags as if for a vacation and boarded trains to Italy, in various phases of denial as to whether they would return. The rails ran south over the bluff, just blocks from the field.

Kate. Courtesy of Keith Brower Brown.

For the next decade, Tempelhof houses Berlin's sole concentration camp and a military airfield, its structures coldly hewn to the administration of violence.

Soviet tanks take the field on a January day. The airport is spared bombing during the invasion. Allied generals land on this tarmac, hauling the captured commanders of the German forces into the terminal building to sign their final order of surrender.

The American military wins oversight of this quadrant of the city, moving its officials into the terminal offices that recently housed the SS. After a few years of shaky truce collapse, the Soviet army cuts off land supply routes into West Berlin, and the Tempelhof runways serve as the landing pad for the Berlin Airlift. Where Prussian soldiers once drilled in a show of military discipline, and brown-shirted masses paraded for Leni Riefenstahl's lens, the Allies land hundreds of planes per day in a spectacle of Western logistical might.

Within a year, the airlift and its spectacle break the siege. The Americans keep much of the airport as a military base, with some facilities resuming duty as a civilian air link to the island of West Berlin, encircled by East Germany.

Two larger commercial airports eventually open on either side of Berlin, and following reunification, neighborhood protests mount against the noise and nuisance of the older relic airport. In 2008, the municipal government shuts down air operations at Tempelhof.

Within two years, under the pressure of neighbors eyeing the unused field, the city reopens the airfield as a vast park for the public. It is tremendously popular among human kite-flyers, rare bird and insect species alike. Soon the park agency cordons off much of the field into islands of protected meadow habitat, launching a barely planned venture in grassland rewilding inside the capital city of Europe's most powerful country.

Meanwhile, developers hungrily eye the vast plain, and plans and proposals swirl for housing and commercial development. In 2014, a city referendum to allow partial development of the field is rejected by nearly two-thirds of voters. Berliners resolve to hold Tempelhofer Feld as open and raw, as it has long stood. One year later, as the federal government admits 800,000 refugees from Syria's civil war, the cavernous terminal buildings are transformed into short-term, open-plan shelters. The short-term grows longer, until eventually the residents are afforded more privacy in semi-permanent structures within and alongside the old airport. Today the field is open.

III

I landed a few miles southeast of Tempelhofer Feld some 82 years after my family departed. Having heard about this city and its weight in the family's past all my life, I was returning for the first time since a week-long visit as a teenager. I was now Kate's age when she had fled. I came wanting a fuller sense of history and family culture by learning this place in intimate, everyday terms. I had little idea what I would find, but I planned to start by researching family history and strengthening my grasp of the German language. I had learned a broken German at home as a kid. Now I hoped for a fluency that would allow the sounds of words to fit my sense of place, like onomatopoeia.

4
A radler is a 50-50 mixture of beer and fruit soda.

Opening of Tempelhof Air Field as a public park in May 2010. CC BY SA. Courtesy of Times on Wikimedia Commons.

Flock of birds at the field, 2013, CC BY. Courtesy of flohserver on Flickr.

Staying with friends in an East Berlin apartment block during my first weeks, I settled into a routine of private research and social hours, stumbling towards passable German. It was June in Berlin; the lightly employed youth of the continent congregated in parks in the shadow of the Wall, over picnics and open radlers.[4] Lines ran long into nightclubs housed in decommissioned power plants. The Berlin I knew from family stories was the terminus of upheaval and loss; the Berlin I met then had been, for at least a decade, a famed zone of conspicuous, defiant leisure. The contrast was jarring, and I didn't know how to make sense of it.

History was everywhere but seemed barely relevant, or largely unknown, to those in the city. In other words, it felt hollow; I often felt myself in a landscape of husks. When I asked Berliners about the history of fraught places, they usually knew its broad strokes, if not its specific sites. The scattered shells of history all around were a backdrop, their meanings like half-memories that could not be recalled fully in the present time.

I played a concert on Schleusenufer, a small island between canals at the eastern edge of the city center. Only later did I learn that its industrial yards had been the easternmost shard of West Berlin, the furthest point east in the West. Nobody had mentioned it to me, and even friends raised in both West and East were unaware of the island's history as a borderland. My venue was cobbled together between rusted shipping containers; next door, a louder club played commercial trance. Reunification and the culture that grew in its wake seemed to have wholly submerged the fatal stakes of the old terrain.

I looked for the *Stolpersteine*, or stumbling stones: a widely known project of Holocaust remembrance initiated in 1992 by Gunter Demnig. In walls or sidewalks all across the city, on cement cubes laid flush like cobblestones, brass plates give the name, birth, and death dates of those who lived there and lost their lives. But after several weeks, without having noticed any stumbling stones on my own, I consulted a directory. There were none with my family name, but I found a stone listed for a Käte, her name like my grandmother's, near where I was staying. The Stolpersteine website offered a curt biography of Käte, giving the occupation of family members, marriage date, date of capture, and what became of her children. I kept thinking how precisely her biography rested on data collected by her exterminators.

After a five-minute search, I found the stone in front of an upscale pharmacy. I laid a few flowers, feeling both heavy and arbitrary in the act. The directory showed nearly 8,000 more stones in Berlin, and over 50,000 across Europe. Within a few blocks of my apartment were almost 100 stones. Each could have been its own research project. To acknowledge them all, let alone bring them richly into the present, would be insurmountable for any one person. And what would be the point? The conversion of Nazi records into cobblestone memorials overwhelmed me with sheer numbers, seeming to preclude the possibility of a personal connection with the past as a whole.

On a July day I went to Mohrenstraße, or the "street of Moors," in the commercial heart of Berlin; its name likely an 18th-century reference to the North African slaves then imprisoned in the area. The epithet "Mohr" was considered derogatory, however archaic, by all the Germans I asked. At this street, I joined in Berlin's Black Lives Matter march; walking, along with 1,000 other people, to demand the street and its subway station be renamed, among other goals. A friend remarked that there had been a campaign to rename the street for many years, but it had gained little traction in the halls of power. That was a shame, she said—but weren't there more pressing, present injustices to tackle anyway? This history may matter to us some, but what does it really amount to? If this conspicuous street in the heart of Berlin kept its name despite years of protest, what hope was there for history to matter in the far corners of the city, where it did not blare from street signs? Fraught history was present all around, but any richer sense of it in daily life eluded me and most of the Berliners I came to know.

A few weeks after my arrival, I moved into a room in a shared house in Tempelhof's Gartenstadt, four blocks from Tempelhofer Feld. My house stood at the corner of a street still named for the Red Baron, in Gothic script. Soon afterwards, a housemate invited me to her partner's birthday party on the feld; a few minutes later I was out on the grass for the first time, lilting to dance music with a half-dozen Ugandan émigrés. The closed airport terminal building hulked across the meadow. Fenced-off, temporary refugee housing sat in its shadow on the tarmac. I grew dizzy in the converging lines of flight: my family's site of exile had become one of fragile refuge.

While I began to learn the history of the field from my perch nearby, I still had little idea how close I was to where my family once lived. I did not think to ask that question until I arrived— testimony to how being in a place, rather than merely reading about it, opens different dimensions of attention. Proximity takes on new meaning when your body has to move across it.

I wrote home to ask my parents where my family had lived. After searching through a small box of old letters, my mother e-mailed the two addresses she could find. One was just eight blocks south of my house, the other less than a mile east. Meanwhile, I searched through federal archives for a great-uncle who stayed behind when the rest of the family left; that was the last we knew of him. I found one final trace: a 1937 address from a Jewish registry in the state records, about ten blocks north of my rented room.

Unwittingly, I found myself at almost the center of my family's past homes, all within a short walk of the field. The coincidence seemed significant. I searched for the family apartments, hoping for a view of their facades or a glimpse into their courtyards. But at each address, I found only postwar buildings. The number of one old address, written on an envelope from my great-grandfather, was skipped over entirely between newer apartment buildings. Whatever had been there before had likely been turned to rubble, and long cleared away. I tried not to make too much of it, but I couldn't stop sulking, feeling crestfallen.

It was as if every trace of my family was gone from Berlin, except one line in the foul archive.

I was right in the neighborhood where it had all happened; it was closer than ever to me. But my sense of the city hollowed of its history was hard to shake. Increasingly I worried I would never find my own sense of history alive in the present.

Then a turn came from an unexpected place. At home alone one night, I watched Christian Petzhold's film *Phoenix* (2014), which tells the story of a survivor of the camps from Berlin who returns to her city in 1946, as so few did, to reckon painfully with the spaces of her past life, her hiding, and her capture. She finds her husband, a gentile, who has also made it through the war alive. Because she has sustained profound facial damage, her husband does not recognize her. She is overcome and does not reveal her identity to him. In a twisted lovesickness fueled by regret, he pays her to live with him and play her former role, in a series of reenactments of their romance before the war. On the park bench they frequented, in the houseboat that was their hideaway, they are reunited—but history has shattered all possibility for the intimacy that once was. These longed-for places have become hollow, trauma and betrayal having rotted their core, an unfeeling new order already springing from the ruin. Watching the film felt close to what Kate might have experienced in Berlin, if she had come back to stay.

The film ended. I felt shaken, without any words. I went out for a walk. The Tempelhof night was cooler than expected, arresting. Breathing in the damp air and shivering, it struck me: this bodily tremor might be some of the feeling of history in the present that I was searching for.

I realized that Kate had felt these same night winds, and she had breathed them on this bluff. One piece of her world was as real and alive in my body as it had been in hers. That meant this history was not an abstraction of entries in an archive—it contained a live, breathing person. Her survival through it allowed me to exist, and to be breathing, here, now. The joy of home and the terror of loss could not be captured in federal records, or readily recalled in everyday life eight decades later. But they had been lived and real, and absolutely *here*.

I could not expect everyone around me to feel the way I felt in contact with history. That would be to claim a kind of singular, exclusive story for the land. But I could learn to tell *a* story, and in putting it to words, I might carry some of the sense I found to others, seeking resonance.

Finally I reached Tempelhofer Feld, which was closed for the night. I peered through the fence. Unlike my family's cleared homes, the field stood as open now as it had been in their time. Kate had passed fifteen years before, so I had no way to know exactly what she thought of this place. But that need not hold the terrain silent.

The field appeared heavy with boots, the runways cracked from the weight of airplanes. Terrible power had been practiced here, then run fallow by the next generation. Grass stood on end, charged with a new sense of what it meant to see the field for the last time. To intimately learn a story of this land is to know its history had happened in a very specific place, for very real lives—which is to say, to know history had happened at all. It seemed to me that articulating such a meaning, in a place, was exactly what geography can do. And it was exactly what I came here for: to come one shiver closer. The meadow lay at rest, its history present and breathing all along. I watched it grow, for the indefinite moment, toward a wilder kind of commons.

•

National Socialist party rally on Tempelhof Air Field in May 1934. Bundesarchiv, Bild 146-2008-0006. CC BY SA 3.0. Courtesy of the German Federal Archives.

Thank you to Nathan Sayre, whose encouragement brought this essay to light; to Alyssa Battistoni and Sharad Chari, whose insights shaped it; and to Sara, Suzi, Eva, Bella, Rory, Thomas, and Julia for showing me this Berlin.

This work is dedicated to Ben Maurice Brown, my father and Kate's son, who passed in my care as I made final revisions to the essay. He carried our family's losses with strength so that I could make this from them.

NICOLE BENNETT is a PhD student in the Department of English at the University of Wisconsin, Madison. She has long benefited from public higher education, attending a California community college before receiving her BA from the University of California, Berkeley and her MA from California State University, Long Beach. Her research focuses on waste as both concept and material object; her master's thesis examined waste in three post-1945 Los Angeles–based novels. While she is deeply interested in postmodern and contemporary American fiction, her broader work concerns the ways in which pollution, contamination, toxicity, trash, and disposability are represented visually and narratively.

BENEDIKT BOUCSEIN graduated in architecture from the Swiss Federal Institute of Technology (ETH) in Zurich in 2005 and received his PhD from its Institute for the History and Theory of Architecture (gta) in 2008. He co-founded the magazine *Camenzind* in 2005 and BHSF Architects in 2007. From 2007 to 2017 he was a researcher and lecturer at ETH Zurich. He is the author of *Graue Architektur* (Gray Architecture; Walther Koenig, 2010), and co-author of *The Noise Landscape: A Spatial Exploration of Airports and Cities* (nai010 publishers, 2017). He was appointed Professor for Urban Design at the Technical University Munich in 2018.

KEITH BROWER BROWN is a doctoral student in geography at UC Berkeley and a National Science Foundation Graduate Research Fellow. He currently serves on the steering committee of the East Bay Democratic Socialists of America. Keith's prior work has been published in *Climate & Development*, *Jacobin*, and *Carbon Trade Watch*.

STEPHEN CAIRNS is an architect, writer, and teacher whose work concerns the interaction of buildings, cities, and society. He is the Future Cities Laboratory (FCL) Director in Singapore, Professor in Architecture at the Swiss Federal Institute of Technology (ETH) in Zurich, and Principal Investigator of the Urban-Rural Systems research team at FCL. He authored *Buildings Must Die: A Perverse View of Architecture* with Jane M. Jacobs (MIT Press, 2014) and edited *Future Cities Laboratory: Indicia* with Devisari Tunas (Lars Müller Publishers, 2017).

MICHAEL CHIEFFALO is a doctoral student at Harvard University, a practicing architect, and former planning commissioner. His research engages with processes of agrarian urbanization, socio-environmental dimensions of factory farming, the diverse built environments of industrial agriculture, and alternate visions of urbanism that foreground agricultural landscapes in form-making. He holds a BArch from Roger Williams University, an MS in architecture from Columbia University, and an Urbanism, Landscape, Ecology–focused MDes with distinction from Harvard.

B. R. COHEN is Associate Professor at Lafayette College. His interests lie at the intersection of the histories of science, technology, and the environment, with particular attention to industrial agriculture from the 19th century to today. He is the author of *Notes from the Ground: Science, Soil, and Society in the American Countryside* (Yale University Press, 2009) and *Pure Adulteration: Cheating on Nature in the Age of Manufactured Food* (University of Chicago Press, forthcoming).

CAITLIN DeSILVEY is a geographer whose research explores the cultural significance of material change and transformation, with a particular focus on heritage contexts. She often uses visual imagery and storytelling to stimulate public imaginary of changing environments and places, and studies patterns from the past to understand what the future might bring. Although much of her work concerns how things (and places) fall apart, she is also interested in practices of repair and maintenance that hold things together. She is the author of *Curated Decay: Heritage Beyond Saving* (University of Minnesota Press, 2017), which received the 2018 Historic Preservation Book Prize (awarded by the Center for Historic Preservation at the University of Mary Washington).

JILL DESIMINI is a landscape architect and Associate Professor at Harvard University Graduate School of Design. Her work has received a Narendra Juneja Medal and an ASLA certificate from the University of Pennsylvania, a Selected Professions Fellowship from the American Association of University Women, and was shortlisted in the Van Alen Institute competitions Urban Voids (2006) and Future Ground (2014). Her current research investigates design strategies for abandoned landscapes and has been published in the *Journal of Urban History*, *Landscape Journal*, and *JoLA*. She has authored book chapters on urban wilds and is co-author of *Cartographic Grounds: Projecting the Landscape* (Princeton Architectural Press, 2016).

ERLE C. ELLIS is Professor of Geography and Environmental Systems at the University of Maryland, Baltimore County (UMBC) where he directs the Laboratory for Anthropogenic Landscape Ecology (http://ecotope.org). His research investigates the ecology of human landscapes at local to global scales and is directed towards sustainable stewardship of the biosphere in the Anthropocene. His recent work examines long-term global changes in human ecology (anthromes, anthroecology), the global synthesis of local knowledge (GLOBE), and 3-D landscape mapping (Ecosynth). He teaches environmental science and landscape ecology at UMBC, has taught ecology at Harvard's Graduate School of Design, and is the author of *Anthropocene: A Very Short Introduction* (Oxford University Press, 2018).

PETER GALISON is the Joseph Pellegrino University Professor at Harvard University. He received his PhD in theoretical high-energy physics and in the history of science from Harvard in 1983. He has received a MacArthur Foundation Fellowship (1997), the Pfizer Award (1998; for *Image and Logic* [University of Chicago Press, 1997]), the Max Planck and Humboldt Stiftung Prize (1999), and the Abraham Pais Prize in the history of physics (2018). His other books include *How Experiments End* (University of Chicago Press, 1987), *Einstein's Clocks, Poincaré's Maps* (W. W. Norton, 2003), and *Objectivity* (with L. Daston; Zone Books, 2007). In collaboration with Robb Moss he directed the documentaries *Secrecy* (2008) and *Containment* (2015); the latter focused on how to guard radioactive materials for the 10,000-year future. Galison partnered with South African artist William Kentridge on the multi-screen installation *The Refusal of Time* (2012). In 2016 he co-founded the Black Hole Initiative, an interdisciplinary center that is the locus for his current philosophical and film work.

MATTHEW GANDY is Professor of Geography at the University of Cambridge. His publications include *Concrete and Clay: Reworking Nature in New York City* (MIT Press, 2002), *The Fabric of Space: Water, Modernity, and the Urban Imagination* (MIT Press, 2014), *Moth* (Reaktion, 2016), and numerous articles in *New Left Review, International Journal of Urban and Regional Research, Society and Space* and other journals. His current research engages the interface between cultural and scientific aspects of urban biodiversity.

JANE M. JACOBS is Professor of Urban Studies at Yale-NUS College, Singapore. She is the author of *Edge of Empire: Postcolonialism and the City* (Routledge, 1996), *Cities of Difference* (Guilford Press, 1998), *Uncanny Australia* (Melbourne University Publishing, 1998), *Buildings Must Die: A Perverse View of Architecture* (MIT Press, 2014), and numerous peer review papers. Trained as a geographer, she has maintained an enduring concern for the relationship between society and space, including the social shaping of urban built environments, the politics of heritage, and practices of everyday habitation at both the city and the domestic scale. Her current research is a history of design innovation in Singapore's large-scale housing provision system, 1960–1995.

EIRINI KASIOUMI is a PhD candidate and a teaching and research assistant in Architecture and Urban Design at the Swiss Federal Institute of Technology (ETH) in Zurich since 2012. Her interests include the urban management of infrastructures and the design and politics of large-scale projects. She has co-authored *The Noise Landscape: A Spatial Exploration of Airports and Cities* (nai010 publishers, 2017) and her doctoral research focuses on the evolution of planning strategies concerning the airports in Paris. She studied architecture in Greece and holds a Master of City Planning from MIT (2010). She has also worked as an architect and urban designer in offices in Greece and Switzerland including at KCAP Zurich.

M. ROMAN-JOHN KOSCIELNIAK is a PhD candidate in Urban & Regional Planning at the University of Michigan. Broadly, he studies the politics, economics, and geographies of American urban decline. His research interrogates the interactions of policy, real estate, and finance constitutive of contemporary racial capitalism. Presently, he focuses on power, property, and speculation in relation to demolition-dependent redevelopment in Detroit. He is also developing a long-term research agenda addressing the political-economy of fringe financial services. He will defend his dissertation, *Ground Forces: Dirt, Demolition, and the Geography of Decline in Detroit, Michigan*, in early 2019.

MAZEN LABBAN is Visiting Assistant Professor of Geography at Rutgers, The State University of New Jersey, and senior editor at *Capitalism Nature Socialism*. He is the author of *Space, Oil, and Capital* (Routledge, 2008) and several articles on energy, mining, waste, labor, and finance published in the *Annals of the Association of American Geographers, Antipode*, and *Geoforum*, among others. Labban is currently at work on a book about urbanization, wasting, and the planetary mine, and another on financial speculation.

CHRISTOPHER MARCINKOSKI is Associate Professor of Landscape Architecture and Urban Design at the University of Pennsylvania and author of *The City That Never Was* (Princeton Architectural Press, 2016). He is a licensed architect and director of PORT, a public realm and urban design practice based in Philadelphia and Chicago. In 2015, he was awarded the Rome Prize in Landscape Architecture from the American Academy in Rome.

NATHAN F. SAYRE is Professor of Geography at the University of California, Berkeley, where he also holds affiliations with the Energy Resources Group, the Berkeley Food Institute, and the Institute for the Study of Ecological & Evolutionary Climate Impacts (ISEECI). His research centers on the political economy and environmental history of semi-arid rangelands, especially in the southwestern United States. He has published extensively on the topics of scale, carrying capacity, scarcity, and the anthropogenic. His most recent book is *The Politics of Scale: A History of Rangeland Science* (University of Chicago Press, 2017).

ÁLVARO SEVILLA-BUITRAGO is Associate Professor at Universidad Politécnica de Madrid, Town and Regional Planning Department. His academic research uses critical theory to explore the social history of planning, with special attention to the various forms of dispossession, displacement, and topocide that inform the production of space under capitalism. He has published widely in the fields of architecture, planning, and urban history, as well as critical geography, politics, sociology, and cultural studies. He participates in academic projects in Germany, Spain, Switzerland, and the US, where he is a member of the Urban Theory Lab at the Harvard University Graduate School of Design. He blogs at www.multipliciudades.org.

WADE SHEPARD is a perpetually traveling writer who perhaps spends a little too much time in new cities around the world. He is the author of *Ghost Cities of China: The Story of Cities without People in the World's Most Populated Country* (Zed Books, 2015), which chronicles two and a half years spent in China's underpopulated new cities. For the past three years he has traveled up and down various corridors of the "New Silk Road" to gain on-the-ground perspective of the Belt and Road Initiative for a new book forthcoming in 2019.

THOMAS SIEVERTS studied architecture and urban design in Stuttgart, Liverpool, and Berlin. After co-founding the office Freie Planungsgruppe Berlin, he was appointed Professor of Urban Design at the Academy of Fine Arts in Berlin and the Technical University Darmstadt. He has served as visiting Professor at Harvard University; the University of California, Berkeley; and the Technical University of Vienna (1967–1999). He has run his own office since 1978, was director of the Internationale Bauausstellung Emscher Park (IBA Emscher Park, 1989–1994), Fellow of the Institute for Advanced Study in Berlin (1995–1996), and President of Europan Europe (2010–2014). Professor Emeritus since 1999, he continues planning, writing, and lecturing internationally. He received an honorary doctorate from the Technical University Braunschweig, a gold medal for service to the city of Vienna, and the Fritz-Schumacher-Preis from the city of Hamburg, among other awards, and has numerous publications to his credit.

JULIA SMACHYLO is a doctoral candidate at Harvard University, an urban designer, and a registered urban planner in Ontario and the UK. Her research responds to the increased awareness and value of natural capital in research and policy, as well as the influence of non-state actors such as environmental organizations, landowners, and the private sector in shaping landscapes. Julia has a BA in geography from Queen's University, a Master of Urban Planning from the Bartlett School of Planning, University College London, and a Master of Urban Design from the University of Toronto.

URBAN-THINK TANK (U-TT) is an interdisciplinary design practice delivering innovative and practical solutions through the combined skills of architects, civil engineers, environmental planners, landscape architects, and communication specialists. Founded by Alfredo Brillembourg and Hubert Klumpner in Caracas, Venezuela, in 1998, U-TT has held the Chair for Architecture and Urban Design at the Swiss Federal Institute of Technology (ETH) in Zurich since 2010. They have been awarded the 2010 Ralph Erskine Award, the 2011 Holcim Gold Award for Latin America, the 2012 Holcim Global Silver Award for innovative contributions to ecological and social design practices, and the Golden Lion at the 2012 Venice Biennale of Architecture.

AUSTIN ZWICK recently obtained his PhD in Planning from the University of Toronto, where he studied contemporary social and economic transitions (or the lack thereof) in Appalachia, focusing on the incursion of the fracking industry and the demise of coal employment. He was appointed Assistant Teaching Professor at the Maxwell School of Public Affairs at Syracuse University in 2018. He is keenly interested in how new technologies can transform patterns of urban and regional economic growth.

FORTHCOMING
New Geographies 11: Extra Terrestrial

> extra /ˈɛkstrə *adj.* (17th c.):
> Added to an existing or usual amount
> or number.
>
> terrestrial /təˈrɛstrɪəl *adj.* (15th c.):
> On or relating to the earth.

First used in 19th-century literature, *extraterrestrial* describes what is "of or from outside the earth or its atmosphere." However, when the term's constituent words are decoupled and dissociated from typical science-fiction references, a curious epistemological device emerges. *Extra terrestrial* reveals those spatial interactions between the surface of the earth and the layered or "extra" conditions added to, and projected from, the earth's surface. Through processes of urbanization, remote sites such as antennas, launch pads, telescopes, satellites, and space probes cultivate an extra infrastructural and technological stratification, not in direct relation to, but rather in evolution from, terra. *New Geographies 11: Extra Terrestrial* explores the historical and technological context of an *extra terrestrial* duality—an entangled zone of infrastructural space found in architecture, landscape, and geography—stretching from earth to space, and conversely, space to earth.

Editors
Jeffrey S. Nesbit & Guy Trangoš